ARCHAEOLOGICAL SURVEY OF SOUTHERN INDIA

THE BUDDHIST STUPAS
OF
AMARAVATI AND JAGGAYYAPETA
IN
THE KRISHNA DISTRICT, MADRAS PRESIDENCY,
SURVEYED IN 1882

ARCHAEOLOGICAL SURVEY OF SOUTHERN INDIA

THE BUDDHIST STUPAS
OF
AMARAVATI AND JAGGAYYAPETA
IN
THE KRISHNA DISTRICT, MADRAS PRESIDENCY,
SURVEYED IN 1882,

BY
JAS BURGESS, LL.D., C.I.E., F.R.G.S. M.R.A.S., &C.
DIRECTOR GENERAL OF THE ARCHAEOLOGICAL SURVEY OF INDIA

WITH
TRANSLATIONS OF THE ASOKA INSCRIPTIONS AT JAUGADA AND DHAULI,

BY
GEORG BUHLER, PH.D., LL.D. C.I.E., &C.
MEMBER OF THE IMPERIAL ACADEMY OF SCIENCES,
AND PROFESSOR OF SANSKRIT IN THE UNIVERSITY OF VIENNA.

GYAN

Published by

Gyan Publishing House
5, Ansari Road
Daryaganj, New Delhi-110002
Phone: 011-47034999, 9811692060
E-mail: books@gyanbooks.com

Distribution Network
gyanbooks.com
India, USA, Canada, UK, Australia, France

ISBN : 978-81-212-2724-7 (HB)
First Published, 1887

2nd Impression 2021

Printed at: Gyan Press, Delhi.

The Buddhist Stupas
of
Amaravati and Jaggayyapeta
Author: Jas Burgess

ARCHÆOLOGICAL SURVEY OF SOUTHERN INDIA.

THE BUDDHIST STUPAS

OF

AMARAVATI AND JAGGAYYAPETA

IN

THE KRISHNA DISTRICT, MADRAS PRESIDENCY,

SURVEYED IN 1882,

BY

JAS. BURGESS, LL.D., C.I.E., F.R.G.S., M.R.A.S., &c.

DIRECTOR-GENERAL OF THE ARCHÆOLOGICAL SURVEY OF INDIA.

WITH

TRANSLATIONS OF THE AŚOKA INSCRIPTIONS AT JAUGADA AND DHAULI,

BY GEORG BÜHLER, PH.D., LL.D., C.I.E., &c.

MEMBER OF THE IMPERIAL ACADEMY OF SCIENCES,
AND PROFESSOR OF SANSKRIT IN THE UNIVERSITY OF VIENNA.

LONDON:

TRÜBNER & CO., LUDGATE HILL

1887.

Plate I.

CHAITYA SLAB FROM THE INNER RAIL AT AMARÂVATÎ.

Scale 1/6 of the original.

PREFACE.

The present volume contains the results of an examination of the remains of the Amarâvatî Stûpa made in December 1881 and January 1882, soon after the excavation of the site by orders of the Madras Government. By that excavation 255 slabs were laid bare, including a number that had been previously unearthed by Mr. R. Sewell, and again reburied for safety; other 44, which he had stored in a shed, and 29 slabs at Bejwâḍâ Library, brought up the total to 329 of all sorts,—some of them mere fragments, with little or no sculpture upon them. To these, by some small excavations, I was able to add 90 more bearing sculptures or inscriptions, and had the time and means at my disposal allowed a systematic examination, still more might have been discovered. The following pages contain a description of specimens of each sort of slab and sculpture, including illustrations of all the larger and best preserved.

The publication of this volume has been very unfortunately delayed, first by the detention of the sculptures at Amarâvatî for twenty months after they were packed, and so preventing their being photographed; secondly, by cataract in both my eyes, which crippled me for a time, and then laid me aside entirely for four months; and thirdly, by difficulties and delays in the preparation of the plates. In a work which was intended to be complementary, so far as the Amarâvatî Stûpa is concerned, to the *Tree and Serpent Worship* of the late James Fergusson, Esq., D.C.L., LL.D., C.I.E., &c., I had counted on much and valuable assistance from him. He was naturally greatly interested in it, and had promised to look over the proof-sheets and suggest any improvements that might occur to him. The first two chapters were submitted to him, but offered no point on which he felt disposed to make any remark, and before the next sheets were ready to submit to him, the hand of death was on him, and deprived me of his ever kindly and considerate criticisms, inspired as they were to the last by a genius so intuitive as his, and a knowledge so wide and minutely accurate in every detail. If the date now assigned to the Amarâvatî Stûpa is earlier than what he had arrived at, his was the genius to assign it to the same age as the Nâsik caves; and had I discovered no inscriptions of the Andhra kings at Amarâvatî, the revised translations of the Nâsik inscriptions and the advances made in Indian chronology since he wrote his work would alone have required a rectification of his date. The discovery of an undoubted inscription of King Pulumâvi—the same Andhra monarch who has also left us inscriptions at Nâsik and Kârlê—puts the accuracy of his bold induction beyond question.

Among the plates are included copies of all the drawings made under Colonel Colin Mackenzie's direction that were not already published in *Tree and Serpent Worship.* Many of the scenes depicted in the sculptures thus illustrated cannot be yet identified, but as our knowledge of Buddhist myth and legend advances, it may be expected that more of them will be explained. With reference to the plates, I cannot better express my own opinion than in the words of Mr. Fergusson in the Preface to the second edition of his work: "The more I study them, the more convinced I am that the plates of this work—I speak of the plates and the plates only, wholly irrespective of the text—are the most valuable contributions that have been made to our knowledge of Buddhist history and art since James Prinsep's wonderful decipherment and translation of the Aśoka inscriptions. These plates present us with an entirely new but most interesting picture of religion, life, and manners in India in the first centuries of the Christian era." The additional fifty-two plates of sculptures in this volume ought to increase the interest, as they add to the information.

In a work dealing with the *disjecta membra* of a great structure, often added to or partly "restored" for three or four centuries, and with little beyond a few fragments of the Outer Rail found *in situ*, a systematic arrangement of the materials and illustrative notices is almost impossible; and when it is remembered that most of the text had to be written under the almost daily interruption of official correspondence, its defects in this respect may perhaps find excuse.

To Dr. E. Hultzsch, now Epigraphical Assistant to the Archæological Survey of Southern India, I am indebted for the translation of the Prâkṛit inscriptions found on the stones. And Professor G. Bühler, LL.D., C.I.E., of Vienna, besides the translation of the Jaggayyapeṭa inscriptions, has contributed to the volume revised readings and translations of the Aśoka inscriptions at Jaugada in Gânjâm, and at Dhauli in Orissa, from the facsimiles which I made in April 1882, and his improved versions will doubtless be appreciated by Orientalists. Lastly, to the publishers I owe the use of a large number of the woodcuts, and I was allowed the use of several of the others by the late Mr. J. Fergusson shortly before his death.

J. BURGESS.

EDINBURGH, 11*th October* 1886.

CONTENTS.

THE AMARÂVATÎ STÛPA.

LIST OF PLATES.

LIST OF WOODCUTS.

REPORT

OF THE

ARCHÆOLOGICAL SURVEY OF SOUTHERN INDIA.

THE AMARÂVATÎ STÛPA.

CHAPTER I.

INTRODUCTORY: EARLY HISTORY.

WHEN any monument of an antiquarian character is discovered in Western countries,—it scarcely matters where, in the great basin round the Mediterranean, or within the limits of the ancient great historic monarchies,—there is little difficulty in relegating it at once to its proper period, religion, and type. So much has been done, especially within quite recent years, for every branch of Classical, Egyptian, Assyrian, Keltic, and other forms of archæology, and so many works have been written on every class of monuments, and the ancient history of the different countries is so fully known, that any well-educated person can, with a moderate amount of study, speedily qualify himself to deal intelligently with any branch of the science or to make original investigations. In Indian archæology the case is very different: we have no history of early times; the Paurânik legends that do duty for history only puzzle or mislead; in numismatics, which has done such service in opening up the histories of other countries, we know little or nothing as yet bearing on that of Southern India; the inscriptions of Northern and Western India have of late been discussed by several able scholars, but for the south and east of the Peninsula, the labours of Mr. F. Whyte Ellis and Colonel Colin Mackenzie[1] in the early part of the century, of Sir

[1] Colonel Mackenzie, between 1796 and 1818, collected over eight thousand (8076) inscriptions, besides drawings and other materials for the illustration of the antiquities of Southern India; but, except the catalogues and brief analyses of the vernacular MSS. by Dr. H. H. Wilson and the Rev. W. Taylor, they have not been examined.

Walter Elliot[1] between 1826 and 1854, and of Dr. Burnell,[2] represent very nearly all that has been attempted; and in architecture, we owe all that has yet been published to Dr. James Fergusson.

Hence it arises that there is scarcely any literature on the subject of South Indian antiquities but what has been created within the last few years, and that is of too local and restricted a character to enable the mere student to qualify himself for entering upon strictly antiquarian research in India with the same confidence and breadth of information as he could readily acquire in any department of Western research. New discoveries are not unfrequently quite unconnected with anything previously met with; there is nothing to guide the investigator to their age and class; and he has to depend on a long and wide experience of styles of sculpture, architecture, palæography, and the like, to lead him to an approximate date. He must also bring together such scattered historical and other fragments of information as can be found to support his conclusions. For the evidence of style, though the most trustworthy, is often more distinctly felt than can easily be so expressed as to carry conviction to those not accustomed to judge of its value or unfamiliar with its principles; for, as the botanist or zoologist at once relegates to the same order of plants or animals forms the most unlike each other to the untrained eye; so, from a comparison—dependent sometimes on minute details rather than marked resemblance—the antiquary is often able at first sight to co-ordinate structures which appear to the inexperienced very dissimilar. But this criterion of style, where it is applied with sufficient care, is an almost unfailing one. Inscriptions are of course most useful, but they have to be used with caution, for we do not always know whether they have not been added at some period of restoration or addition, long after the original work was finished, or whether they belong to some previous structure demolished to make room for that which may be under consideration.

Much, too, that has been written on Indian antiquities is misleading, and some of the largest and most pretentious works have to be used with great caution,[3] and the facts they may contain sifted from the theories and conclusions of the authors.

The remains of an ancient stûpa, or mound surrounded by carved slabs, at Amarâvatî, on the left or south bank of the river Kṛishṇâ, little over twenty miles higher up than Bejwâḍâ, were discovered by Colonel Colin Mackenzie, of the Trigonometrical Survey, in 1797. The vicinity was then almost quite unknown to Europeans, and the neighbouring village was being extended under a petty landholder, who was ambitious to secure both regal and divine honours, and had just made it his capital. The stûpa was being excavated by his orders, for the sake of the bricks and massive stone slabs it was found to contain,

---

[1] Sir Walter Elliot, between 1826 and 1834, collected copies of 595 inscriptions, chiefly in the Canarese districts of the Dekhan, and made another large collection in the Telugu districts, between 1848 and 1854 (*Ind. Ant.*, vol. vi, p. 227). The first were largely utilised by himself in a paper read before the Royal Asiatic Society in 1836 (*J. R. A. S.*, vol. iv, pp. 1–41), which supplied almost the sole material used by Professor Lassen in his *Indische Alterthumskunde* for the history of the Chalukyan dynasties of the Dekhan, and more recently by Mr. J. F. Fleet in numerous translations in the *Indian Antiquary;* but though both collections were deposited with the Literary Society at Madras, no attempt has been made by any scholar in that Presidency to utilise them. Sir Walter's own rough versions were destroyed on the voyage from India.

[2] Dr. Burnell collected fac-similes of important inscriptions for his *South Indian Palæography*, but he contributed little towards their translation.

[3] Few books on the subject were, till within recent years at least, more frequently referred to than T. Maurice's *Indian Antiquities* (7 vols. London, 1800–6), but works with as pretentious titles and of quite as little scientific value have been published within the last decade.

and Colonel Mackenzie visited the place, and perceiving the importance of the discovery, did his best to carry off or delineate as many of the finest sculptures as he was able. But with no history, and little of any other information bearing on the antiquities of the country, it is not to be wondered at that it was not till long after Colonel Mackenzie's time that it was first surmised that the Amarâvatî stûpa was a Buddhist monument. His own belief that it might be Jaina was creditable, considering the state of knowledge at the time.

The earliest mention we have of the Telugu country is in the famous edicts of Aśôka, about 250 B.C., in the second of which[1] he speaks of the neighbouring kingdoms "as Chôḍa, Pâṁḍiyâ, the countries of Satiyaputra, and Ketalaputra as far as Taṁbapaṁṇî (Ceylon)." Here Satiyaputra represents Telingana, probably including also Kaliṅga, or the districts over which the Telugu language is spoken, and which, in modern times at least, extends along the east coast from Ganjam to Pulikat, and thence eastwards to the seventy-eighth meridian, which closely corresponds with its eastern limit as far north as the Pain-gaṅgâ River, where the boundary turns to the eastwards.

The earliest dynasty of which we have any record as ruling this country is that of the Śâtavâhanas or Andhras, who held sway for about four centuries,[2] from the second century B.C. till the end of the second or beginning of the third century A.D. In its palmier days this kingdom must have been the most powerful in the Peninsula. Pliny,[3] in the first Christian century, says, "Validior deinde gens Andaræ, plurimis vicis, XXX oppidis, quæ, muris turribusque muniuntur, regi præbet peditum C.M. equitum MM., elephantas M."

Their conquests extended far to the north and to the western coast; for one of their earliest kings—Simuka Satakaṁṇi—perhaps the first of the dynasty, has covered the walls of a large cave at Nânâghâṭ, fifty miles north-west from Puṇâ, with an inscription recording the great Brahmanical sacrifices he had made, and the rich gifts he had bestowed on each occasion;[4] and his successors, in the Cave Temples at Nâsik, Kârlê, and Kaṇheri,[5] and on their coins, have left evidences that they had extended their power to Mâlwâ and the borders of Gujarât.[6]

Their first capital is said to have been on the Kṛishṇâ, at Śrîkâkulam,[6] about nineteen

---

[1] In the Jaugada, Girnâr, Kâlsi, and Kapur-di-giri copies; in the Dhauli version the part is so weather-worn that it is illegible. See Senart's *Inscriptions de Piyadasi*, pp. 62 ff.; *Archæolog. Survey of West. India, Report*, vol. ii, p. 99; and infra pp. 115, 121.

[2] Wilford has made three dynasties of these Andhra kings (*As. Res.*, vol. ix, p. 101). There is no warrant for this in the *Purâṇas*, except that in the *Matsya*, a second dynasty of "seven other Andhra kings of the race of their servants" is mentioned; but the corresponding passage in the *Vâyu* speaks of "seven contemporary races; as ten Abhîras," &c. Wilson, *Vishṇu Pur.*, Hall's ed., vol. iv, pp. 207, 216.

[3] Pliny, *Hist. Nat.*, lib. vi, c. 22, s. 4.

[4] *Arch. Sur. West. Ind. Rep.*, vol. v, pp. 59–74.

[5] *Ibid.*, vol. iv, pp. 105–114; and vol. v, pp. 75, 76, 78, 82. In the Hâthigumphâ inscription of Udayagiri in Orissa, dated in the 165th year of the Mauryarâja-kâla, mention is made of Sâtakarṇi "protecting the west" and having a numerous army of horses, elephants, men and chariots. This, according as we date the commencement of the era of the Mauryan kings, may have been in 157 or in 92 B.C., and is proof that this dynasty was powerful for at least a century B.C. Bhagvânlâl Indraji in *Actes du Sixième Congr. intern. des Orientalistes, à Leide*, IIIième partie, pp. 149 ff.

[6] Wilson, *Mackenzie MSS.*, vol. i, introd., p. cxvii; there is another Srî-kâkola (*vulgo* Chicacole) on the coast in Ganjam district, at one time the capital of Kalinga, and which is perhaps the Κωκαλα of Ptolemy (VII, i, 12), though he has placed it too near the mouths of the Ganges. In the *Andhra kaumudî*, as cited by Mr. Campbell (*Telugu Gram.*, Int. p. ii), we find it stated that—"Formerly, in the time of Manu Svayambhû, in the Kali age, Hari, the lord of Andhra, the great Vishṇu, the slayer of the Dânava Nishambhu, was born in Kâkula, as the son of the monarch Suchandra, and was attended by all the gods as well as reverenced by all mankind. He having constructed a vast wall connecting Srîsaila, Bhîmêśvara (at Dracharâmam, lat. 16° 46½′ N., long. 82° 7′ E.)

miles west from Masulipatam, and founded, according to legend, by Sumati, a great emperor; by whom is probably meant Simuka,[1] the first of the dynasty. It was afterwards transferred to Dhânyakaṭaka or Dharaṇikoṭa, and thence to other places. Indeed the royal seat was either frequently moved, or else the princes had separate viceroyalties under the supreme king. Thus Ptolemy, the Greek geographer, about A.D. 150, mentions a city in the Dekhan which he calls 'Hippokoura the capital of Baleokouros.'[2]. Its position is not determined, but on the Andhra coins found at Kôlhâpur we have the names of two kings, Viḷivâyakura Vasishṭhîputra and Viḷivâyakura Gotamîputra,[3] and Professor Bhâṇḍârkar has concluded, with some probability, that Viḷivâyakura may be the name represented by the Greek Baleokouros.[4] Again, Ptolemy[5] calls Baithana or Paithana, on the Upper Godâvarî, "the capital of Siri Polemaios," in which we easily recognise Śrî Puḷumâyi or Puḷumâvi,[6] who is mentioned in inscriptions at Nâsik, Kârlê, and Amarâvatî.

In order to approximate as near as we may to the probable date of the Amarâvatî stûpa, it will be necessary to indicate how the chronology of the Sâtavâhana kings, who date their inscriptions only in regnal years, is arrived at, and to supply such other scraps of information as relate to the subject. Now, as I have shown in *The Cave Temples*,[7] the inscriptions of Nahapâṇa, a satrap of Western India, and of his son-in-law Ushavadâta or Ṛishabhadaṭṭa, are dated in the years 40, 42, and 46,[8] probably of the Śaka era, or in A.D. 118–125. Nahapâṇa calls himself a Kshaharâta, and Sâtakarṇi Gotamîputra says that he rooted out this race and subdued their country. The coins of Nahapâṇa and of Chashṭana, another satrap, ruling most probably in Mâlwâ and Gujarât, have both Baktrian-Pâli legends and are of the same type;[9] but Ptolemy mentions a Tiastanes as ruling at Ujjain,[10] who is identified with Chashṭana, and this places him before 150 A.D. Then Chashṭana's grandson, Rudradâman, in an inscription on the Girnâr rock,[11] gives a date "in the year 72," and says he defeated "Sâtakarṇi, the lord of Dakshiṇâpatha" (the Dekhan). Rudradâman's son, Svâmi Rudrasiṁha's coins date from 102 to 117, or A.D. 180–195. Thus we arrive at these approximate dates:—

Nahapâṇa in the Dekhan	about A.D.	110–125
Chashṭana at Ujjain	,, ,,	125–140
Jayadâman, his son	,, ,,	140–148
Rudradâman, his son, in Gujarât	,, ,,	148–178
Rudrasiṁha, his son	,, ,,	178–200[12]

Kâleśvara (the greater), and the Mahêndra hills (50 miles N.N.E. from Kaliṅgapaṭṭam), formed in it three gates," &c. This Andhra Râyuḍu is now worshipped as a divinity at Śrîkâkulam on the Kṛishṇâ, and was the patron of Kunva, the first Telugu grammarian.

[1] This is the name as given in the Nânâghâṭ inscription; in the *Purâṇas* it is corrupted into Śiśuka, Śipraka, Sindhuka, &c.

[2] *Geog.*, VII, i, 33.

[3] *Jour. Bom. Br. R. As. Soc.*, vol. xiii, p. 305; vol. xiv, pp. 153, 154.

[4] *Early Hist. of the Dekhan*, p. 17.

[5] *Geog.*, VII, i, 82.

[6] This was pointed out by Lassen, *Ind. Alterth.*, vol. iii, p. 179; *conf.* vol. i, p. 213 n.; vol. ii, pp. 884, 954.

[7] Pp. 189, 264 ff.; *Arch. Sur. West. Ind. Rep.*, vol. iv, pp. 37, 78.

[8] *Arch. Sur. West. Ind. Rep.*, vol. iv, pp. 102, 103.

[9] *Ibid.*, vol. iv, p. 37 and note.

[10] *Geog.*, lib. vii, c. i, 63.

[11] *Arch. Sur. West. Ind. Rep.*, vol. ii, p. 129; *Cave Temples*, p. 189.

[12] Coins continue the dates of these Kshatrapa kings down to about the year 310, *i.e.*, to A.D. 388. Now Chandragupta, who conquered Gujarât, dates his coins in 82–93, of the Gupta era, which, according to Albiruni, began in A.D. 319; and thus he was ruling in A.D. 401. The accordance of these dates supports the assumption above made, that the Kshatrapas used the Śaka era for their inscriptions.

As Nahapâṇa almost certainly represents the Kshaharâtas uprooted by Sâtakarṇi Gotamîputra, we must place them as contemporaries, and Puḷumâyi, the son of the latter, will thus be contemporary with Chashṭana,—as we should naturally infer from Ptolemy's mention of both. In brief, we have :—

Sâtakarṇi Gautamîputra I.	circa A.D.	114–135
Puḷumâyi Vâsishṭhîputra, his son	,, ,,	135–163[1]
S'ivaśrî Sâtakarṇi, Vâsishṭhîputra[2]	,, ,,	163–170
S'ivaskanda, ? Mâḍharîputra	,, ,,	170–178
S'rî Yajña Sâtakarṇi Gautamîputra	,, ,,	178–200
Vijaya	,, ,,	200–210
Chandraśrî Sâtakarṇi, Vadaśrî[3]	,, ,,	210–215
Pulumâvi III.	,, ,,	215–220[4]

This investigation enables us to place the inscriptions we have of Puḷumâyi and Śrî Yajña from Amarâvatî within the limits of the second Christian century.

There are, however, some other fragments of information, hitherto almost unnoticed, which it may be as well to present here.

In a Tibetan life of the great Buddhist Âchârya Nâgârjuna, the founder of the Mâdhyamika school, who is said to have governed the Buddhist Church for sixty or sixty-two years, we are told that he travelled widely in Southern India, converted Muñja, king of Oḍiviśa (Orissa), and a thousand of his people, did much for the preservation of the Southern congregation, erected many vihâras in Oḍiviśa and other countries, and specially that he "surrounded the great shrine of Dhânyakaṭaka with a railing."[5] Now, could we ascertain the date at which Nâgârjuna lived, this statement would be of considerable value to us. Unfortunately such accounts as we possess on this point are most conflicting.

In the seventh century three states occupied the Andhra country. Kosala extended over a very considerable area of the territory which, less than a century ago, formed the Marâṭha kingdom of Berar, and, as shown by Mr. Fergusson, its capital was probably near Wairâgaḍh or Chanda.[6] To the south-west of it was Andhra, the capital of which Hiuen Thsang calls Phing-khi-lo,[7]—syllables which have not been transliterated into any recognisable

---

[1] Dr. Bhau Dâjî (*Jour. Bom. Br. R. As. Soc.*, vol. vii, p. 117) places "Padumâvî" about A.D. 120.

[2] See *Ind. Ant.*, vol. ix, p. 64.

[3] *Ibid.*

[4] For a full list of the Andhras as given in the *Purâṇas*, see *Cave Temples*, p. 265.

[5] Schiefner's *Târanâtha's Geschichte des Buddhismus*, p. 72; *Jour. As. Soc. Beng.*, vol. li, p. 119; *Ind. Ant.*, vol. xii, p. 88.

[6] *Jour. R. As. Soc.*, N.S., vol. vi, p. 262. The *Matsya Purâṇa* speaks of a dynasty of "S'rî-parvatiya Andhras," which may refer to a petty dynasty of kings ruling perhaps at Chandraguptapaṭnam near S'rî S'ailam. Wilson's *Vishṇ. Pur.*, Hall's ed., vol. iv, p. 208. They are said to have reigned fifty-two years, and are, perhaps, the same dynasty to which the *Bhâgavata Purâṇa* assigns seven kings. Lassen, *Ind. Alterth.*, vol. ii, p. 1212 n.

[7] The resemblance of this to Veṅgi, the name of the capital of the Pallava dynasty in the fifth century, is either accidental, or Vêgi near Elur and fifty-five miles E.N.E. from Amarâvatî does not represent the ancient Veṅgi. Dr. Burnell ingeniously tried to identify the Chinese and Indian names: see his *South Ind. Palæog.*, p. 16 n. In the inscription of Samudragupta at Allahâbâd, Hastivarman, king of Veṅgi, and Svâmîdatta of Peṭhâpur or Pishṭâpur, are mentioned among those conquered by him in Dakshiṇâpatha ;—the latter place being about seventy-seven miles E.N.E. from the former. This belongs to the year 70 or 75 of the Gupta era, or about 390 A.D. *Jour. As. Soc. Beng.*, vol. iii, p. 263; vol. vi, p. 972; *J. Bom. Br. R. As. Soc.*, vol. ix, App. p. cxcviii; conf. *Ind. Ant.*, vol. v, p. 73; vol. xii, p. 34. A class of Brâhmans, widely distributed over the Telugu country, are known as Veṅginâḍus, from Veṅgi, and, with the Vêlanâḍus, form the most important division of their caste in the region. Dr. J. Wilson, *Caste*, vol. ii, p. 54.

Indian form, though Viṅkila, as proposed by M. Stan. Julien, probably approximates to it. Its position was 900 li (150 miles) or so to the south of Kosala, and, if the pilgrim's statements are to be depended on, it must have lain somewhere to the west of the Godâvarî, about Chandur, in about lat. 18° 35′ N. To identify it with Veṅgi, the capital of the Pallava kingdom of the fifth century, is in conflict with the overthrow of that dynasty by Kubja Vishṇuvardhana about thirty years before Hiuen Thsang's visit. The circuit of 6000 li,[1] which he ascribes to the kingdom of Dhañakaṭaka, implies a breadth of at least 150 miles, and embracing Veṅgi and the whole of the area included in the present Kṛishṇâ and Gôdâvarî districts, with a large territory outside of them. The third kingdom was Mahâ-Andhra or Dhânyakaṭaka, whose capital Hiuen Thsang places 1000 li (165 miles) or so to the south of Phing-khi-lo, and near it were two great convents, then deserted.

At the end of his account of Kosala, Hiuen Thsang tells us that in former times a King So-to-pho-ho, for the sake of Nâgârjuna, had established a Saṅghârâma at a place "about 300 li or sixty miles to the south-west of the country, on the Po-lo-mo-lo-ki-li mountain. The solitary peak of this mountain towers above the rest, and stands out with its mighty precipices as a solid mass of rock, without approaches or intervening valleys." Not having visited the place himself, and being extremely credulous and ready to believe any wonderful account, the report he gives from hearsay is manifestly a very exaggerated one and not a little indefinite. He says the king "tunnelled out this rock through the middle," and "at a distance of ten li, by tunnelling, he opened a covered approach. Thus, by standing under the rock, we see the cliff excavated throughout, and in the midst of long galleries (or corridors) with eaves for walking under and high towers, the storeyed building reaching to the height of five stages, each stage with four halls with vihâras enclosed," &c. He informs us also that the name signified "black peak." Fa-hian, in the beginning of the fifth century, also heard of this place when at Banâras, and gives a still more wonderful account of it. He calls it Po-lo-yu,[2] which he explains as meaning "pigeon monastery." This latter would lead us to Pârâvata as the proper name, while Hiuen Thsang's Po-lo-mo-lo-ki-li may be transliterated, as Julien does, into Paramalagiri, or into Parabaragiri, or, as Mr. Beal has it, into Bhramarâgiri;[3] but none of these forms help us to identify the place, though both Chinese spellings seem to point to Parvata as perhaps the true one. To this monastery we are told Nâgârjuna summoned Bhikshus or devotees to reside in it, and stored it with copies of all the canonical books and their commentaries; and as the Tibetan books say that he died at the monastery of Dpal-gyi-ri or Śrî-Parvata mountain,[4] they doubtless refer to the same place. Afterwards, Hiuen Thsang informs us, quarrels arose, and the Brâhmans expelled the Buddhists and took entire possession of the monastery. Now, if we assume, with Mr. Fergusson, that Wairâgaḍh[5] was the capital of Kosala, and that

[1] Hiuen Thsang's indications of the sizes of districts by their circuits is as unsatisfactory as it is peculiar. It would be the most difficult thing possible to get close approximations to the peripheries of districts, and when obtained they afford no idea of the area included; thus a circumference of 6000 li may enclose almost any area up to 80,000 square miles, according to the form enclosed and the character of the boundary-line.

[2] *Fa-hian*, chap. xxxv.

[3] Julien's *Mém. sur les Contr. Occid.*, tome ii, pp. 101–106, and *Méthode*, Nos. 1159, 1043; Beal's *Bud. Records of West. Countries*, vol. ii, pp. 214–217.

[4] Vassilief's *Bouddisme*, p. 201.

[5] *Jour. R. As. Soc.*, N.S., vol. vi, p. 262. Wairâgaḍh, in lat. 20° 25′ N., long. 80° 5′ E., is, according to tradition, a place of great antiquity, founded by a King Vairôchana. It was the capital of a family of Mânâ chiefs, till they were overthrown by the Gonds about the ninth century. The surrounding forest contains numerous foundations of ancient buildings.

Hiuen Thsang's "300 li from the country" are to be measured from the capital, we ought to look for the site of this monastery somewhere to the south-west of Chândâ, or near Mânikdurg and the Varadhâ river. Mr. Fergusson would place it on the Viñjhâsanî hill, near Bhândak, a town which local tradition identifies with Bhadrâvatî, mentioned in the *Mahâbhârata*. The Viñjhâsanî hill, however, does not at all answer to the description given by Hiuen Thsang, though it contains caves which mark it out as an ancient place.

But Śrî-Parvata is the name of the famous Brahmanical temple, dedicated to Mallikârjuna,[1] which stands on a lofty rock overhanging the Kṛishṇâ river, and is better known by the synonymous name of Śrî-Śailam, one of the twelve great liṅga shrines of later Hinduism,[2] about 102 miles W.S.W. from Dharaṇikoṭa and eighty-two miles E.N.E. from Karnul. This is 250 miles south of Mânikdurg and beyond the probable limits of the Kosala kingdom; but it is to be remembered that Hiuen Thsang reports from hearsay, and may easily have been led into a mistake as to its position; indeed, his expression is so ambiguous, that it is doubtful whether the distance was reckoned from the capital of Sh'-yen-toh-kia or from the borders of the Kosala country. The accounts given both by Fa-hian and Hiuen Thsang agree quite as closely with the actual shrine of Śrî-Parvata as Hiuen Thsang's similar second-hand report respecting Ajaṇṭâ does with the fact. No previous attempt to fix the site of this place has been satisfactory;[3] it has puzzled every one, and that now offered is the only one that, with the exception of the rather obscure indication of distance, fulfils the essential conditions in the descriptions. That Śrî-Parvata was the proper form of the name seems proved by the Tibetan, and the identity of this with Śrî-Śailam is well known and recognised throughout Sanskrit literature,[4] while the acknowledged great antiquity of the Hindû shrine, the ancient and very remarkable causeways of very early date constructed from different points up to the top of the precipitous hill, and the character of the place, agree sufficiently with the reports of the Chinese pilgrims.

---

[1] In lat. 16° 7′ N. and long. 78° 55′ E. See *Asiat. Res.*, vol. v, p. 303 ff.; vol. xv, p. 123; *Madras Jour. of Lit. and Sc.*, 3d series, pt. 2 (Oct. 1866), pp. 132–134, 138–139; Hamilton's *Gazetteer*, s. v. Perwuttum. Since this was in type I have personally visited this remote shrine, so difficult of access, and found the almost isolated hill, about 1570 feet high, surrounded on three sides by the river Kṛishṇâ and the fourth partly by the Bhîmanakollam torrent. The present temple dates from about the beginning of the sixteenth century, and in details so resembles the Hazâra-Râma temple at Vijayanagar, that there can be little doubt that they were both built about the same time. The courses of sculptures on the outer walls round the courts are of precisely the same character as those at Vijayanagar. It must have been rebuilt after some destruction by the Muhammadans, probably in the fifteenth century; but of its predecessors there are few if any vestiges now visible.

[2] Wilson's *Hindu Theatre*, vol. ii, pp. 18, 277; *As. Res.*, vol. xvii, pp. 196, 197; Monier Williams's *Hinduism*, p. 178.

[3] *Jour. R. As. Soc.*, vol. vi, p. 313; Cunningham, *Anc. Geog.*, p. 525.

[4] The *Mâtsya Purâṇa* speaks of a family of Śrî-Parvatîya Andhras, which may refer to a petty dynasty of kings ruling either at Śrî-Śailam itself, or across the river, at Chandraguptapatṇam in the vicinity. They are said to have ruled fifty-two years, and are perhaps the same race to which the *Bhâgavata Purâṇa* assigns seven kings. Wilson, *Vish. Pur.*, Hall's ed., vol. iv, p. 208; Lassen, *Ind. Alterth.*, vol. ii, p. 1212 n. Śrî-Parvata or Śrî-Śaila is mentioned in the *Mahâbh.*, iii, 8160; *Śuśruta*, ii, 169, 2; *Bṛih. Sanhita*, xvi, 3; *Mârkand. Pur.*, lvii, 15; *Vâsavad.*, 87, 2; *Bhâg. Pur.*, v, 19, 16; x, 29, 13; *Kathâsaritsâg.*, 65, 66, 73, 105. In the *Mâtsya Purâṇa*, where the names of Durgâ are given, she is said to be called Mâdhavî at Śrî-Śaila; in the *Śiva Purâṇa* the liṅga here is called Mallikârjuna. When Bâṇa was slain by Śiva as he was traversing the heavens, part of his carcase fell at Śrî-śaila in Siddhikshetra, another at Amarakaṇṭaka, and the remainder near Gaṅgâsâgara. *Revâmâhâtmya*, chap. xxix, in Wilson, *Sel. Works*, vol. v, p. 118. In the *Śaṅkarakshepa-Śaṅkarajaya*, "Śaṅkara adores in Mahârâshṭra the Mallikârjuna of Śrî-Śaila;" and in the *Agni Purâṇa*, Śrî is said to have performed austerities there. The shrines are dedicated to Mallikârjuna, a form of Śiva, and to Pârvatî and Bramharambhâ, to the latter of whom a sheep is sacrificed every Tuesday and Friday—a survival of the old bloody sacrifices offered to all forms of Durgâ. There is a *Mallikârjuna Śataka*;—Wilson, *Mack. Coll.*, vol. i, p. 350.

To return from this digression: the king who was the Dânapati or patron of Nâgârjuna, and who, through a device of his queen to secure the throne for her son Suśakti, is related to have died at the same time as the patriarch, is said by I-tsing, another Chinese traveller, to have been of the So-to-pho-han-na or Sadvâhana family, and was called Sh'-yen-toh-kia, while Guṇavarman (431 A.D.), in his translation of Nâgârjuna's *Suhṛillêkha*, calls him Shan-tho-kia. There is no uniform certainty about the transliteration of Sanskrit names from Chinese; thus Hiuen Thsang's So-to-pho-ho and I-tsing's So-to-pho-han-na are translated into Chinese as *In-shen*, the Sanskrit equivalent of which is Sadvâhana, whereas we know that the family name of the Andhra kings was Śâtavâhana or Sâtavâhana. But for the restoration of his personal name from Sh'yen-toh-kia or Shan-tho-kia we have no translation or other datum.

In Tibetan he is called Bde-byêd, which is translated by the Sanskrit Śaṁkara.[1] Târanâtha says he was called Udayana, but tells us that in his youth he was named Jetaka,[2] which hardly approximates to the transliteration of Sh'-yen-toh-kia. Mr. Bunyiu Nanjio suggests Jñâtaka[3] as the probable original form of the name. All that we can as yet determine is, that he was most probably one of the latest members of the Andhra dynasty, and possibly identical with the Siri-Yaño or Śrî-Yajña of the Nâsik and Kaṇheri cave-temple inscriptions, whom we have placed about 180 to 200 A.D. Some manuscripts, however, assign to him a reign of ten or more years longer.

In further consideration of the date of Nâgârjuna, it is to be remembered that the Tibetan books take no account of the second Buddhist council, and place the *Nirvâṇa* or death of Buddha only 110 years[4] before the council in Aśoka's time, 240 B.C. Thus they place the council under Kanishka, the great Indo-Skythian king, 400 years after the *Nirvâṇa*;[5] and so with other dates. Hiuen Thsang, the Chinese pilgrim of the seventh century, also usually employs this chronology.[6] Now Kanishka, who is always placed 400 years after the *Nirvâṇa*, is generally admitted to have ruled about 78–100 A.D., and Pârśvika, the Buddhist patriarch who presided at the great council, was his contemporary. Aśvaghôsha was the second in succession to Pârśvika, and Nâgârjuna the fourth. This removes him a considerable distance from the commencement of the second century, or even into the third. Some accounts mention that he lived when 500 years from the *Nirvâṇa* had elapsed, or about 150–200 A.D., and Târanâtha, the Tibetan historian, quotes statements to the effect that he lived either twenty-nine years from the beginning or from the end of the sixth Buddhist century,[7] or about 180 or 220 A.D. If, as is probably intended, the date of his death is meant, and as the interval between Aśoka's council and A.D. 78 is more than the

---

1 "He who makes happy;"—Vassilief's *Bouddisme*, p. 201; Jäschke's *Tibetan-English Dictionary*, p. 270*b*; *Jour. As. Soc. Ben.*, vol. li, p. 119, or *Ind. Ant.*, vol. xii, p. 88. Udayana is also translated into Tibetan as Bde-spyod, and Bde-spyod-bzaṅ-po, and in one place is transliterated by U-tra-ya-na. Schiefner's, *Târanâtha's Gesch. des Buddhismus*, pp. 2, 71, 72.

2 Târanâtha gives his family name as Śântivâhana, or Ântivâhana, and these corruptions may shake our confidence in the accuracy of the personal names he supplies. Schiefner's *Târanâtha's Gesch. des Buddhismus*, pp. 2, 71, 72, 303, 304; *Jour. As. Soc. Ben.*, vol. li, p. 118.

3 *Catalogue of the Chin. Bud. Tripiṭaka*, No. 1464. Might not the name be Jayanta, for Vijâya, the successor of Yajña Śrî? The Tibetan *rgyâl* is equivalent to the Sanskrit *jaya*.

4 *Jour. As. Soc. Ben.*, vol. i, p. 6.

5 *Asiat. Res.*, vol. xx, pp. 400, 513.

6 Beal's *Bud. Records of West. Countries*, vol. i, pp. 99, 150, 151, 156, 174–175. He seems to use this method as one in vogue in India, but not necessarily correct; sometimes he adopts a longer chronology; *ibid.*, vol. ii, pp. 222, 223.

7 *Vassilief*, p. 201; *Târânâtha*, p. 73.

290 years we have allowed,[1] while it seems more natural to reckon from the beginning than the end of a century, we may assume the earlier of these two periods as perhaps the nearer to the true date. If, as seems probable, Śrî-Yajña or else Puḷomâvi III. was the Sâtavâhana king who patronised him, his rule over the Church may have begun about 137 and ended in 197;[2] or, under the last king, it may have extended to about 215 A.D. For our present purpose, however, it is sufficient to have thus fixed the conclusion of his ministry within a few years before or after A.D. 200.

We now pass to the mention of the Amarâvatî monument by Hiuen Thsang. The Chalukyans had conquered the country about thirty years previously, and Jayasiṁhavallabha, the second ruler of the new dynasty, was on the throne, when, about the year 636, the Chinese traveller passed down from the kingdom of Andhra through a thick forest country to Mahâ-Andhra, which he also calls Tho-na-kie-tse-kia or Dhañakaṭaka, from the old capital, close to Amarâvatî. He describes the state as nearly 1000 miles in circuit, and its capital some forty li (nearly seven miles) round. The country he found thinly populated—possibly the result of the recent conquest; the convents had been numerous,[3] but were mostly deserted and ruined; while of those preserved there were about twenty with a thousand priests or so. And he goes on to say that "to the east of the city, bordering (*leaning*) on a mountain, is a convent called the Fo-lo-pho-shi-lo or Purvaśilâ. To the west of the city, leaning against (*maintained by*) a mountain, is a convent called 'O-fa-lo-shi-lo or Avaraśilâ. These (*or* this) were built by an early king in honour of Buddha. He hollowed the valley, made a road, opened the mountain crags, constructed pavilions and long (*lateral*) galleries, while chambers supported the heights and connected the caverns. The divine spirits respectfully defended it; both saints and sages wandered here and reposed. . . . But there have been no priests (*here*) for the last hundred years, in consequence of the spirit of the mountain changing his shape, and appearing sometimes as a wolf, sometimes as a monkey, and frightening the disciples; for this reason the place has become deserted and wild, with no priests to dwell there."[4] And in the life of Hiuen Thsang by Hoeï-lih, it is added to the mention of the monasteries, that the king who built (the latter), "lavished on it all the splendour of the Baktrian palaces."[5]

It is not quite clear what city is here meant; naturally we might infer that it was the capital, which was then at Bejwâḍâ; and if so, Amarâvatî, if it corresponded to the Aparaśilâ or Western-Rock monastery, would be twenty miles distant; but if Dhañakaṭaka were the city meant, Amarâvatî is to the east of it, and would rather agree to the Eastern-Rock or Purvaśilâ convent; and, indeed, the site of a second stûpa is still pointed out to the west of Dharaṇi-

[1] Indeed, the statement that Kanishka lived 400 years after Buddha simply means that 400 years "had elapsed," and it may have been by twenty or even fifty more.

[2] After the above had been written, I found that Eitel, in his *Handbook of Chinese Buddhism*, has placed Nâgârjuna's rule between 137 and 194 A.D. What are his data is not stated, but it would be very interesting to know, as the coincidence with the results of this independent investigation is remarkable.

[3] In the statement in the *Mahâwanso* (5th cent.), that the great sage Mahâdêva took with him from Pallavabhâgo (the Pallava countries) 460,000 devotees, while 844,000 went from all other parts of India, Kashmir and Kabul to the consecration of the Ruanwelli dâgaba at Anurâdhapura (B.C. *circa* 100), the numbers are of course greatly exaggerated (and Turnour has inadvertently added a million to the number of Pallava bhikshus), but the relative proportion is an evidence that Buddhism was believed to have been, in early times, in a very flourishing condition along the east coast of the Peninsula. Turnour's *Mahâwanso*, p. 171.

[4] Beal, *Bud. Records of West. World*, vol. ii, pp. 221–223; M. Julien, *Mém. sur les Contr. Occid.*, t. ii, p. 111.

[5] St. Julien's *Vie de Hiouen Thsang*, p. 188.

koṭa, which may have corresponded to his second saṅghârâma, though every vestige of it has now disappeared. But neither hypothesis quite meets the statement, because the Amarâvatî stûpa is not on or very near any mountain or high rock; still we must bear in mind that Hiuen Thsang, not having visited it personally and not clearly understanding his informants, has, as in the cases of Śrî-Parvata and Ajaṇṭâ, given an inaccurate report. The capital in Hiuen Thsang's time was doubtless at Bejwâḍâ, and Mr. Fergusson has satisfactorily shown [1] that the reference to mountains may be explained as referring to the road or *via sacra* leading from the capital to the Avaraśilâ monastery, which could be no other than this one at Amarâvatî. Moreover, the names of the two monasteries, as we shall see below,[2] may be otherwise explained than with strict reference to their relative topographical position.

But we are not entirely dependent on Hiuen Thsang for mention of a stûpa at Dhañakaṭaka. The Tibetan translation of this name is Dpal-ldan-'bras-spuṅs (accumulation of grain) or Dhânyakaṭaka, and Târanâtha refers to the great Chaitya at it,[3] in terms which might imply that it had been one of the greatest seats of Buddhism in early times.

Like nearly all local legends and royal genealogies, those of the Andhra country derive the descent of the early kings from Parikshit and Janamejaya at the time of the Great War. To Śâlivâhana or Śâtavâhana[4] is assigned a rule of twenty-one years, but his four successors, Mâdhavavarmâ, Kulaketana, Nîlakaṇṭha, and Mukkaṇṭi,[5] together fill a period of 199 years, the last dying in 298 A.D. Then a Chôḷa dynasty is said to have ruled for 217 years, and was succeeded by a Yavana Bhôja and his dynasty, lasting for 458 years, till A.D. 973.[6] By the race here called Yavanabhôja[7] is apparently meant the Eastern Chalukyas, who, under Kubja Vishṇuvardhana, conquered the country about A.D. 606, and ruled till about 1064. They were preceded by a Pallava dynasty, of whose history as yet we know but little. They ruled at Veṅgi, and were connected, if not identical, with the kings of Kañchi,[8]—

---

1 *Jour. R. As. Soc.*, N.S., vol. xii, pp. 104–109.

2 See p. 24.

3 Târanâtha's *Gesch. des Buddhismus*, pp. 142, 277; conf. Köppen, vol. ii, p. 111; Lassen, *Ind. Alt.*, vol. iv, p. 15. In an inscription in the present temple at Amarâvatî, dated in Śaka 1283 (A.D. 1361), the place is called Śrî-Dhânyavâṭîpura, which is quite equivalent to the Pali form Dhaṁñakaṭaka. Conf. *Ind. Ant.*, vol. xi, p. 97.

4 Born at Sâleyadhâra in the Dekhan. Conf. *Arch. Sur. West. Ind. Rep.*, vol. iii, p. 56; *As. Res.*, vol. ix, p. 161; Wilson, *Sel. Works*, vol. iii, p. 181. Of the Paurânik lists of Andhra kings, these local legends seem to make no mention.

5 On the ground that Mukkaṇṭi has the same meaning, Mr. Sewell identifies Mukkaṇṭi with Trinêtra Pallava (*Lists*, pp. 24, 135; conf. *Ind. Ant.*, vol. vii, pp. 243–247). When Mukkaṇṭi is said to have introduced the eight Brâhmaṇ Gôtras and given them villages at Guntûr, Kocharla, Vinukonda, and Yupputur, it is only ascribing to him what is usually related of the founders of Indian kingdoms. The introduction of the Niyogî or secularised Brâhmans, however, into the district, as writers and village accountants, is ascribed in the Yuppaturu inscription to Trinêtra, and elsewhere this is said to have taken place in 1288 A.D. *Jour. Madras Lit. Soc.*, vol. vii, p. 362; Wilson, *Mackenzie MSS.*, vol. i, p. cxx.

6 *Jour. Mad. Lit. Soc.*, vol. vii, pp. 351–354; Wilson, *Mackenzie MSS.*, vol. i, pp. cxix., cxx., cxxiv.

7 Compare the style, "Mahâbhoja," applied to princes in the Kuḍâ and Beḍsâ inscriptions; *Arch. Sur. of West. Ind. Rep.*, vol. iv, pp. 84, 85, 87, 88, 90.

8 Most of the published information respecting the Pallavas has appeared in the *Indian Antiquary*, see vol. i, p. 362; vol. ii, pp. 155, 156, 161, 272; vol. iii, p. 152; vol. iv, p. 110; vol. v, pp. 50–53, 73, 135, 154–157, 175–177, 318; vol. vi, pp. 25, 30, 61–63, 65, 69, 71, 78, 85, 87, 93; vol. vii, pp. 5–7, 21, 111, 219, 243, 245–247, 303; vol. viii, pp. 1 ff., 23–25, 28, 50, 90, 98, 167–173, 244–246, 273–284; vol. ix, pp. 49, 99–103, 129; vol. x, pp. 36–39, 102, 134, 163; vol. xi, pp. 97, 111, 125–127, 156, 162, 256 f.; vol. xii, p. 187; also Burnell's *South Ind. Palæog.*, pp. 15–17, 35–39, 67, 70, 135, 136; *Jour. Mad. Lit. Soc.*, vol. vii, pp. 8, 20, 202, 207, 319; vol. xi, pp. 302–306; vol. xiii, p. 53; vol. xvi, p. 132; vol. xx, p. 98; *Jour. As. Soc. Beng.*, vol. vii, pp. 110, 121, 496. If the term Pahlava in Sanskrit literature always refers to the Parthians (M. Müller, *H. Sans. Lit.*, p. 54; Weber, *Hist. Ind. Lit.*, p. 188), it seems somewhat strange, that while Andhras, Choḷas, Keralas, and other

possibly ruling the Andhra country through princes of the blood royal or Yuvarâjas. From their copperplate grants we have recovered the names of some of the line ruling in the fourth or fifth century, and a fragment of a large inscription found at Amarâvatî gives a considerable number,[1] but unfortunately only a portion of each line is preserved, and we cannot determine their mutual relations or dates. The dynasty may have ruled for two centuries or more previous to the beginning of the seventh, and in the interval between the Andhras and it there must have been another ruling race[2] represented perhaps by the Purushadaṭṭa Mâḍharîputra, whose inscriptions I discovered at Jaggayyapeṭa.[3] It is said that the last of the Andhras was drowned, and was succeeded by usurping officers,[4] when the kingdom was probably broken up into several portions.

From this examination we have been able to fix approximately the dates of the early Andhra kings whose inscriptions are found at Amarâvatî, and of Nâgârjuna, through whose influence the rail is said to have been erected. The results are in close accordance, and so far mutually support each other. Let us now see how far this agrees with the style of the work as previously investigated by Mr. J. Fergusson. When he wrote his *Tree and Serpent Worship* in 1868, he very justly compared both the style of the sculptures and the alphabet of the inscriptions with those of the Buddhist rock-temples at Nâsik and Kaṇheri, and decided that the Amarâvatî rail stood in point of time between the Sâtakarṇi Gautamîputra cave at Nâsik and the Kaṇheri chaitya; but neither then nor when he published the second edition of the work in 1873 had these early inscriptions received due attention, and almost the only information then available was contained in Dr. Stevenson's paper[5] of 1852, in which the Nâsik inscriptions are ascribed to the early part of the fourth century. As stated above, we now know that the inscriptions of Śâtakarṇi Gautamîputra and Puḷumâyi Vasishṭhîputra at Nâsik belong to about the middle of the second century, and those of Śrî-Yajña Gautamîputra to the end of the same century.[6] With this fresh determination, then, we must necessarily carry back also the date of the Amarâvatî rail; and this is exactly in the line of Mr. Fergusson's argument. For, after discussing the evidence just noticed, he added:—"Notwithstanding all this, there is so much of Greek, or rather Baktrian art in the architectural details of the Amarâvatî tope, that the first inference is that it must be nearer

---

South Indian nations are so frequently mentioned, the Pallavas of Kâñchi and Veṅgi should be passed over. But in the lists in the *Mahâbhârata*, &c., we find the Pahlavas so frequently classed with Drâviḍas, Śakas, Yavanas, Śabaras, &c., and with Abhîras, Śabaras, Mallas, &c., that it may well be supposed that the Pallavas were, in several cases at least, meant, but that the copyists, not so familiar with this southern race as with the classic Pahlavas, assimilated the names, or even misread the former. We know that in some cases they have changed the name also into Pahnavas. The following are the principal references to the Pahlavas:—*Manu*, x, 44; *Mahâbhârata*, i, 6683; ii, 1199, 1871; iii, 1990; vi, 355, 375; *Harivaṁśa*, 760, 768, 776, 781, 782, 1446, 1764, 6441; *Bṛihat Saṁhita*, v, 38; xiv, 17; xvi, 38; xviii, 6; *Mârkand. Pur.*, lvii, 36; lviii, 30, 50; Wilson, *Vishṇu Pur.* (ed. Hall), vol. iii, pp. 291, 294. The only mention I know of them in Bauddha literature is that in the *Mahâvaṁso*, ch. xxix, cited in note 3 above, p. 9.

1 *Notes on Amarâvatî Stûpa*, p. 50.

2 The Śrî-Parvatîya Andhras, already referred to.

3 *Ind. Ant.*, vol. xi, pp. 256–259.

4 *As. Res.*, vol. ix, pp. 45, 62, 102, 110.

5 *J. Bom. B. R. As. Soc.*, vol. v, pp. 1 ff.

6 Dr. Bühler is inclined to date them about 130 years earlier, but his hypothesis depends on the Kshatrapas having used the Vikramâditya era, and on the Gupta era being 128 years earlier than the date assigned to it by Albiruni, both of which require confirmation. Pandit Bhagvânlâl Indraji, Ph.D. (*Bomb. Gazet.*, vol. xvi, p. 620), by dating the Gupta era from the second century, has supported the same theory; but this position, in view of recent researches, is untenable. The Gupta era commenced in 319 A.D.

to the Christian era than the form of the inscriptions would lead us to suppose."[1] With the revised date for the inscriptions we find that this inference is perfectly justified, and we may now with confidence place the date of the rail in the latter part of the second century. The stûpa itself is much older, as is shown both by the sculptures and the inscriptions—especially one in the Maurya character recording the gift of a pillar by the General Mundakuṇtala. The inner rail, again, is probably slightly more modern than the outer one.

[1] *Tree and Serp. Wor.*, p. 172.

1. Buddha, Śâriputra, and Maudgalyâyanâ, from a Gândhâra Sculpture.

MAP OF AMARÂVATÎ IN GUNTÛR
AND THE DIAMOND MINES OF PARTIYÂLA.
WITH THE ADJACENT VILLAGES.

PLATE II.

W. GRIGGS, LITH.

Reduced from the original survey in 1816.

FURLONGS — MILES.

CHAPTER II.

THE EXCAVATIONS AT AMARÂVATI.

THE town of Dharaṇikoṭa is the ancient Dhanyakaṭaka or Dhânyakaṭaka, the capital of Mahâ-Andhra, and lies about eighteen miles in a direct line to the westward from Bejwâḍâ, on the south or right bank of the Kṛishṇâ river, above the bed of which it is well raised. It is surrounded on all four sides by a massive embankment of earth and broken brick and stones, about 650 yards on each side, the west side only being a little shorter and irregular owing to a curve in the river bank. This embankment marks the site of the ancient walls of what must have been the citadel of a city and a place of very considerable strength in early times. A large town no doubt surrounded it. The local tradition, as given by Colonel Mackenzie, runs that:—"The ancient city of Dharaṇikoṭa is said to have extended 3½ miles in length; on the west to the village of Muttayapalem, and on the east to the small pagoda of Pedaṇṭiyâmman, on the road to Vaikuṇṭhapuram. These places are each about 1¾ miles from the centre of Dharaṇikoṭa.[1] On the south the extent is not precisely known, but it is supposed it did not extend beyond Nakkadêvaradinne." Just half a mile to the east is the modern town of Amarâvatî, built on the site of an old village, in the end of last century, by Râja Venkaṭâḍri Nâyuḍu, the zamindâr of Chintapalle, who made it his capital. It was built with streets crossing at right angles, the principal one of very considerable width; and in the early part of the present century, it was a flourishing little town, with a Śaiva temple of some repute which then attracted numerous pilgrim visitors, and it had some trade in weaving, &c. But since the impoverishment of the Zamindârs, through lawsuits among themselves, it has fallen back, the palace is now in ruins, and the place decayed.

To the south of the town, just beyond the outer huts of the lower castes, is the now famous mound which, before 1796, presented the appearance of a very large low tumulus, crowned by a smaller one about thirty yards in diameter and twenty feet high, which had been cased with brick, and was locally known as Dipâldinne or "Hill of Lights."

From a report which Colonel Mackenzie, then on survey duty, had heard in 1797, of antiquities lately discovered at Amarâvatî, he determined to visit the place; and we may as well here give his account in his own words. He says,[2] "I found a circular trench about ten feet wide, dug about twelve feet deep, into a mass of masonry, composed of bricks of sixteen inches square and four inches thick. It is probable that this body of masonry did not extend to a greater depth. The central area was still untouched; and a mass of rubbish was thrown outside of the ditch, which prevented any observation of its original state; but I conjecture that the whole had, previous to its opening, formed a solid circular mound. In this ditch a white slab lay broken, which still exhibited some figures in rilievo, of which Mr. Sydenham took a sketch. Against the outside of the trench, were placed three or four slabs of the same colour, standing, but inclining inwards; on the inside, where these were uncovered, they had no figures, except where the top of one rose above the earth. Without, some sculptures appeared, which lead me to conclude that these sculptures were exposed on that side to view. From the inquiries of my Brâhmaṇs, I could obtain no other account,

---

[1] This would agree well with Hiuen Thsang's circuit of forty li.

[2] *Asiat. Res.*, vol. ix, p. 274.

than that this place was called Dipâl-dinne, or the 'Hill of lamps.' The Râja, about a year ago, had given orders to remove a large stone, to be carried to the new pagoda which he was building, when they discovered the brick work, which induced them to dig up the rest. The white stones were then brought to light, and unfortunately broken; at least we could perceive few of them; and though it was said that some were carried into the temple, the Brâhmaṇ, who was admitted, had perceived only some broken pieces."

In a copy of a brief memorandum in the volume containing his drawings from Amarâvatî, and written perhaps at the time of his visit, he says,—"To the southwards of the village, close to it, is a circular mound of about ninety feet in diameter, which had been cased round with bricks of a large size and slabs of white stone, sculptured so far as I could see by their remains there; for the best stones were carried into the pagoda which Vâsu Reddi was repairing in Ś. 1718."[1]

It was not till March 1816 that Colonel Mackenzie revisited Amarâvatî, when he returned with several European assistants[2] and remained about five months in the neighbourhood, and the assistants for some months longer, making a large series of carefully-finished drawings of sculptures, with a map of the surrounding country. These were all produced in duplicate, and this was most fortunate, for while many of the volumes of his collections left at Madras and Calcutta have been destroyed or lost, the India Office copy of the Amarâvatî drawings has been carefully preserved.

About 1819–20, Colonel Mackenzie wrote an account of the antiquities at and around Amarâvatî, which appeared in the *Calcutta Journal*, and was reprinted after his death, in the *Asiatic Journal* for May 1823.[3] From this the following extracts referring to the stûpa may be worth reproducing:—"About twenty-three years ago (Ś. Ś. 1718) the Râja Vâsureddi Veṅkaṭâdri Nâyuḍu zamindâr of Chintapalle, after visiting the temple of Amarêśvara, proceeded on a religious tour to perform his devotions at the celebrated pagoda of Tirupati; on his return, he felt disposed to change his residence from Chintapalle, and found a new city, so that he pitched on the site of Amarâvatî as the best suited for the purpose from its contiguity to the Kṛishṇâ river, the openness of the country around, and the sanctity of its temple, which is reckoned the first among five principal places of Śiva worship in the country of Telangana."

"To effect his views, he invited Bânyans from Chinapalle, Penugañchiprôlu, Nandigâma, and Betavôlu, as well as Brâhmaṇs and other settlers to all of whom he made suitable advances of money to enable them to erect habitations. While thus engaged preparing accommodation for himself, the employment suggested to his mind the possibility of obtaining bricks by digging for them in the several mounds of earth with which Dharaṇikoṭa and the adjacent grounds abounded. With this view he commenced first at Nakkadêvaradinne, which was then a pretty high circular mound; after digging all round it to the depth of one yard and a half, a few large bricks were all that was found, with broken pieces of the same material somewhat lower. This mound at present measures in diameter thirty feet, and is of moderate height.

"He next directed his search in quest of the same materials to another mound of earth,

[1] A.D. 1796–7; Colonel Mackenzie's clerk has here written 1778, but the mistake is manifest. Mr. Sewell in reprinting this and other papers has done so *literatim* and without calling attention to the errata; I have thought it better to correct mere errors of spelling and misprints.

[2] At one time or another he seems to have had nine European draughtsmen here, Messrs. H. Hamilton, M. Burke, Newman, J. Mustie, C. Barnett, W. Sydenham, T. Anderson, J. Gould, T. Lockwood, and three natives.

[3] Vol. xv, pp. 464–478.

a little higher up, near Balsalâmmâ pagoda, an ancient Śâktî temple: on opening which, at the depth of one cubit, a great quantity of entire bricks were collected, and the search in consequence was continued to a greater depth. The excavation at present forms a small receptacle for water supplied by the annual rains. The search was afterwards continued on the western side of the ruinous fort of Dharaṇikoṭa with similar success.

"While the palace, &c., were yet finishing, the Musalman people who had taken up their residence at the south end near Dîpâldinne, in digging for the same purposes, had occasionally found bricks of an extraordinary size as well as a few fragments which possessed beautiful carvings, which circumstance was reported to the Râja, who eagerly came over to inspect the place, and perceiving that it was the most curious of the several mounds he had caused to be opened, conceived that it might embowel something of value; as most places so marked are generally the receptacles of hidden treasures, he commanded the Musalmans to move elsewhere, as he designed to form a garden there and a reservoir in the centre. Soon after this he ordered workmen to be employed in digging the mound of Dîpâldinne, the upper part of which rose in a turreted shape to the height of twenty feet, which was cased round with bricks of unusual dimensions;[1] the diameter at top measured about thirty yards.

"In digging along the eastern skirts of it, a small temple was discovered, near which lay an image which Vâsureddi caused to be taken into the temple of Amarêśvara, it is supposed for public worship. A small distance west of the above, two pillars were next cleared, which resembled (and perhaps once formed) the entrance to a small pagoda.

"The workmen next proceeded to lay open the western side, in which direction also a small building was discovered, which contained a large pillar lamp in a complete state, having a basin at bottom, and places at top for five wicks or lights. It contained about ten sêrs[2] of copper, which, on being committed to the fire, dissolved into dross, from its having been very much injured and earth-eaten. On the north side of the mound, where at present extends a line of houses, with that part of it left unoccupied and rather low, a Maṇṭapa of four pillars was found, built with bricks: this is supposed to have been a chapel of Jaina worship, from a headless image which it contained sitting cross-legged.

"While forming the reservoir at Dîpâldinne, all the sculptured slabs of various sizes which were found on the northern side were removed to the tank of Śivagaṅgâ, with which the flight of steps on the western side, to the number of twenty, was constructed. Some of the remaining stones have been carried into the great pagoda, part of which are placed as steps to the sanctuary of Amarêśvara, while some are placed in the wall at the entrance of the pagodas of Mahishâsura-mardanî and Sômêśvara. In short, these valuable stones of antiquity have been used in various buildings, both public and private; those in particular applied to Musalman mosques have first been carefully divested of every carving by rubbing them on harder stones, to prevent, as it is said, any pollution arising to Muhammadan faith from idolatrous substances."

The Pindârî raid in March 1816 interrupted the formation of the tank in the centre of the site of the stûpa; "and the death of the Râja Veṅkaṭâdri Nâyuḍu, which happened in August of the same year, put a period to its completion."

Of the mound after the Zamindâr's excavations he writes:—"At the depth of ten feet

---

1 "Length of the bricks 20 inches, 10 in breadth, and 4 thick. Cut straw and leaves appear to have been used in their composition. The earth also of which they have been made must have been potter's earth from the hardness and fineness of the colour."

2 Twenty pounds.

from the top of the mound, stones with a variety of sculptures are seen, which are ranged in two circles, one within the other ;—the space between them is thirteen feet, paved, so far as it is entire, with large slabs of slate stone. The diameter of the inner circle measures 166 feet." . . . .

"On the south side, within the circles, a strong work of masonry is discernible, which may probably be the remains of the interior wall, as the people of the village informed me that a similar work had been observed all round, which has since been cleared away in removing the earth. This mysterious structure is supposed to have four entrances; that only to the south has lately been cleared, which is twenty-five feet within, but becomes narrower as it recedes outward.

"The order in which the sculptures is placed is very regular. They are disposed according to the work they possess; those with pretty large figures form the exterior range; they are a foot in thickness and nearly three broad and rise six or seven feet high. Between every two entire stones are placed two of a circular form one above the other having a small projecting rim at each end, fixed into grooves made on either side of the adjoining stones. These circular stones do not rest upon one another; there is a space between them of two or three inches, and the same may be observed at the bottom; they are not on a level with the base of the adjoining stones. The length of the grooves is according to the dimensions of the stones inserted ;—they are two inches apart; at the extremities an inch or little more in breadth : in the middle the breadth is five or six inches, and three deep.

"The lower circular stones are finished with carvings resembling foliage, and those placed above display a variety of figures in bas-relief. The same observation may be extended to the adjoining stones, with the exception, however, that the lower part of them is semicircular, representing foliage, under which is a border with flowers and figures of lions.

"The slabs composing the inner circle are remarkable for the beauty of the sculptures upon them, which are small, and consist of figures, festoons, and a variety of ornaments, very neatly executed. On the sides are pillars, which are finished either with figures of lions and horses, or of men and women; and over the top is an entablature replete with figures in various acts of devotion or amusement. The inner slabs have been cemented to each other with strong mortar, and supported by a wall of masonry rising to a moderate height in the rear; the adjustment has been very happily executed. Some of these slabs are six inches in thickness, and others nearly nine inches : their shape is chiefly rectangular. All the carvings appear originally to have been painted red and varnished; and so fine was the composition used, that the stones still retain part of the ancient colouring, which, from the length of time they have lain underground, is now somewhat faded, inclining to a copperish red.

"Upon a minute inspection of the several sculptures, in many a story is completely told with clearness and precision, and the characters accurately defined. The passions also are naturally exhibited and strongly marked; and exactness of outline in the representation, as well as in the air and carriage of animals, is happily delineated, and the festoons, foliage, flowers, and an infinite variety of other decorations which adorn these carvings, are altogether excellent. The artists appear to have been skilled in perspective also; upon the whole, neither taste nor elegance are wanting, and in the article of neat and delicate finishing, the carvings of Dipâldinne are far superior to any ancient or modern Hindu production.

"A great many slabs of large size are seen lying on the surface of the reservoir, but it is difficult to say where they were originally placed. On these are chiefly represented a few large figures of men and women, in divisions of two or three, one above another, each three feet high. Some of these are well executed and the proportions are correct.

"A great part of the mound remains uncleared; of the exterior row only the south-east quarter and the entrance in that direction have been opened. The whole of the inner circle has been dug up, and the stones removed for the purposes of building." . . .

"From the extremely careless manner in which the workmen proceeded in opening the mound, scarcely a single stone has escaped uninjured, while a great many have been totally destroyed. The excavation in the centre, intended for a reservoir, is nearly a square, each side of which measures 108 feet; in the middle is a well dug some feet deeper. The intention of digging into the mound, I have been told, originated in a desire of finding treasure, which the late Râja supposed it contained, and with this view the search was continued, but it was not known whether anything was found in it, with the exception of a large store of bricks and the stones with sculpture. . . . ."

"There is not a doubt but that some erection has stood in the centre, from the immense quantities of broken bricks with which the spaces between the two rows of stones are everywhere filled."

Colonel Mackenzie had removed a number of the sculptured slabs to Masulipatam, whence seven of them were sent to the Bengal Asiatic Society's Museum at Calcutta. Other four, including a slab bearing a fragment of an inscription,[1] were transmitted to Madras, and finally, apparently, to the India Office. At least sixteen others also reached London, either before or with those procured subsequently by Sir Walter Elliot; but whether any more were removed by Mackenzie or not we have no definite information. Probably most of those laid bare by his assistants in order to make drawings of them were left exposed,[2] and soon afterwards were used up or burnt into lime, as the others had been by the villagers. The next we hear of them is in 1830, when Mr. Robertson, Collector of Masulipatam, probably from finding some of Colonel Mackenzie's slabs left there,[3] brought down others, and placed thirty-three large slabs in the square of a new market-place called after his own name. From what part of the circle these were taken, or at what expense in the exposure and destruction of others, we have no information. Fortunately they were seen by Sir Frederick Adam, Governor of Madras, when on tour in 1835, and, struck by their extreme interest, he ordered them to be sent to Madras,[4] to be better cared for in the Museum of the Literary Society. This order, however, was not carried out for more than twenty years after.[5] Meanwhile some of the best of them found their way into the Master Attendant's garden, and were taken possession of by him, and only finally recovered by Government in 1880 and sent to Madras by me in 1882.

---

[1] Mr. Sewell says that this had not formed part of the marbles at the India Museum, and had never been seen from the time it was sent to Masulipatam till he discovered it in London (*Report*, pp. 13, n. and 63); but this is contradicted by Prof. H. H. Wilson's statement, made in 1841, that this "slab itself and several specimens of the sculptures" were then in the Museum of the India House.—*Ariana Ant.*, p. 32, n.

[2] I found only one left,—the disc figured in *Tree and Serp. Wor.*, pl. lxxiii, fig. 2, and below, plate xvii, fig. 1.

[3] Among those sent from Masulipatam in 1856 were several which had been drawn by Mackenzie's assistants in 1816–17, *e.g.*, those represented in Fergusson's *Tree and Serp. Wor.*, pl. lxxxi, fig. 1; xcv, figs. 2, 3, ; xcvi, fig. 3; and probably others. Half of another (xcviii, fig. 2) has been obtained since at Bejwâḍâ.

[4] *Madras Jour.*, vol. v, pp. 44, 45.

[5] They reached Madras in 1856, and are described by Mr. Taylor as thirty-nine pieces of sculpture, but many of them small. *Madras Gov. Selections*, No. xxxix, pp. 226, and 250–262. They must soon after have been sent to the India Office.

In 1845, Mr. (now Sir) Walter Elliot, then Commissioner at Guntûr, led by Colonel Mackenzie's paper in the *Asiatic Researches*, vol. ix. pp. 272 ff., visited the site, but found that every fragment of stone above the surface had disappeared. He began to dig, quite haphazard, near the west gate, and the first object that rewarded his search was one of the lions lying prostrate that had surmounted the side of the entrance. He then uncovered some of the stones of the rail standing upright, but not continuously, and penetrated into an apparent restoration of a part of the entrance, as if for the construction of a small temple out of the ruins of the main building. The slabs he excavated were transmitted to Madras, where they long lay uncared for, and exposed to the elements in the green in front of the College. In 1853 the Court of Directors made inquiries respecting them, and they were then placed in the front entry of the Central Museum, more or less exposed to the forenoon sun, but otherwise sheltered.[1] The Rev. W. Taylor was also commissioned to report fully upon them and their inscriptions, and did so in 1856 in his own way; for, having no idea of what was put into his hands, and discarding the Pali alphabet, which had been recovered by scholars of note, he evolved one of his own, and gave transcriptions that are simply nonsensical, while his account of the sculptures is utterly useless except as a list of the stones and their dimensions. The sculptures he appears to have considered as largely of Vaishṇava origin, and some of them at least as belonging to the sixteenth century, and none of them of earlier date than the ninth ! ![2]

Soon after this the marbles were ordered to be forwarded to England, and were mostly sent. They have been described by Mr. Fergusson in the second part of his volume *Tree and Serpent Worship*, illustrated by fifty-four plates, including fourteen from Colonel Mackenzie's drawings, of which the original sculptures have almost all perished.[3] This work, of which the second edition is now exhausted, is one of the most valuable contributions that have ever been made to our knowledge of Buddhist art and early history. It illustrated, for the first time, the architecture and history of a remote period of which we had previously but dim and fragmentary information, and gave a stimulus and direction to further research. The first part of the volume is devoted to a description of the great Tope or Stûpa at Sânchi in Bhopal, and its sculptures ; but a knowledge of the contents of the second division of the work is assumed on the part of the reader of the present account, which, to a large extent, is necessarily supplemental to the earlier work. Those sculptures represented by photography in Mr. Fergusson's description have, since the publication of it, been carefully arranged and to great advantage along the walls of the grand staircase of the British Museum.

There are still in the Madras Museum one or two of the stones taken there by Sir

---

[1] *Madras Gov. Selections*, No. xxxix, pp. 196, 220.

[2] *Madras Gov. Selections*, No. xxxix, pp. 197, 203, 206, &c., 263, 265. A single specimen may be given to show the utter nonsense of this man's versions :—Of the short inscription on the pillar given in Fergusson's *Tree and Serpent Worship*, pl. lxxxix, fig. 1, he remarks : "The two last letters being those which the late J. Prinsep, Esq., rendered *danam*, I so read them at first ; but doubt first began here, as to Mr. Prinsep's rendering." He reads it thus :—"*vohanu petanu-papu tahanunu laphi tahanu chatitacagailayam.*—Pillar raised on place of the burning, accomplished *loss.*" Now half of the first letter is destroyed, but there is little difficulty in making it out, and the whole really reads—*Gadhikasa Haṁghasa sa putakasa sa duhutukasa chetiya thabho dânaṁ*:—"Of Gadhika Haṁgha (Saṅgha) with his sons, with his daughters, the gift of a *chetiya* pillar." It will be seen at once from this that Mr. Taylor had invented his own alphabet for these inscriptions, and this, long after scholars had recognised Prinsep's to be the proper one.

[3] As already noted, only one was discovered in the excavations of 1880: it is that given in *Tree and Serp. Wor.*, pl. lxxiii, fig. 2 ; and part of another (pl. xcviii, fig. 2) was found at Bejwâḍâ.

W. Elliot; but "there was," he says, "a miniature representation of a dâgaba in sandstone, which had formed the summit of one of the single pillars, one of which stood on each side of the entrance within the *pradakshiṇa*. This lay for some time in the entrance of my house at Madras. I told the curator of the Central Museum to send for it when I left that residence." This *dâgaba* seems to have been lost.

The next excavations at Amarâvatî were made by Mr. R. Sewell of the Madras Civil Service, who, in 1876, obtained a grant of money for the purpose, and began the work in May 1877. The results of his operations, with verbatim reprints of all Colonel Mackenzie's papers on the subject, appeared in his *Report* in 1882.[1] In February 1880, the Duke of Buckingham, then Governor of Madras, directed the Collector to complete at once the excavation of the whole site. This was unfortunate; no professional assistance—not even the services of a Public Works engineer—was supplied, and the sculptures had very much to take their chance at the hands of ignorant labourers; the whole area was cleared of earth, and also of any traces that may have existed of the original stûpa above the level of the foundations.

In the end of 1881, on taking charge of the Archæological Survey of Madras, I visited the place and found the site thus converted into a large pit, roughly circular, about seventy-five yards in diameter, but with extensions at the four cardinal points. The slabs and fragments found, inclusive of a number of those unearthed by Mr. Sewell, were 255 in all, and were laid down round the circle. During my stay I discovered about ninety more, and had over 170 slabs packed for transmission to Madras; but their removal was delayed for nearly two years.[2]

[1] Mr. Sewell not having a professional training, his drawings cannot be depended on in details; thus, on his plan showing the positions in which he found the stones, his Nos. 26, 27, 37, and 39—stones *in situ*, whose precise positions ought to have been accurately noted—are extended over thirty feet, while they lay within twenty feet of space; other distances are as much contracted; and of the pavement, which he shows entire over the whole area excavated, and consisting of slabs of equal breadth, only patches formed of very irregular slabs really exist.

[2] As if some fatality pursued these sculptures, after lying for nearly two years more at the Madras Central Museum, the late Curator, without informing the Archæological Survey, proceeded to have as many as possible of them fixed up in one of the rooms according to his own notions, and they have accordingly been embedded in partitions of Portland cement, covering up every part of them except the sculptured surfaces. A few rail discs appear *between* uprights of the outer rail, but further arrangement there is none; and as the slabs cannot be disengaged from the encrusting cement, any rearrangement is now hopeless.

2. Lower border of a rail slab from Amarâvati (*Tree and Serpent Worship*, Plate lxi, fig. 2).

CHAPTER III.

THE STÛPA AND ITS REMAINS.

THE removal, in 1880, of all the débris and other remains of the stûpa within the area of the rails—much of it thrown into and quite filling up the tank dug in the centre by Râja Veṅkaṭâdri Nâyudu—destroyed for ever the chance of recovering any precise dimensions of the central pile, which even a few bricks *in situ* might have fixed. We are therefore obliged to fall back on the imperfect observations of Colonel Mackenzie and what we know of other kindred structures, in order to form some idea of what it originally was.

We know of but two very distinct types of stûpa. The more common is exemplified in those of Manikyala, Sâñchi, Sarnâth, and of Anurâdhapura in Ceylon; they have a circular basement, supporting a hemispherical dome, usually with a ledge or path of some breadth round the spring of the dome, and are surrounded by a stone rail. The second class is best represented by the great stûpa at Boro-Budur in Java, in which the central dome is reduced to comparatively inferior dimensions, but is raised on a very lofty platform formed by three circles of smaller stûpas surrounding it in descending tiers, and these by a series of five concentric rails, each on a lower platform than the next inside it, the whole standing on an ample basement. This is manifestly a later development than anything we have in India, though this Amarâvatî one has had a double railing. And we gather from Colonel Mackenzie's account and from indications among the remaining fragments that the inner rail as well as the outer one was carved on both sides. The slabs were in some cases thin, and set back to back and cemented with mortar; and at the west gate there are evidences that there was an entrance through this circle: similar arrangements are also traceable at the north and south entrances. Inside this rail, and at a distance of about 12 feet from it, Mackenzie found a solid mass of brickwork, 8 feet thick, running round a considerable portion of the south-west quadrant, and he was informed that it had been observed all round the circle. This in all probability marked the basement of the stûpa supporting the terrace, and was doubtless faced with sculptures. Whether the dome rose directly from this, and was nearly 125 feet in diameter, or whether it was contracted by other terraces above this, we have no clear evidence. Colonel Mackenzie states that when he first saw it the central or higher portion of the mound was still untouched, and rose in a turreted shape to a height of 20 feet, with a diameter of about 90 feet at the top, and had been cased round with bricks. This would give a height of from 36 to 40 feet above the level of the procession path between the rails; and as the rails were completely covered over with fallen bricks and débris, indicative of the ruin of an immense pile of building, the great dome may well have been more than twice the height of the central ruin, as seen in 1797, and of much larger diameter. The inference this points to is, that if there was any terrace above the first, there could hardly have been more than one of any great breadth, and that the dome was perhaps stilted on a drum, and rose to a very considerable height, all faced with sculptured marble slabs. This at once reminds us of those very elaborately carved panels, which must have been numerous here, forming the chief sculptures of the inner rail, and representing richly carved dâgabas, chaityas, or stûpas, twenty-four of which

PLATE III.

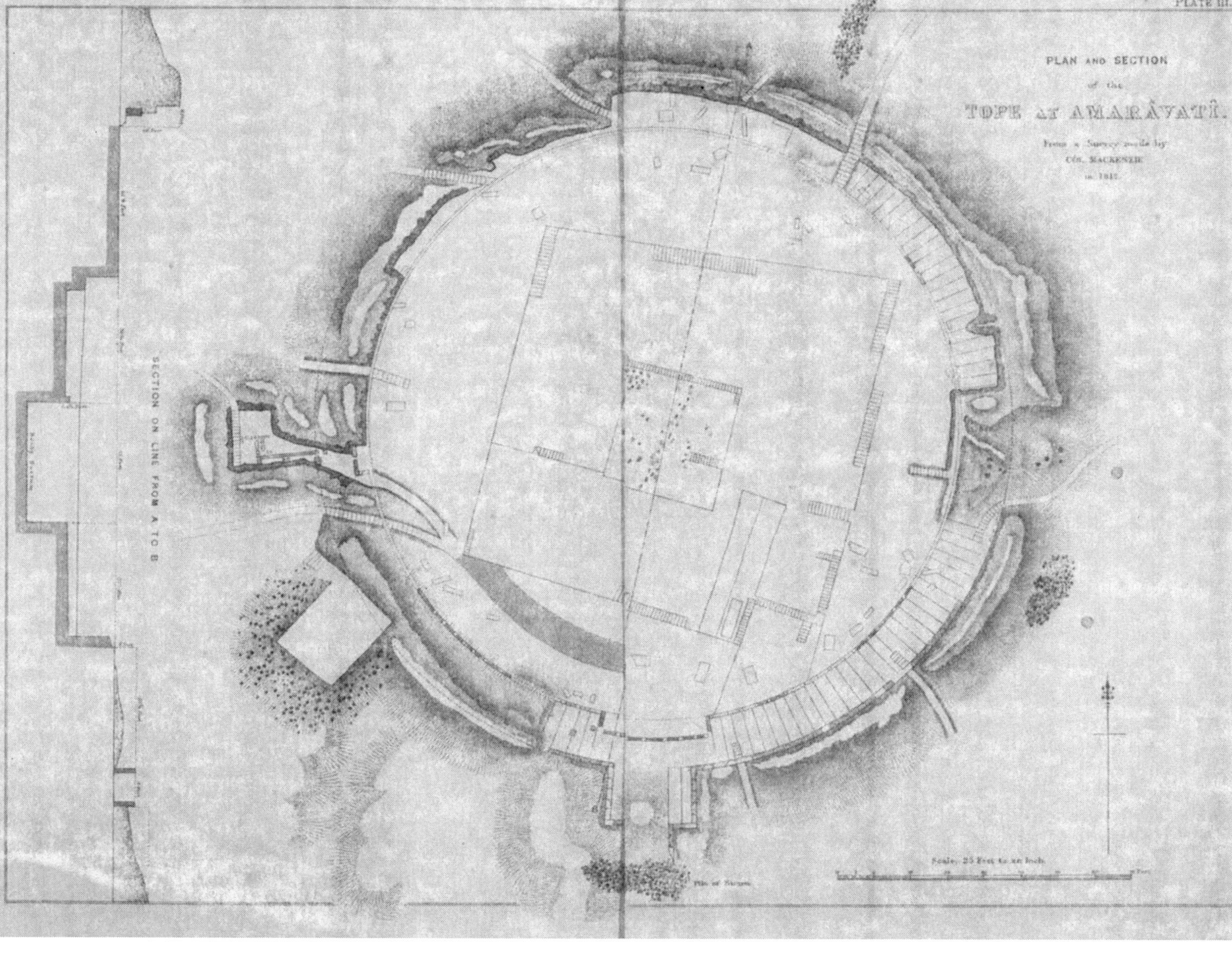
PLAN AND SECTION
of the
TOPE AT AMARÂVATÎ.
From a Survey made by
COL. MACKENZIE
in 1817.
SECTION ON LINE FROM A TO B
Scale, 25 Feet to an Inch.

were drawn by Colonel Mackenzie, and of which ten are now in the British Museum. They were at once recognised by Mr. Fergusson as "miniature representations of the building itself and of the different parts quite sufficiently correctly drawn to be recognised." "These," he adds, "are particularly interesting, as they are the only pictures now known to exist that enable us to realise what the appearance of these monuments really was as they were originally erected." One of the peculiar characteristics of these dâgabas, which had not previously been met with elsewhere, is the existence of five steles or pillars on each face. Now my exploration of the Jaggayyapeṭa stûpa has revealed that these five lofty pillars (*âyaka kaṁbho*) had been set up on each of the faces of the stûpa. The central one is usually crowned by a miniature dâgaba, and it appears to have been one of these which Sir W. Elliot found at the west entrance, and which has been mentioned above. On the whole, we may accept these sculptures as fair representations of this great stûpa when in its completed form. How many terraces it had cannot now be determined, but we seem warranted in assuming that the base was about 138 feet in diameter, and that the dome was over 90 feet, leaving a margin sufficient for two terraces of about 11 feet, or three of 7 feet each. Like the smaller one at Jaggayyapet, it was probably formed of layers of earth, each a few feet in thickness, carefully levelled, and covered over by a well-laid flooring of large bricks. This mode of constructing these stûpas prevented any great lateral thrust, and enabled the builders to carry them up to a very considerable height. The floorings were so carefully jointed that no appreciable quantity of water could percolate through them to swell or otherwise disturb the strata of earth, and the circumference was protected by a thick casing of excellent brickwork, and faced with slabs of a beautiful greyish white limestone or marble, covered with the richest sculpture.

Surrounded by a double sculptured rail, the outer one about 13 feet high, and the stûpa rising to a height of perhaps 100 feet, this great marble dome must have had a very brilliant effect, while round the outside were numerous small chaityas,—miniature copies of it,—the monumental records of the hierarchy in whose charge it was; and in a wider circle around were the monastic buildings and dwellings of the yellow-robed fraternity of monks, with the wet season retreats of mendicants from all quarters. On the fortnightly festival occasions, and more especially at the *dipavali* season, the whole surface of the dome was covered with festoons of flowers, and flags fluttered from the square capital on its top, while at night it was dotted over with hundreds of lamps, that covered it with a blaze of light which, amid the darkness, made of it a hill of lamps, and gave it the popular name, still handed down, of Dîpâldinne.

Plate II. is copied from the survey of the locality around Amarâvatî made by Colonel Mackenzie in 1816–17. It has already been published in Fergusson's *Tree and Serpent Worship*, but is necessary to the proper understanding of the relative position of the places mentioned in the text, and is reproduced on a slightly reduced scale, and with some corrections of the spellings, partly from another copy of the same in Mackenzie's volume of drawings. The old ramparts of Dharaṇikoṭa are to the west of and higher up the river than Amarâvatî, and the sites of the several mounds are plainly marked. A group of stone circles or circular tumuli to which Colonel Mackenzie drew attention is found to the west of Dharaṇikoṭa, but by far the most numerous groups are round the foot of the hills to the south-east. The villages of Mogalur, Battulapâdu, Nakalampet, Gani-Atukur, and Partiyâla form a small block on the north side of the river, belonging to H.H. the Nizam. This tract was long famous for the production of the famous diamonds of Golkoṇḍa. The mines have long been deserted as no longer productive, but the old pits are to be seen in every direction.[1]

Plate III. is reproduced on a reduced scale from the same work, being also copied from a drawing in the Mackenzie Collection, and represents the plan and section of the monument as it existed in June 1817.[2] At that time the slabs marked in black were either standing or lying in such a position that their original site was easily identified; their number indicates how much of the outer rail was then almost entire; and the paving-stones of the procession path round a large part of the east side of the circle were also *in situ*.

The central building had then quite disappeared, the bricks having been largely utilised in building the new town, the slabs in repairing and building temples, and making steps for tanks. The Râja then began to search for treasure, and in the centre of the stûpa was found a stone casket, inside which was a crystal box containing a small pearl, some small leaves of gold, &c. These were afterwards recovered by Sir Walter Elliot and sent to the Madras Museum. Then he determined to convert the hole formed by this excavation into a tank, but the work was abandoned before completion. Most of the excavated earth, however, was thrown on to the procession path and the outer rail, and so to a certain extent protected them, until Sir Walter Elliot in 1845 made further excavations, and secured a large number of the slabs. The dimensions of the tope have already been given, and this plan will help to illustrate the description.

Plate IV. shows the condition of the place since early in 1882, after the excavations made by order of the Duke of Buckingham. The stones then in position were very few, and mostly broken, showing that in the interval since 1816, if not since 1845, much of the circle had been dug up and the slabs probably burnt into lime. The other stones then lay scattered about, near where each had been found.

Part of the pavement in the north-west quadrant remained undisturbed, and I found that it was laid upon a mass of broken marbles which had borne sculptures. This is a clear proof that there must have been, at some date much later than the outer rail, a partial restoration of the stûpa, when many of the sculptures belonging either to it or to others in the neighbourhood were broken up and used in this way. On the south-west, whence the stones seemed to have been most recently removed, there were small supports of brick and lime raised against where the rails had stood, as if to support them. This was also traceable elsewhere in parts where the flagstones of the procession path had not been quite destroyed and torn up. Behind the line of the rail, a little to the east of the north gate, among others a large slab was dug up at some depth, bearing an archaic sculpture of a man and boy (Pl. li, fig. 2), and not far from it I found pieces of broken sculpture supporting the backs of the rail pillars. To the south of the west entrance lie five massive blocks of brown granite, which have at one time been pillars of the outer rail; the upper halves of all are broken off, but one of them is still over 7½ feet in length, and all are 3' to 3½ feet broad above, and carefully polished. Beside them were found the cross-bars, very much lighter than those used elsewhere in the circle where the uprights are limestone, being plain lenticular slabs, let into the edges of the granite pillars, and considerably more apart than the others. It is hard to say to what age these may belong, whether they may be part of

---

[1] See *Asiat. Res.*, vol, xv, p. 126; Yule's *Marco Polo*, vol. ii. pp. 346, 349.

[2] A woodcut of this, to the scale of 100 feet to 1 inch, was also published by Mr. Fergusson in his *Handbook of Architecture* (1855), and in *Jour. R. As. Soc.*, N.S., vol. iii, p. 136.

PLAN
of the
STÛPA AT AMARÂVATÎ.
From a Survey made
in 1881.

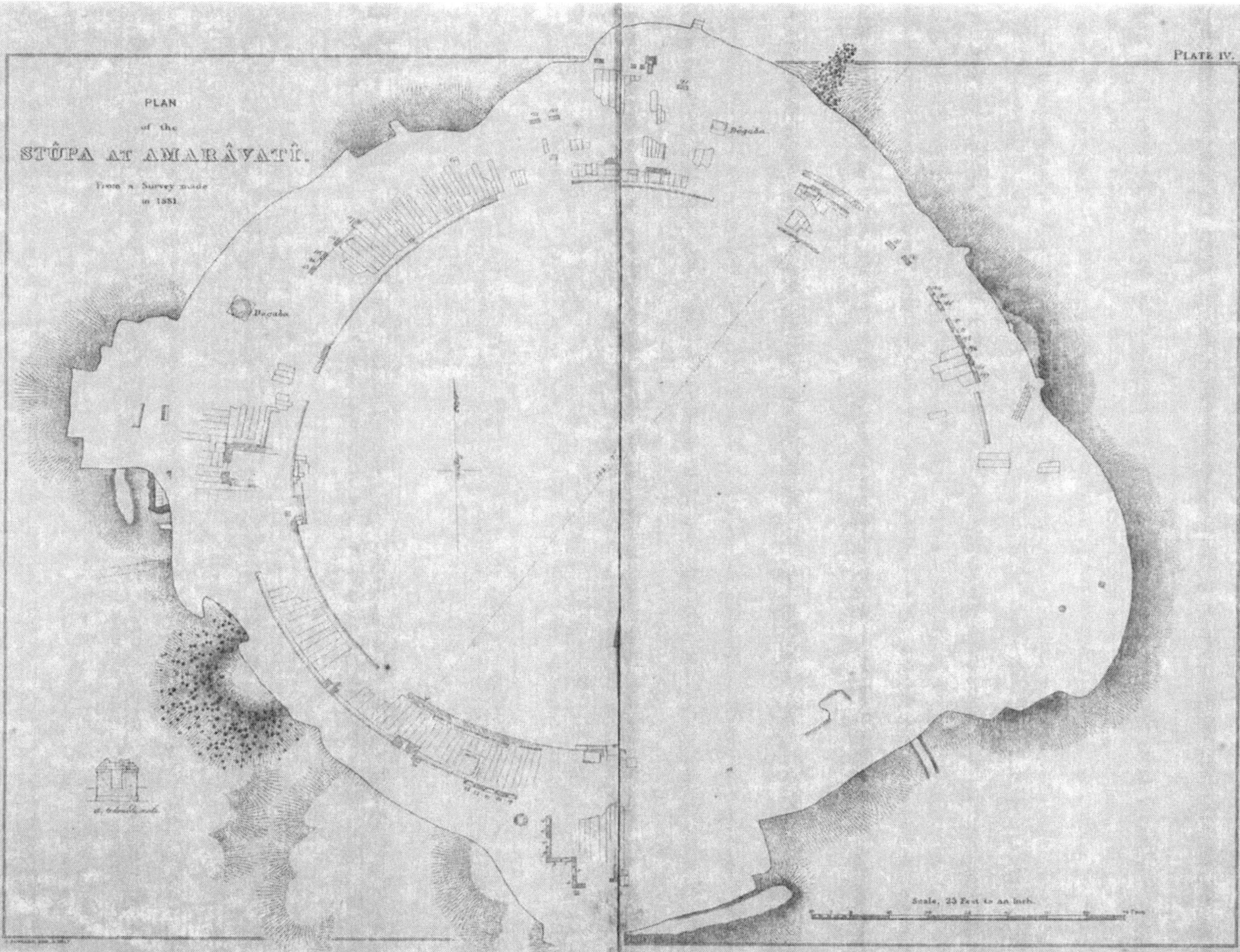

an early rail, that was gradually displaced by the one of which we know most, or whether they were inserted to fill up a gap made at some later period. I incline to think they are very early; and just at this point in the circle it is that more archaic sculptures are found than anywhere else round the circle: indeed, it is only here that those slabs with archaic pilasters bearing winged figures on the capitals are found. These latter are so very like those of Jaggayyapeṭa and the vihâra cave at Pitalkhorâ, that there can be no doubt they are of the same age, and much earlier than the common style of sculptures here. The granite pillars may have been the commencement of an early rail never completed, but in place of which the outer marble one was afterwards erected.

At the west gate are the remains of a small room or shrine built of brick upon the platform, and which may have abutted against the inner rail. The bricks used in its walls are so much smaller than those belonging to the original stûpa that it must be referred to a much later period. A little to the north of this is the base of a small brick stûpa, the top of which had been destroyed; but on excavating to a slight depth in it, I found a small earthenware pot, containing some fragments of burnt bones. The pot was fractured in excavating, but was sent to the Government Museum at Madras. Between the west and south gates are the remains of two small brick and lime erections on the outer side of the path and abutting against the rail. It is hard to conceive what they have been intended for unless it were for lights. Still nearer the south gate is a brick and lime basement, like that against the rails, as if to support some slabs; and lying over it were found some of the most richly carved of the slabs, but they appeared rather as if they had been thrown down there from the inner rail than as part of an erection that had fallen to decay.

Close to the south gate was the base of another very small brick dâgaba; and at the side of this gate was also a fragment of brickwork. In the north-east quadrant was found a narrow water-channel, also carefully laid with large bricks.

At various points round the inner circle were found portions, often of considerable length, of the brickwork that had supported the inner rail. This circle was 162′ 7″ in diameter inside, and was built of very large bricks of good quality. The inner rail stood on this, and may have been from 1′ 2″ to 1′ 4″ in thickness. The mass of brickwork forming a wall eight feet thick inside this, which Colonel Mackenzie left exposed, had, as was to be expected, all been carried away; but its outer diameter would be 138 feet,[1] and inside 122 feet. The turreted mound above was about 90 feet in diameter at the top, but probably most of the bricks had been removed before Colonel Mackenzie saw it, so that it may have been originally with the outer casing of marble close upon 100 feet in diameter. The height we are less able to estimate, but it may have been from 80 to 100 feet, inclusive of the square capital on the summit.

In the inscriptions this building is called the *Mahâchaitya*, or "Great Chaitya of the Holy One (*Buddha*) belonging to the Chaitika School." A chaitya, as has been explained,[2] means primarily a "funeral pile," a "heap," and then a "monument" and "altar." They seem to have been introduced, perhaps at a very early date, by non-Aryan tribes, and are only an advance upon the burial tumulus surrounded by a rude stone circle, of which many examples are to be found in the neighbourhood of Amarâvatî. Chaityas of a superb

---

[1] By some mistake, probably of the draughtsman, this is the diameter marked as that of the inner rail on Colonel Mackenzie's rough "Sketch" plan, which Mr. Sewell got reproduced.

[2] *Cave Temples*, p. 174.

*

character are spoken of as existing in Gotama's own times, when he sometimes repaired to them to rest and teach.[1] *Stûpa* has much the same meaning, and is applied almost solely to the larger chaityas, or those not under a roof. To render them proper objects of worship it was necessary they should possess a relic of the Buddha, or of some of the great teachers of the sect.

The Buddhist teachers soon began to differ on minor points, and the Church was early split into two great schools—the Mahâsaṅghikâs or School of the Great Congregation, and the Mahâsthavirâs or School of the Great President. The Mahâsaṅghikâs soon after split into five schools—the Chaityikas, Chaityaśailâs or Pûrvaśailâs,[2] the Avaraśailâs, the Haimavatâs, the Lokottaravâdins, and the Prajñaptivâdins.[3] The first are said to have arisen from the teaching of an ascetic who lived on Mount Chaityaka.[4] May not the name of Pûrvaśilâ, given by Hiuen Thsang, then be in this way properly applicable to this shrine—not specially from its situation, but from its belonging to the Pûrvaśailâ school? And in the same way the other saṅghârâma, wherever it was, may have belonged to the sect of the Avaraśailâs.

3. External Elevation of the Great Rail at Amarâvatî.

The outer rail, probably the most elaborate and artistic monument of the kind in India, was formed of upright slabs about ten feet in height above the level of the inner paved path,[5] and connected by three cross-bars between each pair of uprights, the ends being lenticular in section and let into mortices cut in the edges of the upright slabs or pillars. These supported a coping or frieze about two feet nine inches high; and a brick support about

[1] Thus we find mention of the Udena chaitya, Gotamaka, Sattambaka, Bahuputta, Sârandada, and Châpâla chaityas, all at Vaiśâlî.—Rhys Davids, *Buddhist Suttas*, p. 40.

[2] The Pûrvaśailâs were followers of Mahâdeva, an early teacher (Burnouf, *Intr. à l'Hist. du Bud. Ind.*, 2d ed., p. 398; Vassilief, p. 229; *Târanâtha*, pp. 175, 271, 273). They were known in Ceylon as Pubbaselîyâs (*Mahâwaṅso*, p. 21).

[3] Some accounts add three more to these schools, but some of the sects soon disappeared again.

[4] One of the five hills—Vaihâra, Varâha, Vṛishabha, Ṛishigiri, and Chaityaka—of Râjagṛiha is so named in the *Mahâbhârata* (ii, 799, 811, 815, 843; Lassen, *Ind. Alt.*, vol. ii, p. 85, n.); but some of the Buddhist names —Vaibhâra, Vaipula, Gṛidhrakûṭa, Ṛishigiri, and Paṇḍava—differ from the Brahmanical (*Jour. As. Soc. Ben.*, vol. vii, p. 996; vol. xvi, p. 958); and as the Buddhists do not give this name to any of the Râjagṛiha hills, it is very probable this Mount Chaityaka was elsewhere.

[5] The sculptured inner faces of the slabs are about 9 feet 1 inch in height, but the brick support at their bases has to be taken into account.

a foot high ran along the line of their bases. The annexed woodcut,[1] representing a small section of it as reconstructed by Mr. Fergusson from the slabs now in the British Museum, will help us to judge of its external appearance. The lower part or plinth outside, according to Mr. Fergusson, was ornamented by a frieze of animals and boys, generally in ludicrous and comic attitudes ;—and unless the thin slabs bearing these rather archaic sculptures were used in such a position, it is hard to see where else they could have been employed. Some of them, however, look as if they had once formed coping-stones, perhaps to an earlier rail, and had been split and trimmed to adapt them for a different purpose—perhaps to form this frieze. The pillars, as usual, represented octagonal shafts, almost *in plano*, ornamented with full discs in the middle and half ones at top and bottom; and in the intermediate spaces, always divided vertically into three, were figure-sculptures of considerable variety. On the cross-bars or rails were full discs all different and all carved with the utmost care. The coping was ornamented outside with the long wavy flower roll carried by men, and with various symbolical figures inserted over it or on it.[2]

As we shall see, the inside of the rail was much more richly carved; the coping or frieze was one continued bas-relief; the central discs both of the rails and of the pillars were filled with sculptures of great elaboration and beauty of detail, representing scenes of sacred legend and of everyday life or history.

Allowing 26 feet for each gateway, the roll of each quadrant would measure 125·3 feet, and as a pillar and its accompanying cross-bars occupied together on an average 5 feet 10 inches, we find that twenty-two pillars with sixty-three rails would be required for the quadrant. Then the inner area of the gates measured 26 feet wide by 16 feet, and had three pillars on each side and one at each outer corner, while the vestibule just within the entrance measured 13 feet wide by 8 feet 3 inches, and had two more on each side, that is, twelve pillars for each gate. This gives a total of 136 upright slabs or pillars for the whole rail, with 348 cross-bars carved with discs on both sides; and on this rail rested 803 lineal feet of massive coping, also carved on both sides.

The inner rail, still more elaborately carved, was altogether only about 6 feet high, and formed an almost continuous screen of the richest sculpture, its circumference being 521 feet, or, allowing for the entrances, 470 feet of carving. Within this again was the stûpa itself, measuring 435 feet in circumference at the base, and doubtless entirely faced with slabs of rich sculpture up to the capital. No other shrine that we know of in India presented such a profusion of sculpture, and in quality it was unequalled by any. Well might Hiuen Thsang say that it "displayed all the magnificence of the palaces of Baktria, and the thick woods with which it was surrounded and a multitude of sparkling fountains made it an enchanting retreat."

As has been pointed out by Mr. Fergusson, both sides of the outer rail were carefully carved, but with this difference, that the sculptures on the outer side were rather more conventional and uniform in design. Each pillar bore on both sides a circular boss or disc on the centre, with two others—rather more than half circles—above and below, leaving a band of about two-fifths their diameter between each pair. The two half-discs on both sides of the pillars were carved in concentric bands of leaves, and often surrounded by a border of beautifully carved creepers; and below the lower and above the upper were bands of

[1] From Fergusson's *Ind. and East. Arch.*, p. 100, by the kind permission of the author.

[2] Fergusson's *Ind. and East. Arch.*, pp. 100 ff.

animals and flowers. On the outer sides, so far as we can learn from the very few instances left, the upper band frequently, if not always, bore a small dâgaba in the centre, and elephants reverently approaching it from each side. The spaces between the discs on this side were usually filled with conventional sculptures, the lower with dancing dwarfs or *gaṇa* between borders of large leaves, and the upper representing the dâgaba, Buddha, the Nâga, &c., and attendants on worshippers. On the inner sides, the central disc and spaces above and below it were filled by the most varied sculpture, scenes from the life of Buddha, from the Jâtakas or fables of his previous births, from the history of the sect and of the country, domestic and mythological. It is only in the paintings of Ajaṇṭâ and Bâgh, that we find anything comparable to the rich variety and excellence of art displayed in these sculptures.

The cross-bars which connect the pillars are also richly sculptured, the outer and inner sides bearing discs carved in concentric rings of leaf pattern, except the central one, which on its inner side forms a medallion filled with figures in every variety of attitude and combination, and representative of scenes that interested the Buddhist mind. The massive coping, which lay over the tops of the pillars, and into which they were morticed, was 2′ 9″ high, rounded on the top and carved on both sides—the outer with a long wavy roll of flowers, borne up by human figures at intervals, varied with figures of *dâgabas*, the *bodhi* tree, the Bauddha *chakra*, *triśula*, and other religious emblems. The inner side was filled with sculptures of scenes full of life and movement.

It would add to their interest if we could explain fully the scenes and personages represented in these sculptures, but this can hardly be expected yet, though our knowledge of Buddhism is advancing so rapidly that we may expect that before many years most of these scenes will be identified with confidence. Their publication affords the only hope of obtaining information respecting them, for it is only those widely read in Buddhist legends that can be expected to throw light upon them. The Ajaṇṭa frescoes, if also published, might be expected to reflect light on these, and to receive it in turn from them. Much, however, may be learnt of the feelings represented, and of life, manners, and customs of the age from these pictures when carefully studied, even though we fail to say precisely who the persons are, or what made the incidents represented so interesting to the Buddhists of seventeen hundred years ago.

4. Buddhist Sculpture from Gândhâra.

CHAPTER IV.

THE SCULPTURES OF THE OUTER RAIL.

Our first example of these sculptures (Plate V.) is one of the outer rail pillars, 2 feet 10 inches broad, and altogether 9 feet 4 inches in length, of which about 16 inches have been sunk in the earth. This is probably one of the stones taken to Masulipatam by Mr. Robertson. It was long in the garden of the master-attendant there, and has suffered severely, about a third of it from the top having been destroyed. On the outer side, it will be observed, the lowest band, 5 inches broad, is carved with elephants and a very large stag, between two mythological monsters or *makaras*,[1] with a long snout, gaping mouth, two feet, and the tail of a fish, which are almost universally represented in early Buddhist sculptures at the ends of bands of carving. The animals are spiritedly carved, and the interspaces filled with scrolls of foliage. Over this is a half-disc 19·3 inches high, or about 2¼ inches higher than a semicircle, with a central knob in a calyx surrounded by two concentric bands of petals with the points turned inwards, and outside them three bands of leaves each with a beaded margin, the outer one surrounded by a fillet of flowers and creepers 2½ inches broad, the ends of it terminated by *makaras*. On the shoulders of this disc the triangular space is occupied by an opening lotus bud, and over the whole extends a large leaf carefully corrugated, with curling edges, on which, in three wide and shallow flutes, stand as many fat *gaṇa*, *yakshas*, or dwarfs, the central one dancing. A similar corrugated leaf crops out above and below the large central disc, which is every way similar to the half one below, but has only one *makara* in the lower part of the surrounding fillet. What was above this is not easily made out—possibly it was a throne bearing two footmarks, or with the *bodhi* tree behind it and an attendant on each side, with two others in each of the side compartments.

The inner side, as will be seen from the plate, is much richer in figure carving. The lower band has two lions in the centre among foliage, with *makara* terminals. The lower half-disc is similar to that on the other side, only differing in minute details, as is the case in almost every example. From the lotus buds in the corners the whole of the space between the discs is filled with figures in three compartments. These are not easily explained; the three compartments probably represent so many episodes in the same story. In that to the left, a râja or chief is seated on his throne, behind which, in a recess supported by two pillars, are two attendants with fly-whisks or *châmaras;* below—a dwarf clasps his footstool; on his left are two men in attitudes of supplication, one with a lower garment tied at his waist; and seated in front to his right is a man with a cloth wound round his body and a high turban. In the central compartment we again recognise the râja in the centre, his right hand uplifted as if expressive of a strong determination to carry out some purpose, and holding some object like an elephant goad in his left; the man with the cloth and turban is

---

[1] The *Makara* is really the Hindu *Capricornus* or *Ægoceros*, the tenth of the zodiacal constellations, and, as Hyginus (on Germanicus) and Isidorus inform us, some of the ancients represented this creature with the tail of a fish (*e.g.*, on several coins of Augustus), so the Hindu *makara* is usually represented with the tail of a fish or dolphin. It is the dragon of Chinese and Burman ornament.

addressing him respectfully, while behind stands the other wearing the loin-cloth, and beyond them is a horse caparisoned for a rider and an elephant. The queen, the only female figure on the slab, very scantily clad, as was apparently the custom among Andhra ladies, holds her husband by the left arm, and behind her are two pillars, one bearing a *chakra* and the other a different symbol. The third compartment to the right presents a scene in front of a gateway surmounted by an arch, on two pillars of the antique type found at Pitalkhorâ and Jaggayyapeṭa, and on some of the earlier slabs here, with animals on the capitals. The chief stalks across the scene, placing his left foot on some round object between the triple head of a large male nâga and three other hoods representing females. The Nâga, in human form, also appears rising from the same place and supplicating the râja. Behind the latter is the man in turban and cloth, and in front the other with the loin-cloth with some triple object carried over his shoulder on a pole or handle, and apparently appealing strongly to the râja. Two figures appear in the gateway, holding up their hands with outstretched forefingers as if in surprise, some of them with similar objects to that carried by the last. Outside the gate and behind the robed figure are two more spectators, one of them bearing a like object on his right shoulder.

The central disc does not show any connection with these. In the midst a chief sits on his *sinhâsana* or lion-throne, holding up his right hand as if speaking. Behind is seen the sacred *bodhi* tree, and two men ply the fly-whisks. Three seated in front seem to be engaged in debate, and the other fourteen stand or sit in attitudes of respectful attention. All are men and wear the large turbans and heavy earrings that characterise the Andhra figures painted in Cave X at Ajaṇṭâ, and those carved in the façades of the chaityas at Kaṇheri and Kârlê.

The three compartments above this central medallion are too much injured to be made out. In the centre were two figures on a throne, and two men lie below or in front. In the left section has been an elephant with housings, and some figures below it.

Plate VI.

The next example (Plate VI) is a large fragment of a pillar, from between the south and west gates, 3 feet 1½ inches broad, and which stood about 5 feet 9 inches out of the ground. In excavating in 1880, it had been badly hammered on the top and down the edges, and broken across.

The lowest portion of the carving on the front (fig. 2) is a band of animals; on the left a *makara* gaping after a sort of lion or *Vyâla* with horns; and on the right a similar *makara* pursuing a tiger. In the centre is a flower, and the interspaces are carved with leaves like the discs. The corners over this are filled to the level of the top of the circle with foliage, and the space between this line and the bottom of the next medallion is divided into three panels filled with human figures. The left one has been badly damaged. In the right of it is a door, at which stands a child, while a woman is rushing excitedly in, looking back at something now broken away. Just behind her is another, with her back to the spectator and her hand raised to her face. In front, to the left, a woman lies or has fallen, but partly rests against another who sits on her knees. Behind these has been a fourth, with her back to the spectator; and above is left the head and arm of a figure, perhaps flying, who seems to threaten those below.

In the central panel are a dozen figures; the principal one is a tall male stretching up his left hand, while in his right, held off from his side, he holds a short sword, pointing downwards. All the others seem to be females and children, in a state of the greatest alarm at this threatening figure. In the lower right corner is a child, on whose head the mother, stooping on one knee, lays her right hand, while she looks back at this man. Against her back falls a younger woman ; against her a third, who leans her hand upon the shoulder of the first. Above the man's outstretched arm a face is seen, bent to one side as if in pain or grief. On the other side, behind the sword, is a child on its mother's knee, who crouches in the corner. Beyond his arm is another rushing off with her child, and behind her are two other females. In the upper corners of the panel are two trees. This story is vividly told, and may perhaps yet be identified among the Buddhist legends.

The third or right side compartment seems also to belong to the same story. The central personage is again a man, standing or dancing on a fallen figure ; both his arms are thrown up, and he swings an infant by the leg in each hand. On each side, standing on tiptoe, are two others, the one to the right having a battle-axe. The corners under the central medallion are filled with foliage.

The central disc had a florid border round it, but here again another very interesting scene has been ruined, perhaps not very long ago. In the fragment left of it, a râja sits in the centre on a *siṁhâsana* or lion-throne, his left foot doubled up before him and the right on a footstool. On each side sat others, and in front on the floor four men. The one in front of the footstool has his left arm round his neighbour's neck, as if constraining him to some action, and points with his right hand to the scene on the right. The two figures to the left are in the act of supplicating the throne. To the right stands a man with his arms akimbo ; a second pulls him back by the right arm, and another, kneeling, holds him by the right leg, as if to prevent him from leaving. The head of this figure is gone, with all the other portions of what must have been an animated scene.

The back (fig. 1) has suffered still more than the front. The lower band is carved with elephant-headed *makaras*, two elephants attacked in front by lions, and foliage. The half-disc below is separated, as in front, from the central disc by a space divided into three panels or flutes, with a dancing *gaṇa* or *yaksha* in each. The central disc is shattered, as if pounded with a hammer or stones.

Plate VII.

Another pillar, found *in situ*,[1] is represented in Plate VII, fig. 1. It is about 9′ 3″ in height, of which about 8 feet was exposed to view and the rest sunk in the ground. The breadth is 2 feet 8½ inches, and it has been very much injured—the defacement across the middle having occurred probably long before the Râja of Chintapalle's times.

The lower band contains only the usual *makaras* and two tigers careering to the right, and separated by a sort of conventional open bud with three petals. The lower disc is unusually high, being 28½ inches, or about 7-10ths of a complete circle ; the concentric circles are carved with great elaboration of detail, and surrounded by a neat fillet of leaf pattern. The corners are filled up in the usual way with lotus buds and large wavy leaves. Between this and the central disc the area is as usual divided into three compartments, in which probably the same figures are repeated. In that on the left two men seem to be just issuing from a gateway following a Nâga chief, whose attitude, with his left hand uplifted and the right drawn up to his collar, may imply some excitement or determination. He and his followers

[1] No. 30, on the plan in Plate iv.

seem to be advancing rapidly. Two dwarfs or *yakshas* are just in front of them, and beyond is a man with his hands in the attitude of respect or supplication. The second scene represents two tall figures in company, the arm of the one laid on that of the other, who holds up his left hand as if addressing him and pointing him onwards. One dwarf runs before carrying some round object, and the other follows holding up his joined hands in petition. A man with a high turban runs after the first tall chief, holding a short spear in his left hand, and apparently laying the right on the chief's shoulder, who does not seem to notice him. Another man behind this lifts his right hand as if about to strike the chief. In front and beyond the second tall man is another man. The third panel is damaged by the breaking away of part of it: in it a Nâga chief appears as if in great excitement, throwing up his arms, and with the one dwarf before and the other behind him carrying a large round object, and looking up at a man following with a *sittar* in his hands. Beyond him are two others, of whom one seems to be intent on the scene in the second panel, and may perhaps belong to that group.

The lower portion of the central disc is entirely destroyed, and some of the faces left have suffered injury since the slab was packed at Amarâvatî. What is left above shows that it was one of a class of representations not unfrequent among these sculptures. Examples may be seen in *Tree and Serpent Worship*, plates lxvii, lxviii, lxx, lxxi, figs. 1 and 2, and lxxii, fig. 2,[1] all from Colonel Mackenzie's drawings, of which the original slabs have disappeared. There can be no doubt that it was one of the characteristic emblems of the religion at Amarâvatî, and consisted of an empty throne[2] with two cushions upon it, and *chauri*-bearers standing behind, while on the footstool, broken away in this case, were the *pâduka* or footprints of Buddha.

From the back of the throne rises a pillar supporting a double *triśula* or trident, next perhaps to the *svastika* the most frequent symbol on Buddhist sculptures and inscriptions, and which is found to this day in a slightly modified form in the *vajras* or torques so common in Nepalese and Tibetan monasteries and chaityas. The sides of the pillar supporting this *triśula* are always represented as in flames, and, as Mr. Fergusson has remarked, this seems to be the counterpart of the Agni-liṅga of Śiva which we find represented in the Brahmanical writings and cave temples.[3]

5. Vajra from Nepâl.

"The appearance of the great fiery liṅga," according to the *Liṅga Purâṇa*, "takes place in the interval of a creation to separate Vishṇu and Brahma." "Upon the liṅga the sacred monosyllabic *Oṁ* is visible."[4] As this Agni-liṅga is the form in which, according to the Brahmanical mythology, Śiva asserted his superiority to the other two gods, it may be that the Buddhists similarly represented the superiority of their theology by the flaming *triśula*.

Another example of this symbol, so frequent among these sculptures, is represented in the accompanying woodcut (No. 6), from a disc on one of the central bars of the rail, drawn

[1] Woodcut No. 6 below.

[2] An empty throne may seem a strange symbol of a religion, but to the Buddhist it was not inappropriate: the Buddha had disappeared entirely in Nirvâṇa; his seat was empty. From the theistic point of view it is oddly symbolical of God dethroned—no king in the kingdom of the Bauddha *Dharma!*

[3] *Cave Temples*, p. 437; *Arch. Sur. West. Ind. Rep.*, vol. v, p. 25.

[4] Introd. to Wilson's *Vishṇu Purâṇa*, p. lxviii; *Tree and Serp. Wor.*, p. 208.

by Colonel Mackenzie.[1] Here it is represented, not on a throne, as it most frequently is, but behind an altar. The sacred feet or *pâduka* are represented in front of the altar. Two *chauri*-bearers and a third attendant stand by the flaming pillar, and a male worshipper is seated at each side with the unusual number of eight snake hoods rising from behind his head: the usual number is either seven or five. In the original drawing, a woman or Nâginî sits behind each with the single snake hood which always distinguishes the female of the race wearing this strange appendage. That they are the Nâga people we read of in Bauddha legends can hardly be doubted; but whether they were a tribe who had adopted the cobra as their *totam*, or why they are distinguished by this strange adjunct, is perplexing.

6. Worship of the Triśula Emblem on a Fiery Pillar.

In the example in Plate VII, the *bodhi* tree is conjoined with it, and appears rising from behind the *triśula* pillar. Behind the throne and on each side the pillar are two men with high headdresses bearing fly-whisks or *chauris*. To the right are five females and two men in the attitude of worship, one of the latter with a robe thrown over his person, and he has an old wrinkled face—probably representing some old priest; the other kneels in front of him and has a high headdress—now damaged. On the left side are nine worshippers, all men, with the high Andhra headdress.

The three panels above the middle disc are much injured, but seem to contain only one scene. In the centre a figure sits cross-legged, and a man and woman kneel before him, while another woman stands to his left and a man at his right hand, all in the attitude of reverence or beseeching. His left hand rests on his thigh, while the right is raised as if addressing those about him. He wears bracelets, necklaces, and heavy ear-rings, and has a turban. The background is not easily made out, but, from the presence of flowers on it, it is perhaps meant to represent that the scene is laid in a garden. The blossoms appear, however, on what is more like a flame than bushes, and perhaps the sculpture is intended to picture some Bauddha miracle. Two other figures stand behind, one on each side. In the left compartment a dwarf and two tall men face towards the central figure,—one in the Andhra costume with his hands clasped in reverence, the other wearing a tunic and short drawers, and perhaps holding a rod. On the right were four figures, probably all women, also facing towards the central seated figure and in reverential attitudes.

The back of this pillar is represented in fig. 2, and, like the front, the lower border contains two *makaras* and two lions with a flower separating the latter. A long leaf also issues from the mouth of each of the *makaras*. The central disc and lower half one are each beautifully carved with concentric rings of petals, the small areas in the centres being marked with minute circles to represent anthers. The corners are filled up each with a bud and large leaves, and the lower area divided into three shallow flutes, each containing a dancing dwarf or *yaksha*.

[1] Fergusson's *Tree and Serpent Worship*, pl. lxxii, fig. 2. The woodcut in the text is from the same author's *Ind. and East Arch.*, p. 46, and in his first paper on Amarâvatî in *Jour. R. As. Soc.*, N.S., vol. iii, p. 161.

The area over the central disc has a *dâgaba* in the central panel crowned with an umbrella, and having a worshipper on each side. In each side panel are also two men approaching to worship, and followed by a dwarf: that on the left side, however, is broken off.

PLATE VIII.

The next rail pillar (Plate VIII) probably belonged to the area within the north gate, close to which it was found.[1] It is 2 feet 9 inches broad and 7 feet 3 inches high, of which the lower 22 inches on the outside and 24 on the inside have been below the surface. On the outside (fig. 1), over a plain belt 6 inches broad, is a band 7 inches deep, with a *makara* at each end, and the intermediate space filled with beautiful flower pattern. Over this is the half-disc, 16 inches high, with a rich border of creeper ornament. In the corners are opening lotus buds and a broad corrugated leaf. Then in the three panels are capering dwarfs, one in each side compartment and two in the middle one. The disc above these has been of a different pattern from most of the others. In the centre was a three-headed monster, or rather a triple-bodied animal, apparently winged, but the heads are broken off. This animal is not unfrequently represented, however, on these sculptures.[2] The arrangement of the circles of petals differs much from the usual style, and instead of the outer border carved with creepers, we have five twisted cords contracted together at eight points round the circle by round or square clasps.

The front of the slab (fig. 2) has at the bottom the usual bands of leaf pattern, differing of course in detail from the others, and terminated by *makaras.* Over this is the half-disc with a border of leaf pattern, but much worn, and over it are three small panels filled with figures. Unfortunately the left one is so much damaged that it is scarcely possible to make out what it has been intended to represent. The most distinct figure is a woman kneeling perhaps in front of another figure seated. Beyond her appears a small figure holding up some object, and beyond this a tree and a larger figure. In the central panel a man is seated under a tree and a peacock spreads its tail before him; at his left sits his wife on a low cushion, and beyond the peacock are two figures, perhaps doing reverence towards it. In the right side panel a râja rests, apparently half asleep on his seat, his knees supported by his cloth tied round them—rather a favourite arrangement for one seeking to support himself in this position. Two females attend with fly-whisks behind, and an oval object between them, which one is tempted to think is a fan, but which is curiously marked. Seated in front is a man with a sword across his knees, and another kneeling to supplicate something from him.

The central disc has been carved with much care, but is unfortunately very severely damaged. In the lower segment are two wading birds among lotuses and water-plants. Above has been a chief seated with one of his wives on a throne; each has a foot on the stool in front and the other drawn up on the seat, and she has apparently been addressing him. Another female, perhaps also his wife, on the right leans back in her seat with her right foot on a small hassock and the left drawn up on the seat. Both these wear two very heavy rings on each ankle, and apparently very little clothing. Indeed, in many of these sculptures the clothing is almost as scanty as that worn by some of the wilder tribes in the Eastern Ghâṭs to the present day; and it is not improbable that in early times, before the

---

[1] No. 171 on the plan, Plate iv. [2] *Tree and Serp. Wor.*, pl. lvi, fig. 1; pl. lxxxviii, fig. 3; pl. xcviii, fig. 1.

invasions of the Dekhan by more northern races, the use of clothing was not felt to be so necessary as it has come to be in later times. Nor did this imply any looser state of morals then than among ampler clothed races; it may even be that they were purer then than in later times, when contaminated by invading and conquering tribes. In front of the throne a female offers some object, and beyond her another has been seated; but the rest of the scene is quite destroyed.

Plate IX.

The next slab was found lying on its face on the outer verge of the procession-path, on the north-east of the circle.[1] It is 7 feet 8 inches long, but one edge has been broken away, and most of the face of the central disc on the front. It is much abraded, but the central and lower half-discs on the back, with three capering *yakshas* or dwarfs between, are still fairly preserved (fig. 1).

On the front (fig. 2) the three panels of sculpture are a good deal injured; in that on the left we have a man and woman seated fronting each other, and apparently engaged in conversation. Beyond them stand five persons, probably all females, looking on—one with a somewhat peculiar head-dress. In the central panel a man with a high head-dress is striding across the scene; a female kneels before him with her hands raised to her face; another beyond her raises her hands as if in terror or to stop him; and beyond these are other two. Behind the man also is a fourth female with a peculiar head-dress. Of the third panel we have only portions of three figures left, two of them at least females, and looking towards the left, as if belonging to the scene in the centre. Of the middle disc only a fragment is left, showing some women, either asleep, or, judging from the position of one of them, thrown down by some assault, as in the scene represented in Plate xii, fig. 2.

Plates X, XI.

Fig. 1 represents the face of a very plain pillar, the one side being quite smooth. This one shows further varieties in the carving of the discs upon these rail pillars, scarcely two of which are perfectly alike in all respects. The patterns also beneath the lower half-disc and round it and the central one supply examples of the ever-changing variety of these floral ornaments.[2] The space between the discs illustrates the general design which runs through all, dividing these spaces into three panels by raised arrises.

The next (Pl. x, fig. 2) is the lower half of another rail pillar, 2′ 10″ broad, 10 inches thick, and about 5 feet high, of which 1′ 9″ has been under ground. It was found close to the north gate, and is split, and half of one of the pieces has been broken across.[3] On the back is one of those beautiful bands of purely decorative sculpture formed of flowers arranged with rare taste, and always varied. Round the lower half-disc is a similar border, with flowers, birds, and tigers interspersed among the convolutions of creepers, and above are three dwarf or *Yaksha* figures in the usual flutes; but the slab is broken through the lower margin of the central disc.

The front has also a decorative band below with *makaras* at its extremities, and the

---

[1] No. 198.

[2] Good examples of this style of ornament in Buddhist sculpture will also be found in woodcuts 2, 19, 29, in the present volume. They have been taken from Messrs. Trübner's illustrated edition of E. Arnold's *Light of Asia.*

[3] No. 157 of the original numeration used in Plate iv.

disc is bordered by an ornament which bears a close resemblance to that on the jamb of the door of the Nâsik Chaitya cave, and to some examples at Sanchi.[1]

The three flutes above contained three groups; that on the left shows a man amply clothed, and kneeling in worship to the *pâdukâ* or footmarks of Buddha, at the base of one of the flaming pillars, while another, in the robe of a Bauddha ascetic, stands over him holding a cloth in his hands. In the central panel the feet and pillar are again represented, the latter having apparently been crowned with the Bauddha *triśula*. A man approaches it from the left, and behind him is an object like a huge snake with an unusually deep mouth, depending from above, but possibly meant for the root of a *vaḍ* or *asvâttha* tree bifurcating on a rock. The same object is also represented on a somewhat larger scale in the first panel, where the rocky background is strongly marked. The recurrence of this object plainly indicates that the two scenes are closely connected. Another man approaches from the right, carrying some object like a flask with a round body and long neck, but the figure is destroyed by the fracture of the stone. The third panel contained four figures, one being a woman with heavy earrings and bracelets. They stand in attitudes of reverence, but their heads and the rest of the sculpture is broken away.

The piece represented on Pl. xi, fig. 1, is another upper portion of a pillar, 2′ 6″ broad by 3′ 1″ high and 11 inches thick, which has been carved with quite unusual care, for even the centre of the upper half-disc has been utilised for one of the scenes. Part of one of the tenons which held on the coping-stone is still left on the top. The upper frieze has a curious dwarf figure at each end, and the intervening space is divided into four by the stems of creepers, and in each space is a pair of animals—tigers, bears, the mythical animal before noticed, &c. The upper half-disc is bordered by a very rich band of flowers and birds, and contains in the middle the *bôdhi* tree with the *pâdukâ* or footprints, as symbols of Buddha, on an altar by the trunk of it. Three men are seated on each side, wearing the Andhra turban, and two on each side below, in a horizontal position, are paying worship to it. Under the disc the three flutes or panels are filled with figures, apparently all belonging to the same scene. In the middle one is a sort of lofty palanquin with an arched roof, and in it an elephant. This "divine car" is borne by a number of small dwarf figures, and numerous other larger ones are represented round it and in both the side divisions, flying through the air, one bearing an umbrella and another a flag, as symbols of royalty.

This is just another representation of what we find in the central compartment on the coping-stone[2] sent to Calcutta by Colonel Mackenzie, and figured in the accompanying cut (No. 7). It represents the Bodhisattva or future Buddha descending from the Tushita heavens to be born of Mâyâ, the consort of Suddhodana. "Without being touched," says the *Lalita Vistara*, "a hundred myriad instruments, divine and human, sent forth ravishing melody. Hundreds of myriads of Dêvas with their hands, shoulders, and heads bore the grand divine car. A hundred thousand Apsaras led the choirs of music, and proceeding behind, before, on right and left, praised the Bodhisattva with their songs and concerts."[3] The future Buddha descended as "a pure white six-tusked elephant, with rose-coloured head, having teeth like a line of gold, and all his members and their parts with his organs without

[1] *Cave Temples*, p. 274 and Pl. xxv; *Tree and Serp. Wor.*, p. 114, woodcuts 17 and 18.

[2] See Fergusson's *Tree and Serp. Wor.*, Pl. lxxiv. The section figured here is to the same scale as those on the plates, viz., one-tenth of the original. The other two sections of this slab are figured at pp. 64, 65.

[3] *Lalita Vistara*, chap. v.

any imperfection," [1] and entered into the side of his mother Mâyâ. This is taking literally what most of the earlier legends represent only as a dream; but it illustrates the mode of growth of the legendary history of Gautama.

7. The Descent of the Bodhisattva.

The rest of this slab, which probably contained the other scenes usually associated with this one,[2] is broken away. The back of it (Pl. x, fig. 3) bears on the upper portion a *bodhi* tree with the feet of the Buddha on a slab or low altar at its foot, and two elephants approaching on each side to honour it. The half-disc has a rich border, and below have been human figures, but they are almost all broken away. It was found a little to the south of the preceding stone.

Fig. 2, Plate xi, represents another portion of the top of a rail pillar, much injured on the left side, and measuring about 4 feet high by 2 feet 4 inches broad. On the frieze are two lions within the convolutions of a creeper which issues from the mouth of a *makara* at the right end. The margins of the half-discs are carved with a series of rosettes, and the breadth of the slab below seems to have been divided only into two compartments, but so much is broken away that we cannot determine satisfactorily what the scenes were intended to represent. Part of a building appears on the left, and near it a number of people engaged apparently in a struggle. On the right, two women are entering through a door into the presence of a chief seated with two women at his feet, and other two in attendance behind his seat.

The next (figs. 3, 4) is the base of a pillar found near the north gate. It is about 5 feet high and 2 feet 10 inches broad, and has formed part of one of the pillars at the angles inside the gate, the mortices for the cross-bars being on one edge and on the back. This narrows the space for sculpture on the back to 22 inches, and on this side the lower band is of flowers as usual. Just over this was an empty seat or chair, and on a high footstool the *pâdukâ* or footmarks of the Buddha. A man stood on each side with a fly-flap, but both figures are considerably injured.

On the inner side, the band of flower ornament, between two scaly *makaras*, is tastefully manipulated. The richly carved half-disc over it is also surrounded by a border of long broad leaves delicately corrugated.

Above, the width is divided into the usual three flutes. In the left one, a woman with heavy anklets passes her right hand over her head, and with the left apparently holds a

---

[1] *Ibid.*, chap. vi; conf. Beal's *Rom. Legend*, p. 37; Bigandet's *Leg. of Gaudama*, vol. i, p. 28; Rhys Davids' *Bud. Birth Stories*, vol. i, p. 63; S. Hardy's *Man. of Budhism* (2d ed.), p. 145; Rockhill's *Life of Buddha*, p. 15. An elephant is also the first of the objects in the dream of the mother (or mothers) of the Jaina Tîrthaṁkara Mahâvira.—Stevenson's *Kalpa Sûtra*, pp. 25 and 42.

[2] See below, pp. 64, 65, and woodcuts 17, 18.

kneeling boy by the hair, while he supplicates her with his hands, but averts his face. Another figure passes behind him, but the upper portion is broken away.

In the centre, the same boy seems to tell his story to a stout male figure seated on a stool or *bhadrâsana*, with his hand in an attitude indicative that he is replying. Another small figure squats by his side, and a larger one beyond the first boy; others also stand in the background, but they are only partly left on this fragment. In the third scene, the boy follows the man, who is walking away, with the second boy before him; and two men in the background follow.

Plate XII.

The upper portion of another pillar (Figs. 1, 2) has been carved in a very masterly style; on the top is left a fragment of one of the tennons that kept the coping in its place. The uppermost band on the outside (fig. 1) has the *bodhi* tree in the centre, with a pair of feet on a low altar below it, and approaching it from each side are two winged animals, like those we find in the oldest western caves at Bhâja and Pitalkhorâ. The half-disc below this is surrounded with a belt of creeper foliage, and with a large lotus bud filling up each corner. The space below is divided as usual into three panels; in the central one is a *Dharmachakra*, or wheel of the law, on a pillar behind an altar, and two men waying *châmaras* over it. In each side panel is a man and woman, scantily clad, doing *pûjâ* to it.

The inner side (fig. 2) has, in the upper belt, two groups of three tigers in different attitudes, and foliage between; at the ends were makaras, now much worn. The upper disc is richly carved, and surrounded by a band filled with birds in varied positions; and the three panels below have three groups of exceedingly life-like figures. On the left are seven figures, of which three at least are women, looking at a cobra's hole, into which a woman in front points at the snake, and a stout man stands behind it. In the central panel a man stands with his feet far apart over a prostrate female, and another has fallen back just in front of him, and holds up her hands as if imploring mercy, while he holds a bow in his left hand, and has the right drawn back to his ear, as if he had just let fly an arrow. Three figures appear behind, perhaps all women, and the one to the right seems as if making past the fallen one. In the right side panel are two women and a very lanky girl supplicating towards the warrior, while four other figures appear behind them. Another very spirited version of this same story is given on a broken cross-bar (Fergusson's *Tree and Serpent Worship*, Pl. lxiii, fig. 1), with the snake and all the figures here, but with many more women.

Below, the central disc is broken across the upper part, leaving only a fragment of it. Perhaps the scene was similar to the one above, for in the middle we have a chief's head, who holds up a discus or other missile in his right hand, and to the right, in front of him, are several women in attitudes of supplication or timidity.

Fig. 3 represents another upper half of an outer rail pillar, about 4½ feet long, and is probably one of Sir W. Elliot's marbles that had been left at Madras, and is unfortunately much damaged. The upper band of sculpture has a *makara* with a human head at the left end, a *bodhi* tree in the centre, and an altar at its foot; one person is approaching and another leaving it, and in separate areas, divided off by a creeper, is a winged lion on each side between it and the *makaras*. The upper half-disc has a broad but weather-worn flower border. Below it the right-hand panel is partly broken away, but the heads of two elephants are seen, one of them bearing a rider, and two men appear below in front.

The central panel contains two seated figures, apparently in close conversation or debate; each of them has his feet on a cushion, and by the side is a man squatted, perhaps taking part in the debate. Behind are four men standing; two appear to have short cropped hair, and the other two have it gathered back in a knot, projecting from the crown. The figures in this and the other compartments have been carved with much artistic skill, and in a style which differs from the general one in these sculptures. The group here depicted bears a close resemblance to a painting in Cave I. at Ajaṇṭâ,[1] though this is much the older; but the mode of dressing the hair may also be compared with examples in the far older painting in Cave X. at the same place.[2]

The left division contains six men; among them, apparently one of the chief persons in the scene just described, with two companions, approaches a gate, and is met in it by another with two attendants. The clothing of all is scanty, but the figures are well proportioned.

Of the central disc only a fragment is left, but it contains parts of twelve figures, all men, round a chair having the usual representation of a relic-shrine. Behind them are a stone building, a thatched hut, a tree, and part of a gateway. Some of the faces are broken off, but all seem to have the same short-cropped hair as in the upper portion of the slab.

Along the upper margin is a portion of an inscription (Plate lvi, No. 8), which has been thus read and rendered by Dr. J. G. Bühler of Vienna:—

Vinayadhirasa[3] Aya-Punavasusa atevâsiniya uvarayiniya Samuḍiyâya[4] atevâsiniya Malaṁyâ[5] pâḍakâ[6] dâna[ṁ].[7]

"A *pâḍakâ*, the gift of Malâ, the female disciple of . . . Samuḍiyâ, the female disciple of Aya-Punavasu (*who is*) firm in the Vinaya."

The next figure (fig. 4) represents the lower portion of a narrow rail pillar, such as were used at corners at the returns of the gateways. It has a rich band of flowers 5½ inches broad, exclusive of the fillets above and below, and a *makara* only at the right end. The half-disc is 15½ inches high and 30″ wide, the outer border being of half-blown lotus blossoms. Above this the whole breadth of the slab, except a narrow marginal fillet, has been occupied with one scene, of which a large portion has been destroyed, but, like the last described, it has represented the worship of some relic on a seat. Seven men kneel before it, and at least six others have been represented standing in reverential attitudes.

The back of this pillar has been split off, and there are mortices for the rail discs only on one edge, but it is not clear whether it was an angle pillar or stood beside some pillar at one of the gates. This stone was one of those at the Bejwâḍâ Library.

---

[1] *Cave Temples*, Pl. xliii.

[2] *Ibid.*, Pl. xxix.

[3] *Vinayadhirasa*: the epithet is intended to indicate that Aya-Punavasu was a master of the doctrines and firm in the practice of Bauddha discipline. Aya-Punavasu may correspond either with the Sanskrit Ârya-Pûrṇavasu or Ârya-Punarvasu.

[4] *Samuḍiyâ* corresponds with the Sanskrit Samudrikâ. I am unable to restore and explain the mutilated word preceding this name.

[5] The reading *Malaṁyâ* is probably a mistake for Malâyâ or Malâya. A female name in the genitive is required after the second *atevâsiniya*.

[6] The reading of the second letter in *pâḍakâ* is uncertain. The epigraphic peculiarities of this inscription are a total neglect of the difference between long and short *i*, the absence of most *anusvâras*, and the adoption of a peculiar cursive form of the initial *a*.

[7] See Hultzsch, *Zeitschrift d. Deut. Morg. Gesell.*, Bd. xxxvii. S. 561. The Madras Museum authorities have built this slab with others into a wall and covered the corner of it with cement, so that the final letters can no longer be examined.

The accompanying woodcut[1] (No. 8) represents another of these angle pillars, 1′ 9″ broad, and though unfortunately the lower portion is broken away, what is left of it is about 5′ 8″ in length. It is one of those excavated by Sir Walter Elliot and now in the British Museum, and may be introduced here as one of the best examples of the kind. The sculpture here, as remarked by Mr. Fergusson, tells its story "perhaps more graphically than almost any other on these pillars." "A king is seated on his throne, to whom a messenger with clasped hands brings intelligence or solicits orders. In front of him a part of the army is seen defending the walls of the citadel, and on the left hand the moveable force is sallying from the city gate. In front the infantry, in attitudes of great excitement, are seen advancing to the fight, and the rear is brought up by horsemen and elephants, all remarkably well drawn and foreshortened. In the foreground one of the enemy falls on his knees to beg pardon and mercy," which is possibly the information being communicated to the king. Had the lower portion of the pillar been preserved, "we might have seen the result of this sally. It no doubt was successful, and as women appear in the fragments that remain, the whole ended probably in triumph." According to the Hindu system of polity, "a perfect army always consists of four arms, elephants and horsemen, chariots and infantry." Three of these are represented here, but the chariots are absent, but, as we shall see in the case of another battle-scene on a coping stone, they are sometimes represented in these marbles, though they are not so prominent as in the Sânchi sculptures. "Taken altogether," Mr. Fergusson remarks, "this pillar, both in its decorations and its sculptures, is one of the most elegant at Amarâvatî, and it would consequently be extremely interesting if its inscription told us something of its story."[2]

8. Outer Rail Angle Pillar.

This is in two lines at the top, and reads (Pl. lxi, No. 56):—

Loṇavalavakasa Saṁgharakhitasa cha Mariti[sa] cha
bhariyâyo Saghâya cha Saghadâsiya cha Kumaḷaya cha dânaṁ.

"A gift of Saghâ (Saṅgha) and Saghadâsi and Kumaḷa (Kumâḷâ), the wives of Loṇavalavaka, Saṅgharakhita, and Mariti (?)."

PLATES XIII, XIV.

There is a portion of another pillar of the outer rail, about 5 feet high and 2′ 9″ broad, among the stones left for so long at Bejwâḍâ (Pl. xiii, figs. 1, 2). But except the decorative

[1] From Fergusson's *History of Indian and Eastern Architecture*, p. 101, by permission of the author. The same slab appears also in *Tree and Serpent Worship*, pl. lxi, fig, 1.

[2] *Tree and Serpent Worship*, pp. 196, 262.

carving, which on the front especially is remarkably fine, the sculpture has been almost entirely destroyed. On the back has been a seat, with the *pâduka* upon it, and a cushion on the back. Female attendants stand on each side; and in the side compartments have been male figures standing on the heads of two monsters of unusual description; they only occur in one other known case, represented in Fergusson's *Tree and Serpent Worship*, pl. lxx.

The margin round the half-disc in this instance is formed of a triple band of small flowers twisted together into ropes, and the three held together at intervals of about 30° by square and circular clasps alternately.

Plate xiv, fig. 1, is a fragment from the centre of an outer rail pillar, which has apparently been devoted to illustrations of sacred rites. It is 2′ 10″ broad by 2′ 2″ high. In the lower right-hand corner has been the adoration of the feet (*pâdukâ*), surrounded perhaps with flames, and of the *bodhi* tree, and a Deva from above is joining in the rite. In the left corner is perhaps a fragment of the worship of another tree.

The disc is surrounded by a very rich flowered border, with two *makaras* on the lower edge. It has contained one of those curious pillars, of which we shall meet with other examples on a larger scale, bearing the wheel, &c. The top in this case is broken off, but perhaps bore either the sacred wheel or a repetition of the three harpy-like figures which appear twice in the shaft at short intervals, and which seem to have been a favourite ornament or symbol and often repeated. In front of the pillar is a chair or throne, with a round object, apparently a cushion, on the seat, and another against the back of it; below are the *pâdukâ* or feet, and at each side is a deer couched—a favourite cognizance, repeated under the throne of many of the colossal images at Ajaṇṭâ—usually with the *chakra* or wheel between them. The pillar rises close behind the seat, and is octagonal at the base, but is surrounded by circular bands or *tori*, with the groups of three mythic animals between; and the capital is square. A *chauri*-bearer stands on each side behind the chair, and over twenty other men, all with high turbans, perhaps râjas, are seated round worshipping this pillar, or the wheel or other object with which it was crowned.

There are some fragments which I excavated under the level of the platform, close to the south gate, and among them five pieces of a fine pillar of the inner rail, beautifully carved. How these came to be broken and buried it is hard to say. But wherever I dug under the level of the platform fragments turned up, and some of them apparently of even later age than the rails, indicative apparently of a later restoration or appropriation of the shrine for worship, possibly Brahmanical. (See Plate xiv, fig. 1.)

One piece is the right side of the lower half-disc of a pillar, the corner over which is filled in with a beautiful honeysuckle pattern preserved on the second fragment. Two fragments of the band below the central disc show a man in the middle compartment moving violently to the right; a figure kneels before him with a large triple-hooded snake by his side, and behind him is a figure with the right hand uplifted and carrying something over his left shoulder on a rod or staff.

In the right-hand panel stands the Buddha holding out his almsbowl. A man with a *jaṭâ* headdress, a cloth over his shoulders, and his left foot advanced, and resting on a lotus, is about to place something held with both his hands in the bowl, while a female just behind him joins her hands in reverence. Other figures have been destroyed; and of the central disc only a small fragment was found containing parts of some worshippers.

The piece represented in Pl. xiv, fig. 3, is another fragment of the upper portion of one of these pillars, measuring about 3′ 6″ by 1′ 8″. The back has been split off, and only a corner of the face is left. The upper band has been ornamented with animals in pairs, with divisions formed by a creeper plant. At the right end are perhaps two lions, then two bullocks; thirdly, two mythic animals, found also in other early sculptures; and the fourth and last are broken off. The half-disc under this has been beautifully carved, and with a pretty floral border, of which only a fragment is left. The compartments below have been filled with figures, but only the heads of five remain, one of them a female supplicating a man for some favour. On the left was a chief with attendants. The headdresses are somewhat peculiar. The stone was found on the outer edge of the pavement on the north-west.

Plates XV, XVI.

Among the Mackenzie drawings there are some hitherto unpublished that may as well be included with these.

The first we give (Plate xv, fig. 1) is a pillar slab,[1] 2′ 7½″ broad and about 6 feet 5 inches high, exclusive of what was beneath the pavement, which these drawings often omit, and represents only a large broken fragment. The lower band of decorative work is still varied from any yet met with; the *makara* at the left end is changed for a monster with the head of an elephant and the tail of a dolphin, and the heads of four lions look out from the bights or scrolls of the creeper and foliage between. The half-disc is ornamented with a five-hooded Nâga, with a small *chhatra* over the central hood, and nondescript objects on each side, perhaps intended for lamps. The borders round the discs are unusually full of animals—lions, elephants, and even men. These, and indeed much of the purely decorative sculpture on the Amarâvatî slabs, is distinctly identical in kind with the painted decorative work on the ceilings of the Ajaṇṭâ caves, which is so rich and varied, and so deserving the attention of artists.

Of the three compartments between the discs, the side ones are repetitions of the same scene. A young chief, with high turban and heavy ear-rings, on horseback, and attended by five divine dwarfs or *yakshas*, three of whom are perhaps intended to bear up his horse's feet, the other two flying above to do him honour. This supporting of the feet of a horse by *yakshas* recurs where the Prince Siddhartha is represented (Pl. xli, fig. 1) as leaving Kapilavastu on the horse Kaṇṭhaka Aśvarâja, to become an ascetic. The central scene represents an empty chair or throne with a cushion against the back of it, which is surmounted by the Buddhist triśula, and behind it a tree. On each side are two women with the usual heavy anklets and scanty clothing. It is to be noted that the young rider in the left compartment turns round to salute with respect these symbols of religion.

Above the central disc has been another seat, footprints below, and attendant figures on each side; but the greater portion has been broken away.

The next we give (fig. 2) is the lower portion of an outer rail pillar, 3 feet wide by about 5 feet high. The lower band is carved with two *makaras* and two lions rushing towards each other, divided by leaf ornament. The lower disc is 23 inches high, being considerably more than a half one, and is bordered by a neat creeper pattern.

Besides the usual lotus flower, the corners are filled up to the level of the top of the

---

[1] Drawn by Mr. M. Burke; the next is by Mr. H. Hamilton, who was evidently a better draughtsman. Mr. Burke's drawings, however, though not to be depended on for minute details of features and proportion, seem faithful representations of the general features of the scenes.

half-disc with other graceful leaf patterns, and the sculpture arranged in the usual three flutes. In the left-hand one is a lady lying on a couch, with two women sleeping on foot-stools. Other two figures appear beyond the bed, but their faces have been broken off; and a woman is seen above on a cloud flying towards the first.

In the central scene three women appear in a balcony, one of them having an infant, while a man with a regal headdress and his wife speak to them, and two other persons clothed about the chest and neck stand behind. In the third scene a prince—probably the same as in the second—lies on a couch, while a woman on a seat in front appears to have put into his bosom the infant. Another woman kneels and offers her a cup. At the head of and beyond the bed are four attendants, one with the *chauri*, another with what appears to be a dish, and a third with an object resembling a large horn. What scene in Buddhist legend this is intended to represent I do not recognise. Is it a case of "*couvade?*"[1] This curious practice is in vogue among the Erukalavaṇḍlu or people of the Erukala or Yerukala tribe, that wanders about the Kṛishṇâ, Godâvarî, and Nelur districts to the present day;[2] it is probably little known in India outside the Telugu country. When a child is about to be born, the husband goes to bed, and as soon as the infant is born it is at once placed beside him. But this does not explain the other two connected scenes, and one is at a loss to find an explanation for them in Bauddha legends. The publication, however, of this drawing ought to direct the attention of those engaged in the study of the *Jâtaka* literature to the subject. But the local colouring given to them by the third scene may possibly incline us to identify it with some local legend connected with the Andhras,—possibly the surreptitious transfer of an infant into a higher family.

Of the central disc only a fragment is left. The figures in it are mostly, if not all, women, with the large earrings, rich girdles, heavy bracelets and anklets, and scanty clothing of the Andhra race; and the object engaging their attention is a peacock, to which the two principal figures in the foreground, attended by a *chauri*-bearer, are paying marked attention. This does not suggest any connection with the story in the *Nachcha Jâtaka*,[3] and perhaps without the complete scene it will be difficult to identify it.

The next drawing (fig. 3) is of the lower portion of one of these pillars, 2′ 8″ broad, and, on one side, about 6 feet high,[4] but it is broken through the central disc in an irregular line, carrying away the middle and left side of it. It is thus impossible to make out the scene it represented. Some great man seems to have occupied a seat in the centre; in front sits a woman on a low seat, with her back to the spectator, displaying her coiffure. On her left sits a man who seems to be speaking either to the central figure or to the second on her right. He is dressed in a *chaddar*, and has a stick in his lap. Another on the woman's right is similarly clad, and has a bludgeon or javelin lying on his thigh, and makes a humble obeisance to the woman. Behind him is an almost nude figure seated in an

---

1 Tylor's *Researches into the Early History of Mankind*, pp. 293–302; *Primitive Culture*, p. 84. This curious custom prevailed in Corsica, Diod. Sicul., v, 14; among the Iberians in the north of Spain, Strabo, iii, 4, 17; among the Tibarēni on the coast of Pontus, Apollonius Rhodius, *Argonautica*, ii, 1009–1014; Valerius Flaccus, *Argon.*, v, 148; and among the Miau-tse in the south-west of China, Yule's *Marco Polo*, vol. ii, p. 75; *conf.* Lubbock, *Origin of Civilisation*, pp. 10–12; Max Müller's *Chips*, vol. ii, pp. 274–281.

2 *Ind. Ant.*, vol. iii, p. 151; vol. v, p. 188; vol. viii, p. 106; vol. ix, p. 210; Hodgson's *Essays*, vol. ii, pp. 112 ff.; Cust's *Mod. Lang. of the E. Ind.*, p. 78.

3 Fausböll's *Jâtakas*, No. 32; Rhys David's *Birth Stories*, vol. i, p. 292; Schiefner's *Tibetan Tales*, by Ralston, p. 354. Compare also plate viii, and p. 32, *supra*.

4 Drawn by C. Barnett.

attitude of lively attention. Beyond these last two are five men; one, with a cloth over his left shoulder and covering the right front of his person, looks toward the last mentioned, holding his right hand open with thumb and forefinger touching, as if making some explanation; next him is a tall man with high headdress and little clothing, holding up his joined hands in respect to the figure in the centre; a third, next to him on the outer side, stands in the same attitude, but is clothed like the first; behind them are two more, not well seen; one of them appears to carry a present. Above these is the corner of some separate panel. On the left side of the disc are left a dwarf figure paying respect to the central one, and fragments of two others.

The area below this disc is bordered above and below by leaf decoration, and is divided into three compartments. In that to the right is a tree, indicative of an out-door, if not a forest scene. A man is leading by the wrist a woman with an infant in her left arm, both having their hair done up in a long pointed knot sticking out from the head. On the man's right is a smaller female, and in front are four people on the ground; one with his hair in a high knot is held by the wrist by another kneeling beside him and looking into his face; a third kneels to the right with his hands joined, and the head of the fourth is seen over this last.

In the central panel a seated chief is attended by two *chauri*-bearers; a person in loose robe, perhaps a monk, stands to the proper right, and in front of him is seated a man who holds up a cloth in his right hand to the chief, while another kneels on one knee and addresses him. This figure has bracelets and anklets and long loose hair, and is either hunchbacked or the draughtsman has mistaken some object below the throne for this deformity. On the right of the picture a lady is seated, and holds up her right hand as if taking part in the conversation. Beyond her is another figure with joined hands.

In the third scene we have apparently the same individual on his seat, but the headdresses of the *chauri*-bearers are different. A figure stands on each side as before, but the one on his right appears to have laid off the cloth. One with an upper garment is seated in front on the spectator's right, and a smaller figure in the centre talks to him, while a stout man wrapped in a sheet presents some offering to the chief.

The disc below is bordered by a representation of a stout rope or cable, and the decorative band beneath contains two makaras, two lions, and interspersed foliage.

Plate xvi, fig. 1, represents another lower portion of a pillar of the outer circle,[1] and measures 2′ 11½″ by about 3 feet 8½ inches. The lower band between the *makaras* is unsymmetrically divided into four spaces, two filled with flowers and two with pairs of lions. The lower disc had a rich border of flowers, and the space between the discs divided into the usual three flutes, and filled with figure sculpture. In the left panel a young man turns apparently to remonstrate with, or refuse the petition of four dwarf figures who appeal to him; beyond him is a woman whose head and right hand are broken off; facing her is a short, stout figure with an abundance of clothing, and behind him is another woman.

In the central area, a man and his wife are seated on a couch; a man behind and a woman to the left of it bear offerings, and the latter also a fan, while in front of her, and at the chief's right knee, stands another woman making some offering on which he lays his hand. Both these women have cloths thrown across their chests. In front of the couch are three dwarf figures, two of them females, and a dog which the male is feeding, while

---

[1] Also drawn by Mr. M. Burke.

one of the females urges it forward by the tail. In the third or right-hand scene are two men and a woman, who have apparently just come out of a gate which is festooned with flowers, and before them are a male and female dwarf, the latter carrying a vessel filled with small objects like fruits. Only a fragment of the border of the central disc remains above.

The next of these pillar slabs we have to notice (fig. 2) is a fragment 2′ 8¼″ broad and about 5 feet high, but on only about 3 feet of this is there any carving.[1] The lower disc is in this case 20 inches high, or three-fifths of the circle, so that the inner circles are shown complete. The border is varied as usual, and the band below has three lions couchant among the convolutions of foliage, and *makara* terminals.

The three scenes above the disc are all injured along the upper border. The right-hand one contained a chief seated, a woman brings him some vessel; in front is perhaps a monk seated and a female also bringing him a vessel or offering, while another moves in an opposite direction, also carrying some round object.

In the central scene the chief sits with an attendant on each side, one doing him reverence. In front sit three men with cloths cast about their bodies, and the one in the middle without any headdress, and holding some object or weapon which is not easily recognised. The other two face the spectator. In the left-hand panel have been three monks seated, and a number of men attended by a small dwarf making offerings to them.

Plate xxxii, fig. 1, is a drawing of the lower portion of another pillar broken through the middle,[2] and thus destroying much of the scene in the central disc. What is left of it appears to be filled with women only. One seated is playing on the *vînâ;* behind her another is seated on a small raised platform with a companion behind; perhaps four in front are taking part in some sort of dance; one is seated to the left with some object in her left hand, while another kneels and offers her a parcel. Below this are three scenes: in that to the right is an ox-cart, covered, and with the driver looking towards a man and woman standing in the foreground, and to whom two figures with more than the usual clothing are kneeling, one of them at least being probably a monk. Behind these are three others. In the central scene is a man squatted on a seat with a woman seated on each thigh, in a way that more resembles a Brahmanical than a Buddhist sculpture. A woman stands behind on each side, and another sits to the proper right of the middle group. In front are the two monk-like figures again dressed in *chaddars*—the one apparently handing to or receiving from the other something perhaps in a bag, over the head of a dwarf and two smaller figures behind the second.

In the third scene we have the same two individuals as in the first standing at the door of a dwelling in a wood, represented by two trees, two deer, and a couple of lions; two smaller figures stand with joined hands in front of the men and beyond the lions; and a woman wearing a petticoat follows them bearing a load on a pole over her shoulder.

These, together with the examples in Mr. Fergusson's *Tree and Serpent Worship*, supply all the specimens of the pillars of the outer rail at Amarâvatî that are likely ever to be recovered, unless some of the ruinous small temples built by Venkaṭâdri Nayudu in the end of last century, and now ruinous, should be pulled down and the large slabs embedded in their basements be extracted. Those published show what a magnificent series they must have formed when entire, and what interesting scenes they depicted, now so injured, even in the examples left, that we may never be able to read more than a few of them aright. And the same remark applies to the other portions of the building yet to be described.

---

[1] The drawing is by T. Anderson, July 1817.

[2] Drawn by M. Burke.

CHAPTER V.

THE CROSS-BARS OR RAILS.

THREE cross-bars filled up the space between each pair of pillars of the outer rail, the ends being lenticular in section, and let into mortices in the edges of the pillars. The front and backs of each bar bore circular discs, which were carved—on the outside always with rosettes or concentric bands of petals, which for convenience have been called lotus flowers—in all respects resembling the discs on the rail pillars, and with the like continual variation in little details, which saves them from monotony. The inner sides of the upper and lower bars were also carved in the same style, but often with a border of creepers or foliage round the outer edge. No mere description could give much information respecting the beauty and variety of the patterns, but the specimens given in the plates will supply a good idea of this. The middle bar, probably in all cases, was carved on the inner side with figures representing vividly some scene in Bauddha legend or worship, or some local tradition, and the few examples of these that are left are peculiarly valuable. Some eleven in all are given in *Tree and Serpent Worship*, and we have only a few new ones to add.

The first two ordinary discs (Plate xiii, figs. 3 and 4) are placed together because they illustrate how variety is sometimes secured by varying the proportions of the elements of the pattern quite as much as by any difference of detail. The second has two more concentric circles than the first, and is surrounded by a pretty leaf border.

In Pl. xiv, fig. 4, we have another of these discs, which had been for some time at Bejwâḍâ. It presents quite a different pattern, is 2′ 8″ in diameter, but nearly half the sculpture has been destroyed. The central boss is much the same as in the upper and lower rail discs, and is surrounded by circles of petals to about 13″ diameter, but the outer area is divided by leaves into four compartments. The upper one contains two figures raising a tray bearing some object or relic, and others dancing around. All are in the air, and the scene suggests the translation of the *pâtra* or almsbowl, or, perhaps in this case, the curls of hair which Siddhartha shore from his head, and which Sakra caught, and ascending with them to the Trayastriṁśa heavens, paid divine honours to them in company with the other Dêvas.

In the right-hand picture the chief figure is a horse, whose feet are borne up by *Yakshas*, and an umbrella carried before it: this is a scene represented in some of the very earliest sculptures here. The men, or more probably Dêvas, seen beyond the horse, hold up their right hands in approbation, and it would seem to represent the preparation of the horse Kaṇṭhaka for the Prince's escape. The legends say that the *Yakshas*—Patrapada and his companions—bore up the feet of Kaṇṭhaka when Siddhartha mounted on him to leave his home.[1] But we shall meet with other sculptures of this scene in the sequel.

The lower scene on this disc was perhaps the worship of the *bodhi* tree by a number of women, but this and the whole of the left-hand scene is much injured. The donative inscription in the upper left-hand corner is also much abraded.

Fig. 5 shows another fragment of one of these discs, also among the Bejwâḍâ collection. It has been surrounded by a border of creeper plants, and in the centre sat a chief upon a

---

[1] See below, and woodcut No. 22, p. 80.

couch, with a companion seated at his right hand, and a sword or some similar object laid across his knees.

A figure, almost naked, with a crooked knife, horn, or small bag tied to his back, kneels imploringly at the corner of the seat, and another stands behind him also in a beseeching attitude, with some object on his back hanging by a strap across his chest, and depending very low in a broad oval end. He holds a pole with a large broad blade as of a paddle over his shoulder. Beyond him stands a third, with his hands joined, wearing a turban, and at his back something like a round cylindrical basket, out of which rise what appear to be lance-heads. Four women, one of them a *chauri*-bearer, fill up the remainder of the background. Two men stand behind the second petitioner, one wearing a sort of blouse, with a strap across his shoulder supporting a lance or other long instrument on his back. There are also two horn-shaped objects behind the heads of these two men. Below all these is a man sitting, with three or more round him, as if engaged in some quiet conversation. What this disc might have been when entire we may judge from the number of figures and action in this small fragment.

Of the Mackenzie drawings two hitherto unpublished ones of sculptured cross-bar discs are given in Pl. xv, figs. 5 and 6. The first represents a cross-bar 3′ 1¾″ long, bearing a broken disc, exhibiting a struggle, in which a man with a spear is seen rushing out of a building along with another having a short heavy crooked knife. They are attacking some seven unarmed men, some of which have fallen, and the man with the knife has his foot on the back of a half-prostrate figure. Six spectators look on the scene from balconies behind.

The other (fig. 6) is of more interest, being nearly entire, and the scene, in a disc 2′ 6½″ diameter, more intelligible. Seen through a doorway on the right are two men or huntsmen in blouses, one bearing on his head what appears to be two elephant tusks. In the centre of the scene to the left a chief or râja and his queen are seated on a throne. A huntsman, wearing a short kilt, kneels in front and presents the tusks which he has just brought in At the sight of them the lady leans over as if fainting, her husband expresses astonishment or disgust by the action of his right hand, and with the left helps to support her, while an attendant holds her from falling over, and another at the other end of the seat brings a vessel, perhaps with water to revive her. A female dwarf seems to urge the hunter to withdraw, and another looks anxiously up to her. Behind the seat or throne are six attendants bearing *chauris*, &c., all looking towards the lady or queen. The sculpture appears to depict distinctly the *Jâtaka* of the queen who ordered the death of the great Chhadanta elephant, which had been her husband in her previous life,[1] and is now struck with horror at her wickedness.

Plate XVII.

The disc represented in fig. 1 of Plate xvii is a fine example of one of the middle rails.[2] It was found a little to the west of the south entrance, and is the only stone drawn by Colonel Mackenzie's draughtsmen that was found in the recent excavations; all the rest had been removed or destroyed since 1817. The drawing was published by Mr. Fergusson (*Tree and Serpent Worship*, Pl. lxxiii, fig. 2), and a comparison of the photograph with it testifies to its accuracy. The scene represented is a curious one, and a portion of what was almost certainly another sculpture of the same story is preserved for us in a drawing[3] of an

---

[1] *Arch. Sur. W. Ind. Rep.*, vol. iv, p. 45 and plate xvi. [2] Drawn by Mr. H. Hamilton.
[3] Drawn by Mr. T. Anderson.

outer rail pillar in the same series, where it occurs in what is left of the middle disc (*ibid.*. Pl. lxvii.)

There is little doubt that it represents the transference or translation of the *pâtra* or begging-dish of Buddha to the Tushita heavens, where it is fabled [1] it was to be worshipped by all the Devas with flowers and incense for seven days, and Maitreya Bodhisattva, the next Buddha, on seeing it would exclaim with a sigh, " The alms-bowl of Śâkya Muni has come." After this it returns to India, when a sea-dragon or Nâga takes it to his palace till Maitreya is about to assume Buddahood, when it will finally be conveyed to him by the four heavenly kings, Dhṛitarâshṭra, Virûḍhaka, Virûpâksha, and Vaiśravaṇa, who preside over the four quarters, and who first presented it to Śâkya Muni. It is here represented as borne aloft on a tray with all the Devas dancing round it, the Apsaras being behind the Devas. In the other representation (*Tree and Serpent Worship*, Pl. lxvii) the Nâga king, who is immediately to receive future charge of it, is represented as among the throng that accompanies it. Duplicate sculptures of this kind, with slight variations only in the scenes, were doubtless common; we have already noticed at least another.

Mr. Fergusson very justly remarks on this scene that the violent dancing represented is not characteristic of the pure Aryan races of India, but is distinctive of the aboriginal or mixed races of the east of the peninsula. And there can be little doubt that Brahmanism had not at the date of this Stûpa influenced the manners of the people in the Telugu districts to anything like the extent it has in later times; indeed, it is very probable that the now degraded and wandering tribes of this region were in that age, if not the ruling race, at least in a much more influential position than now. The instance of the *couvade* appearing among these sculptures may be cited in support of this.

The next two examples (figs. 2, 3) are of inner faces of upper or lower rail discs; the first was found about the middle of the south-west quadrant, and the other near the west entrance.

Fig. 4 presents another middle disc, found near that given in fig. 2, and is fortunately in very fair preservation.. It represents the worship of the pillar surmounted by the *triśula*, a feature that is so unlike anything we know of in Bauddha mythology, that, were it not for the monks that seem to take so prominent a part in this instance, and the frequent occurrence of this symbol, we might refuse to accept it as having had any connection with Buddhism, and suppose that it was a representation of some cult prevalent among the Telugu tribes before the advent of Buddhism among them. It is one of those obscure points to which as yet no allusion has been recognised in Bauddha literature. We have already (p. 31) referred to this, with an illustration from the marbles now in the British Museum.

The pillar is here represented as rising from the back of a throne or seat, having two cushions at the back. It tapers upwards and is marked with lines running spirally round it, and it stands against a background or slab with what seem intended for flames issuing from the sides of the pillar, which is surmounted by the *triśula* in the form it assumes on the slabs which we suppose to have formed part of the casing of the central *dâgaba*. Though they have perhaps no connection, one can hardly help recognising a certain resemblance between this pillar symbol and the sacred tree of the Assyrians. It evidently is being honoured with worship. A *chauri*-bearer attends at each side—wearing brace-

[1] *Fahian*, chaps. xii and xxxix.

lets and armlets, and with the hair gathered into a sort of high top-knot—indicating perhaps that they are nobles and thought it an honour to take part in worshipping this object. Behind them are several men with the upper garment or sheet drawn over the left shoulder as the monks wear it. Five men in front, not in monks' habits, kneel and worship, and beyond them, to the left, is a monk standing as if directing them or repeating the *mantras* proper to the occasion. On a platform or raised seat behind the last, and in front of a building, stands a man playing on a harp, and at his back perhaps a Bhikshu or beggar. On a similar platform on the right side, and also in front of a house, are five monks—two of them seated, worshipping this *triśula*-crowned pillar.

9. Buddhist Triśula from Amarâvati.

The *triśula* and the *vajra* (which is closely connected with it) have not yet been satisfactorily explained. The second is probably derived from, if not a form of, the first,[1] and is closely analogous to the classical *fulmen* or thunderbolt, but having a different and far more important place in the popular mythology. The essential parts of the Bauddha *triśula* (as shown in the accompanying woodcut, No. 9), are—the circular disc, often carved with a rosette or lotus in the centre and ornamented border; three prongs—the outer ones usually divided into three at the tips; and two "wings" at the sides—sometimes of considerable size.

10. Triśula Symbol from Sâñchi.

The circle is often set upon a square pedestal with curved legs or struts attached to the lower part of the circle, as in examples given below (Pl. xlviii, fig. 2), and in the accompanying woodcut from the Sâñchi Stûpa (No. 10)—where, however, the middle prong of the upper part is shortened and crowned with another symbol —the shield. The occurrence of the *triśula*, shield, *svastika*, &c., at the commencement and end of the earliest of the Junnar, Bhâjâ, Beḍsâ, Kuḍâ, and Kârlê cave inscriptions, testifies to their ancient use as fortunate symbols. The later explanations[2] of mystics or paṇḍits are not necessarily of any authority.

Plate XVIII.

Plate xviii, fig. 1, represents the inner side of another of the upper rails from the south-west. The disc, 2 feet 4 inches in diameter, is surrounded by a border of creeper or *velt* pattern, and on the upper right-hand corner of the flange is carved a small *svastika*.

---

[1] See *ante*, p. 30, and *Arch. Sur. West. Ind. Rep.*, vol. v, p. 12.

[2] Fergusson's *Tree and Serp. Wor.*, p. 115; Remusat, *Foe-koue ki*, pp. 91, 92. The sign [symbol] or *nandipadam* (bull-symbol) bears a very close resemblance to this *triśula*, and appears on early Bauddha and Jaina inscriptions and on the coins of the Indo-Skythic kings, *e.g.*, on those of Gondophares, Zeinonises (Jihunia), Ooêma Kadphises (Hima Kapiśa), Hooerkes, and Basudeo. Conf. Prinsep's *Antiquities*, vol. i, p. 82, pl. iv, figs. 1 and 6; p. 113, pl. vii, 2; p. 209, pl. xix, 9, 17; p. 227, pl. xxii, 1, 2, 3, 6; p. 352, pl. xxviii, 5; &c.; Wilson's *Ariana Antiqua*, pl. v, No. 20; pl. viii, 17; pl. x, 5, 9, 12–21; Gardner's *Coins of Greek and Scythic Kings*, pp. 104, 106, 110,

Fig. 2 is an interesting central bar of the rail from near the north gate, bearing a disc 2 feet 8 inches in diameter, crowded with some twenty-five figures, several of them unfortunately much defaced. In the background is a building with an arched roof, and forming apparently three sides of a square. The ends have the 'Chaitya window' arch, showing that this was a common feature of the architecture of the day. The lower storey is hidden by the figures in front, but from the two ends of the upper one spectators look out on the scene below, and the windows shown along the inner sides appear to be screened by thin cloth or 'chick' mats to obscure the light, and prevent people from outside prying upon those within. The four finials on the cross roof connecting the wings are just such as we find continued down to the time when the Rathas at Mahâbalipuram were carved. Among the figures there appear to be two groups, the one to the left principally, if not entirely, of females, the other to the right, consisting exclusively of males. The principal figure in the second group is a tall man in front, leaning apparently against a horse which an attendant holds by the bridle; he rests his right hand, with a large bracelet upon it, against his side and looks towards the lady who forms the central figure in the other group, while behind him one attendant in a sort of blouse bears the *chhatri* or state umbrella, and another holds a couple of spears. Between these last is seen a figure as if coming out of the house, and beyond the horse is still another coming through a gate on the extreme right. Three men also to the left of the umbrella-bearer, one of them wearing a blouse, with their hands joined in respect, wear similar headdresses, and may belong to the same party, though the respectful salutation would indicate that they are not of the retinue. The other figures seem all to have their attention centred on the lady, who is seated on a chair with her left hand resting on the back of it, while the right is in an attitude indicating a reply to some request: a woman is rubbing her left foot. One stands in front addressing her respectfully, and to whom she seems to listen and be about to reply. Three sit below with offerings, and two or more of those behind have borne the like, one of them entering from a gate or door on the extreme left. A *chauri*-bearer is seen behind the chair, and at the lady's right stands one listening to her, and whose face has not been knocked off. The whole scene is an animated one, and may be understood to represent a visit or interview of some chief to a female of rank, perhaps a petty ruler like himself. It is disappointing to find that the inscription, which is so perfectly legible on the roof of the building behind, is of so little interest (Pl. lvi, No. 11). It reads—

> Gahapatisa Budhino putasa Makabudhino sapi-
> tukasa sabhaginikasa sabhâriyasa
> deyadhama parichakâ be suchiya dânâ.

"Of Makabudhi (Mṛigabuddhi ?) the son of the householder Budhi with his father, with his sisters, with his wife—the meritorious gift of two cross-bars with circular panels." [1]

The next (fig. 3) is a cross-bar from the north-east quadrant,[2] and has been very much injured, and the inscription at the upper left corner mostly broken off, leaving in the first line *-ṇiya*, perhaps of *bhikhuniya;* in the second *-rikaya* of *kumârikaya* (?); and in the last *ṇa* of *dâna*, 'gift.'

111, and 174, 112, 124–128, and 175, 155, 160; *J. R. As. Soc.*, vol. vi, p. 457. Among the Sânchi sculptures it once appears on an altar under a Bôdhi tree, as if it were an object of worship, but otherwise it appears in sculptures chiefly as an ornament. *Tree and Serpent Wor.*, pls. xvi and xxv, and pp. 129, 130.

[1] Dr. Hultzsch (*Zeitschr. d. Deutschen Morg. Gesellsch.*, Bd. xxxvii, S. 556, and Bd. xl, S. 344); *suchi* is an inserted bar.

[2] No. 182 in *Notes on the Amar. Stûpa.*

Here we have the worship of the sacred tree, with the seat in front, and under it the footstool and *pâdukâ* or footmarks. A tall *chauri*-bearer plies his whisk on each side of the tree behind the seat, and some twenty-seven other figures, all men, in various positions, seem mostly engaged in the worship. Some of those in front kneel to the *pâdukâ*. The worship of sacred trees is a prominent feature of Buddhism. It was under a tree that each of the legendary Buddhas as well as Śâkya Muni was said to have attained enlightenment; so also among the Jainas—each of their Tîrthaṁkaras has his special sacred tree. Of the last seven Buddhas, Vipaśî had the *Pâṭali* for his *bodhi*-tree; Śikhî had the *Puṇḍarîka* (a species of mango); Viśvabhû had the *śâla* (*Shorea robusta*); Krakuchchhanda had the *sirîsha* (*Acacia sirisa*); Kanakamuni had the *Udumbara* (*Ficus glomerata*); Kâśyapa had the *Nyagrodha* or Banyan; and Gautama or Śâkya Muni the *Pippala* (*Ficus religiosa*) as his *bodhidruma*. These trees are frequently represented over the heads of images of the respective Buddhas, and also separately as objects of worship. Like the Chaityas, legends are told of their being worshipped also by *Yakshas* or other divine beings, and even by elephants and deer. In the woodcut (No. 11) is an example from the Gândhâra sculptures of the worship of one of these trees by a group of men, and by *Yakshas* flying overhead, while the bust below may be intended to represent a Nâga rising out of the earth or supporting it, just as in the Cave sculptures the *Padmâsana* or lotus-throne of Buddha is often represented as borne up by Nâgas rising out of the earth. In the second (No. 12), representing a disc from the Bharhut Stûpa, we have the worship of the *Nyagrodha*, or sacred Banyan tree of Kâśyapa, the Buddha who preceded Śâkya Siṁha, by two women whose husbands stand beside it and hang garlands upon its branches. In the third woodcut (No. 13), taken from one of the coping-stones of the Bharhut rail, we have a very early example of the worship of a *Bodhidruma* by spotted deer. The offerings to it are flowers, represented on the altar in front. Such an object at any place where a Buddha had preached or passed through any phase of his life would be called a Chaitya, just as a Dâgaba would be. This feature of Buddhism is still practised in Buddhist countries, and the like practice prevails largely

11. Worship of a Sacred Tree by Men and Devas, from a Yuzufzai sculpture.[1]

12. Worship of the Bodhidruma or Sacred Tree.[2]

---

[1] From Trübner's illustrated edition of E. Arnold's *Light of Asia*, p. 19.

[2] *Ibid.*, engraved from the photograph in Cunningham's *Bharhut Stûpa*, pl. xxx, fig. 1.

among the modern Jainas, who also erect temples under their sacred trees, for the worship of the footprints of their Tîrthaṁkaras.

13. Worship of a Sacred Tree by Spotted Deer, from Bharhut.[2]

The next example (fig. 4), from the north-east,[1] presents another object of worship: the *dâgaba* of a very early and plain type, with a multiplicity of umbrellas rising out of the capital like a bunch of flowers, some eighteen in all, the uppermost being much the largest. On the left six tall women approach it with reverence, one bearing an offering. In front of them are two smaller-sized men. Before the *dâgaba* kneel a woman and man in worship, and to the right are five men, two beating drums hung from their shoulders, and two with flutes.

Plate XIX.

Plate xix, fig. 1, represents a central cross-bar disc 2′ 9″ in diameter, the back of which has been split off.[3] It has been much battered, but is of great interest as representing a well-known and easily recognised scene in Bauddha legend—the *Chhadanta Jâtaka*. This sculpture needs only to be compared with the painting of the *Jâtaka* in Cave X. at Ajaṇṭâ, executed probably about the same date, to trace the resemblance in details though the arrangements are different. The same variety of attitudes among the elephants, and the tall plants among which they move, are prominent features of both representations, while the rocks are represented in the usual conventional way. The king of the herd is several times represented, but owing to the injuries done to the sculpture it is now impossible to be sure of them all. First he appears to the right of the centre, happy in his wild haunts, among lions and other feræ, and waited on by his herd. Above this he appears again, stumbling over the pit in which the hunter who seeks his life is concealed, and whose head just appears out of the ground below, about to destroy him. Then to the left he is seen kneeling and allowing the hunter to saw off his tusks. At the top of the panel the huntsman is seen with a pole over his shoulders, bearing off a pair of tusks at each end of it. All this is in accordance with the legend.[4]

Fig. 2 represents the remains of a disc, found close to the east side of the south entrance, which has contained numerous figures, but much of it is lost. In the right is a gateway near a thatched hut, beyond which are some three figures. Then in the upper portion an inner apartment is represented, containing a man or boy lying on a bed with an attendant beyond, while at the foot of it are two men, one of them seated on the couch and

---

[1] No. 190, in *Notes on the Amarâvatî Stûpa.*

[2] From *Bharhut Stûpa*, pl. xliv, fig. 2; a very similar scene occurs on another coping-stone, in which two lions appear along with the deer; *ibid.*, pl. xliii, fig. 1.

[3] Mr. Sewell, who excavated the stone, says he got it "at the southern clearance;" but on his plan it is placed in a position corresponding to 40 feet north of the east point of the circle.

[4] See *Arch. Sur. Surv. West Ind.*, vol. iv, pp. 45, 46, and pl. xvi; *Cave Temples*, p. 288.

with a short sword, as if about to murder the youth. The lower right half of the slab is entirely gone, but it evidently contained some object of respect, perhaps a person. The man seated in the centre with high turban and heavy earrings and bracelets pays respect, and around him sit a number of women wearing the round *tilaka* or caste-mark on their foreheads.

Figs. 3 and 4 are two more examples of the upper and lower discs. The first, found to the north of the western entrance, is 2′ 4½″ in diameter, and has had an inscription on the lower left corner in clear-cut rounded characters, but only the concluding syllables of three lines are left. A small *dâgaba* has been scratched on the central knob, and the lotus has a richer creeper border.

The second, found to the south of the east entrance, is 2′ 6½″ in diameter, and further illustrates the varieties of this ornament. The central knob, as in the majority of cases, has been broken.

14. Buddha teaching, from a Gândhâra sculpture.

CHAPTER VI.

THE COPING OF THE OUTER RAIL.

The upright pillars of the rail having the cross-bars fastened in between them, the whole was then surmounted by a coping about 2 feet 7 inches high and 13 inches thick, formed of blocks 8 or more feet in length, and rounded on the top. Tenons on the head of each pillar were let into the under edge of these blocks, so as to preserve them in position and bind the whole together.

These coping-stones were carved on both sides, the outer always with a long wavy roll, upborne by men at distances of about 24 or 25 inches apart, with sculpture in the spaces where the roll falls down between the men. This roll is generally represented as if it were covered with lace in stripes wound round it, and of great variety of pattern; and sometimes it is so carved as to represent a very thick rope, or a very long coil of flowers enclosed in a net bag.

Plate XX.

The stone represented in Pl. xx is 8′ 8″ in length, 2′ 7″ high, and 13″ thick, and was found on the north-east of the circle. The top is rounded, and the stone has a slight curvature, corresponding to a radius of about 90 feet. On the back or outer side (fig. 1) the wavy roll occupies a depth of 20 inches; below is a border 2⅝ inches deep, carved with flowers and winged animals, and above is a similar band carved with flowers only. The roll is upborne as usual by a man, but a woman also occurs along with him here in a different position in each case; first to the right kneeling, as if to pull up two ropes that run all along under the roll; then half standing up, straining to lift; then as lifted upon the man's thigh; and in the last as if falling off behind him.

A band compresses the roll always over the men's heads, and ornamental leaves project from the band. Where the roll descends it is covered alternately by a square and a round shield, with a lower fringe of very thick cords, and each shield has been delicately sculptured, sometimes with scenes, and at others with geometrical or florid decorative work.

In the bights over the roll are a series of emblems; first, on the right, is a *dâgaba* or *chaitya* with the multiple *chhatra* over it, a five-hooded snake in front, the sacred wheel on the right, and some symbol, now destroyed, on the left. The second has, as it were, the drum of a *dâgaba*, with a band round the middle of it, and three dwarfs or *yakshas* capering on the top of it. The third has the divine bird Garuḍa or Târkshya, the vehicle of Vishṇu and enemy of the snake race, holding a large five-headed cobra or *Nâga* in its beak and talons: what the two small circular discs above its wings are is not clear. The Garuḍa appears also in the Kaṇheri sculptures as one of the enemies from whom Avalôkiteśvara delivers,[1] and on his enmity to the Nâga races is founded the Bauddha drama of *Nâgânanda*, attributed to Śrî Harshadeva, king of Kanauj (A.D. 606–649).[2]

---

[1] *Cave Temples*, p. 358.

[2] *Nâgânanda, la Joie des Serpents*, par Abel Bergaigne (Paris, 1879); *Nâgânanda*, by P. Boyd (London, 1872), act iv.

The third of these sculptures represents a platform supported by three dwarf *yakshas*, and bearing the triple animal busts we find on pillars as objects of worship. The fourth compartment, partly destroyed, contained the sacred *bodhi* tree and worshippers, with the same round discs (perhaps the sun and moon) as in the second.

The inner side of this slab (fig. 2) is richly sculptured, but difficult to interpret. In the lower right-hand corner an interior is represented with a mother and child on a bed, attended by two other women. Whether this is intended to represent Yaśôdharâ and Râhula, the wife and infant son of Siddhârtha, on the night he left to become an ascetic, may perhaps be doubtful. Outside the buildings to the left, leaving what may represent the city gate, is a man on horseback, with an attendant holding it by the rein, and beyond are two spectators, while above them are *yakshas* or other demigods. At the top of the slab, to the right again, are five men in the dress of monks, worshipping before the empty seat (*vajrâsana*) and *pâdukâ*, so often presented, that the idea is forced on us that, for some reason or other, Buddha himself was not represented at the earliest date of these sculptures as an object of worship, but only under the symbol of the empty seat and the footmarks.[1] Between this last and the first-mentioned scene are six lines of inscription on two roofs, but they are unfortunately much worn in parts (Pl. lvi, No. 6). They read—

Râjagirinivâsikasa
Chetikâ navakamakasa
therasa bhayata-Budharakhitasa
atevâsi . . (varu)rikaya bhikhu(nî)na Budharakhita(ya)
sudhutuka . . . ya Dhamadinaya Sagharakhi-
tasa cha dânaṁ.

"The gift of Dhamadina (Dharmadattâ) and of Sagharakhita (Saṁgharakshita) . . . . . of the mendicant Budharakhitâ (Buddharakshitâ) with her daughters . . . . [the pupil] of the venerable Thera Budharakhita residing at Râjagiri and superintendent of the building operations of the *Chetikas* (Chaitikas)."[2]

The scene in the middle of the slab is another of the worship of the *Vajrâsana* or seat of Buddha, with the feet in front, and behind it the *bodhi* tree, surmounted by the triple umbrella. The bare heads of two men, probably monks, appear over the back of the seat, and between it and the tree to the left is a female *chauri*-bearer; to the right two men, wearing turbans, stand before a door, in front of them are two others, and a monk seated worshipping. In front of the "feet" is a basket containing some offerings, and to the left a woman performing the lowest obeisance, while behind her are three other women and two children, or perhaps a little boy and a dwarf woman. Above in the air, flying past the tree and saluting it, are Vidyâdharas and Apsaras or heavenly sprites.

To the left is another large scene, in which the principal figure is a lady, attended by a fan-bearer, and another holding an umbrella; two others stand before her, another enters bearing a dish from a door in the right, and a fourth appears in the background. Seven more women are seated on the ground around the chief lady, playing various musical instruments or singing.

At the left end of the stone is a two-storeyed building, shown, as most buildings are in

---

[1] Compare the *Dasaratha Jâtaka*, where Râma sends his straw shoes, which are placed on his deceased father's empty throne, and by their striking together the ministers knew when injustice was done.

[2] *Zeitschr. d. D. M. Gesellsch.*, Bd. xl. S. 346.

these sculptures, in a sort of perspective, which best suits the purpose of the sculptor to show what is going on within, and which is otherwise perfectly intelligible. In the lower storey is a group of seven men, all seated in conversation ; one in the left rather turns away from another with an oval symbol on the front of his turban. But in the right side of the building the second again appears, distinguished by the same emblem, in close conversation with another man.

In the upper storey, the front is divided into two compartments, and represents a zenana : in each of the front divisions a woman is seen seated, one apparently in grief ; and through the end two are seen seated facing each other.

In this and most of the houses represented in these sculptures, it may be remarked that the architecture is distinctly wooden ; and as they doubtless represent the style of houses in use at the period when the Stûpa was constructed, they afford sufficient proof that the domestic architecture of Southern India continued to be, even down to the beginning of our era, almost, if not exclusively, of wood, or formed on existing wooden models. That it was so generally in India previous to the third or fourth century B.C., has long since been proved by the late Mr. Fergusson ;[1] but, as we see here, the domestic architecture continued to be wooden, at least in some areas, till a much later date, as it still continues to be in Burma, China, and Japan. Buildings not distinctively architectural, such as the walls of towns, were, as we also see in these sculptures, mostly built of brick.

PLATE XXI.

The next slab (Pl. xxi, fig. 1) is one of the largest, 10′ 8″ by 2′ 7″ and 11½″ thick. It was found on the bank, quite outside the circle, and was said to have been dug up to show to some collector, and got much injured from the exposure. The back is covered with the usual roll ornament upborne by five men, and with a rope running loosely along below it. Opposite the men's shoulders on each side a band compresses the roll, the surface of which is carved in the usual style. The four points where the roll dips are covered by shields, two circular, one square, and one formed of a band encircling the roll with the mouth of a *makara* at each side. The first of these shields to the left is carved with a *bodhi* tree having the *Vajrâsana* or diamond throne at the foot, and attended by a tall man and woman on each side, each holding some object, perhaps a *chauri*. Over this is a *chaitya* or *dâgaba* with two tall worshippers. The second shield is square, and has been carved with some arabesque pattern now rubbed off, and with the usual fringe below. Above it is the seat in front of a pillar bearing the sacred wheel or *chakra*—the emblem of the Bauddha doctrine, with two *chauri*-bearers in attendance. The third shield contains two seated and two standing worshippers, paying honour to what seems to be a relic-casket placed on a tripod stand. Over this again is the *chaitya* and worshippers. The cincture formed with *makara* heads is under a short octagonal pillar bearing three half-figures, perhaps of *yakshas* or other supernatural beings, with their hands joined as if in adoration.

This stone had lain long exposed, and the inner side (fig. 2) has been very seriously battered and defaced. On the extreme left are the vestiges of a male figure apparently floating in the air, as the Buddhist Arhats claimed the power of doing, with a male and several female figures beneath looking at him ; two or more females also sit upon the ground.

[1] No scientific archæologist or architect has questioned Mr. Fergusson's conclusion. General Cunningham, indeed, in one of his *Reports*, vol. iii (1873), p. 98, promised to adduce evidence against it, but has not done so.

But so little of the scene is left, and that so injured, that nothing more can be made out. To the right are a number of buildings, curious as exhibiting the style of architecture of the times, and, except a piece of brick wall, perhaps largely constructed of wood. A comparison of all the representations of buildings in these sculptures might enable us almost to reconstruct the civil architecture of the second century.

The buildings entirely cut off the figures to the left from the scene on the right. The centre of it is occupied with a pavilion or *vṛiksha chaitya*,[1] round the stem of a sacred *pippala*[2] tree; at the foot of it is a throne with the footprints, and two men inside the *chaitya* was paying worship to it, while other two are approaching from the left, one of them wearing a massive broad collar. To the right is a chair, with the flaming pillar bearing the *triśula* or trident of the Buddhists, and men seated round it in front worshipping, while one approaches it in an attitude that may be intended as threatening, but his uplifted right hand being broken off, this is uncertain. On the left of this large scene is a *vimâna* or celestial car, empty, but with the bearing pole distinctly carved under the side next the spectator; before it sit two or three fat dwarfs or *yakshas*, and behind them a mythological animal, perhaps a sort of lion or tiger, is crouched on the ground with another *yaksha* standing by it, perhaps being saddled. Beyond these *yakshas* a horse is also being attended to by another *yaksha;* preparations are being made for a start. Just above, the *vimâna* is represented ascending with two persons inside, borne by *yakshas* under the side poles, and the horse and lion career with their riders in front of the car through the air towards the *vṛiksha chaitya*, and to the right of the tree which rises above the *chaitya* and up to the round of the top of the stone the procession is again represented, but with three riders before the car. Then on the ground, the *vimâna* is again presented, empty with the *yakshas* around, one of them blowing a *conch* shell, and the tall figure with uplifted hand is probably one of the travellers by the car. A fat dwarf beyond him appears to have been represented as hurling a piece of rock at the throne and pillar.

The third scene is much destroyed. In it a prince is represented seated, with a man on either hand, and female attendants bearing the umbrella and *paṅkha* or fan behind him. Two men enter from the right, one of them saluting the chief, and in front a man is going out while one seizes him by the leg. The other figures are too much injured to enable us to trace the action of the scene; but there is nothing about the central figure to identify him with Buddha or Siddhârtha.

Over the top is an inscription, the last portion of which is destroyed; it is, however, only a donatory one, without historical importance (Pl. lvi, No. 13 *a*, *b*). It reads, so far as legible:[3]—

. . . . . gahapatino Idasa duhutuya gharaniya Kaṇhâya duhutuya upâsikâya Kamâya saputikâya sabhatukâye sabhaginikâya bhikunikaya cha Nâgamitâya . . ya . kaya . .

"[*The gift*] of the laic Kamâ (Kâmâ) the daughter of the housewife Kaṇhâ (Kṛishṇâ) the daughter of the householder Ida (Indra), with her sons, brothers, and sisters, and of the nun Nâgamita . . ."

Plate XXII.

The next piece (Pl. xxii, fig. 1) measures 9′ 3″ by 2′ 7″ and is a foot thick. It was found considerably to the east of the last, but appears to bear connected scenes. Unfortunately

[1] Pali, *Rukkhachetiyaṁ*. [2] *Ficus religiosa*. [3] Translated by Dr. Hultzsch.

the inner side is much weather-worn, though the outer is in the most perfect preservation, showing with great clearness the texture of the covering of the long roll in its wonderfully minute details; and even the ropes or smaller rolls that are always represented under it are carved with the same forms of surface ornament. The fastenings that usually appear above the heads of the bearers are here omitted, but the "ties" or cinctures round the roll at the shoulders of the bearers are rich and of varied pattern. Near both ends of the slab is a *dâgaba* with a rich abundance of *chhatris*, perhaps of natural vegetable forms, and with attendant worshippers. That at the left end is mostly broken off, but the other is carefully carved on the dome, bears the five-hooded *nâga* in front, the *chakra* on the left, and some similar object on the right, while it is upborne by three *yakshas;* the first had no bearers. Under it is a square shield on the roll, sculptured with some scene of strife, such as we have already noticed. A man with a club or sword has knocked down a woman and tramples on her, another kneels at his feet beseeching mercy, and he is aiming a blow against one of other three women who stand up. The second space from the left is filled by a Nâga, his hands joined in worship, with large ear-rings, and the five hoods of the snake over his turban. The lower folds of the snake on which he sits are carved with great minuteness to represent the scales. A female on each side brings an offering of food to him. Below is a round disc representing a sort of pillar, apparently of wicker-work, bearing some object—probably a relic—to which two women kneel in worship and a Nâga râja stands on each side.

The middle emblem is the tree, with six people, men and women, making offerings to it. One man on the left pours something out of a jar at the foot of it, and another on the right, with his wife behind him, bears similar vessels. Below is a small square disc, on which is carved a woman seated, and before her a man with a horse; a woman stands beyond, perhaps addressing the sitter, and two are behind her. To the right of this, besides the bearer of the roll, a man with a peculiar oval symbol on the front of his turban kneels on one knee and tries to lift the roll. The next downward bend of the roll contains a throne with a round cushion on the back, and from behind it rises the *chakra* pillar—the Wheel resting on three lions on the capital, while the three animals so frequently represented on symbolical pillars are carved round the middle of it. Two men act as *chauri*-bearers. The shield below is circular, and contains the throne and tree, with two kneeling worshippers in front, two standing at the sides, and two attendants behind. The border of flowers above and of flowers and animals below this frieze has been carved with great taste and vigour, and deserves attention.

The inner side (fig. 2) is too weather-worn to be quite intelligible, but enough remains to show how well it must have been sculptured. The action is vigorously represented. At the extreme left are buildings with a doorway, beside which a man sits on a platform. From the door, apparently, have come out a number of people, among whom is conspicuous a Nâga râja and two other male figures, while behind them are seven others, perhaps all women, and at least five of which have the single snake hood which marks a female or Nâginî. To the left of the males a small female bears an oblong object in her left hand, and the first of the men points forward over her head. Behind all, and from a balcony above, three women look down on the group.

A fresh scene appears to commence just to the right, where we have the Nâga râja again standing with his hands joined in salutation towards two men on a horse, whose forefeet a *yaksha* seems to bear up; it is represented as coming out of a wilderness. Above on a platform stands a tall female, just behind a man on horseback, and with her are two other people. To the right and in front of the last horse are two lion-like animals flying through mid-air, each accompanied by his attendants. The foremost of them seems to have come upon a number of dwarfs, with poles and perhaps burdens. Just below the last are two men, one of them sitting under a tree and apparently in close debate. To the right, and just on the edge of the next scene, are again two men; the one, having seized the other, is carrying him off, or else, like Narasiṁha in Hindû mythology, he is tearing out his entrails.

In the next scene is a man in the upper corner on horseback, surrounded by a crowd of attendants, one bearing a halbert similar to those represented in Cave X. at Ajaṇṭâ. Under this, and rushing to the left, is another horseman in full career, a *yaksha* rushing along under the forefeet of the horse, and a runner holding on by its tail. This is interrupted by an indoors scene, in which a chief is seated on his throne, with numerous men on his left and women on his right, and below in front a man and two women supplicating most energetically. At the door a man is also seen walking out. Beyond this to the right we again meet with the horseman and his attendant holding on by the tail as it springs through the air. Beneath are five dwarfs or *yakshas* running with him, and bearing two long rods. There can be no doubt that this is the same as the horseman last mentioned previous to the occurrence of the indoor scene.

The inscription over this sculpture is too much weather-worn to be legible.

Plates XXIII, XXIV.

Many of the pieces of coping are only fragments. One of these (Pl. xxiii, fig. 1), about 4 feet in length, has on the back two bearers, both running towards the left, and the interval over the roll between them is filled by a *dâgaba* with a single *chhatra* over it, and two worshippers. Under it is a circular shield or medallion, with a double border round it, and containing the *bodhi* tree, with the seat bearing the footprints, and a worshipper at each side. The inner face (fig. 3) is carved on the left with four elephants, one at least having a female rider, and below them a lady on horseback and several attendants, with a horse in front led by a small male figure. They have arrived at a door which is shut, but in the entrance of which stands a woman. A line here marks off the commencement of a new scene, in which Buddha is seated on a throne, his right hand held up in the attitude of blessing; an attendant sits at each side, and round him stand or sit a large number of women in the attitude of reverential attention.

The next (fig. 2) was found just to the west of the south gate, and has formed part of the coping at one of the returns there. It has been split up the middle, and perhaps partly used to build into some later work. A dwarf is represented as drawing the roll out of his mouth; immediately in front of him is a wheel mounted on a pillar, at the foot of which stands an *âsana* or seat. Below it and on the roll is a medallion bearing a *dâgaba* and worshippers.

Another fragment, found near the south gate, is represented in fig. 4, in the upper portion of which the flaming pillar supporting the *triśula*, and with the footprints on a lotus, is being worshipped by a devotee. A man with a short knife in his right hand rushes towards it, stretching out his left hand with the forefinger raised in an emphatic manner. Beyond him are two other men, and to the right of the pillar is a tall female with a vessel on her head. Below the man with the knife again appears attacking a man on an elephant. He seems to have brought down the elephant, which he presses on the neck with his left foot, while he seizes its rider by the back of the head, pressing himself against the elephant at the same time by his right hand laid on the coping of a wall. Other figures appear behind. To the left of the wall several monks are seated, but nothing more is left of the scene.

The slab given on Pl. xxiv, fig. 1, is 7 feet 3 inches long by 2 feet 7 inches high, but the inner side had lain long exposed, and but little of it can now be made out. It must have represented some great contest, of which only fragments are intelligible. At the left end are seen the feet of a large elephant in front of a wall. Farther to the right and above are two chariots, one pursuing the other, and one of the occupants of the fleeing one apparently hurling a spear at his pursuer. Below a horse is well represented, falling dead while in full career and his rider in the act of dismounting as it falls; behind an elephant has seized with its trunk another horse by the neck, and the rider, driven against the elephant's forehead, is making his escape as best he can. Other figures of men and animals can just be traced in violent action.

An inscription ran along the lower edge, but is mostly broken off. Of what is left we can read—

. . . . ma . . sapâtukasa[1] Ajakasa unisa savaniyuta deyadhammaṁ.

"A coping stone the common meritorious gift of Ajaka with his father . . . ."

The outer face (fig. 2) is in much better preservation, and from the terminal *makara* being at the left end, it appears to have been one of the coping stones near the north gate—not far from which it was found. The *makara's* mouth is held open by a man who seems to be thrusting the roll down its throat, while a female on its back is perhaps assisting him. One of the usual bearers is just behind him dragging the roll forward. The first shield or clasp on it is round, and carved with four *triśulas* round a circle; the second is square and carved with two *makaras* and two winged lions, &c. Over the first clasp were three men engaged in a wild dance, over the second are three dwarf *yakshas* bearing a tray on which three busts of mythical animals are placed.

PLATES XXV, XXVI.

The next stone (Pl. xxv, fig. 1) measures 6′ 11″ by 2′ 7″, and also represents a slab from some corner or gate; but instead of the *makara* at the right end, we have a very fat curly-headed dwarf or *yaksha* holding the end of the roll over his neck. Of the three clasps or shields on the roll, two are round and one square, carved with four-faced *triśulas* and flower pattern. The symbols are a plain *chaitya* or *dâgaba* with bunches of flower-shaped umbrellas; the *dharmachakra* on its pillar, with the *vajrâsana* bearing the footmarks on the seat, and two attendants having *châmaras;* and the sacred tree, with the *vajrâsana* bearing the footprints, and two worshippers.

The inner side (fig. 2) is somewhat weather-worn, but very curious. Seven elephants, with two riders apiece, come out from the gate of a city, each bearing what there can hardly

[1] Read *sapitukasa*,—Hultzsch, *Zeit. d. D. Morg. Gesel.*, Bd. xxxvii, p. 559.

be any mistake in calling a relic-casket. Inside, to the right, in an enclosed apartment, are twelve men round what may be a table with eight dishes upon it,—though possibly it may be meant for some other object. In another apartment on the same level are half-a-dozen men in conversation; but the slab seems to have been broken here. Below in the foreground are twelve or thirteen women, some playing on musical instruments and others dancing—the scenes being unmistakably the representation of a *nâchh* or dance.

Many portions of coping have been found at different points round the circle split vertically, and sometimes so cut otherwise as to show that at some period many of these slabs were broken up and used for repairs or other building purposes.

Close to the south gate I found two fragments of a coping stone which together measure 2′ 10″ by 2′ 10″, and about 6″ thick, —the slab having been split. The accompanying illustration (No. 15) presents the two pieces placed together. What remains of the sculpture consists of part of a building or perhaps a gateway in the left corner, and a tree behind it, while in front are several figures, sculptured with much minuteness of detail. The lowest, to the left, is a young female with a pleasant face, and pendent ear-lobes borne down by heavy ear-jewels. She wears a full robe down to her ankles, and is descending the steps from a door of the building behind her, bringing some vessel in her hands. The hair is parted in the middle, with a central lock drawn back. The next to the right is also a female, and holds some object with both hands, as if showing it to some one; she has a heavy ring in each ear, bracelets, and a double necklace. Behind is a third figure bearing a dish or a present in the left hand. In the background are two others, one of them bearing something in his left hand against his shoulder. In front of the other is a sixth and evidently more important male personage, with very large ear-jewels dragging down his ears, several necklaces round his neck, and a high turban. He looks down to his proper left at something now broken away. To the right of this, above, is a figure with the wrinkles of age strongly marked on the now injured face; and the body seems to be clad in a full robe, part of it passing over the head and under the chin. In front of the left shoulder of this last another head appears, with a high prominence on the turban, but the features are destroyed. He is seated just in front of the tall male, at whose feet is another man with a full *laṅgoṭi* about his loins, lifting up his hands in reverence to the seated figure. To the right was another, seated on a cushion, with his back to the spectator. The next figure, at the top of the panel and to the right, is clad in a tunic, and apparently carries some object before him. Probably half the scene, however, has been destroyed.

15. Fragments of a Coping Stone.

The next piece (Pl. xxvi, fig. 1) is 3 feet 10 inches long above, and 2 feet 7 inches high by 14 inches thick. Part of the left end of the inner face is chipped off, but enough remains to show that it represented Buddha seated under a tree, with *chauri*-waving attendants, and teaching a crowd of nobles, two of whom also stand under a tree. A vertical division is made by a rusticated pilaster, to the right of which has been a figure of Buddha seated before a background, perhaps of flames, but out of which come flowers in bloom; at the side are Bhikshus worshipping him, and other figures below, perhaps demigods, adoring him. These two scenes may be compared with that in the left end of the ante-chamber of Cave XVII. at Ajaṇṭâ.[1]

The outer side of this stone has the usual roll ornament, which the bearers are represented as tripping along with very lightly. It is minutely carved, and in the bight is a *dâgaba* with two worshippers. Below it is a medallion carved with the *chakra* and throne, also with two worshippers.

The next (fig. 2) is a much-injured piece. On the right has been the flaming pillar, then a building or wall running along to the left, but broken to make room for a gateway of the Sâñchi pattern, with a seat in front of it, and in the entrance just behind the seat a *triśula* over a disc, and flames proceeding from each side. Behind the building to the right of the gate is an elephant and a horse, and to the left two men riding on an elephant towards the gate. In front are several men, and a low domed building, from which runs a partition up to some brick walling beyond. By the side of this sit three persons, and others were in front, with one in a recess beyond.

The next again (figs. 3, 4), though small, is perhaps of its original dimensions—2′ 1″ broad by 2′ 9″ high. On the outer side is a large *makara* with a dwarf riding on its head and the end of the roll in its mouth. On the inner face (fig. 3) a râja is represented come down from his throne to salute four Bauddha priests who are entering by the door, while an attendant touches their feet with his forehead, and a dwarf page is at the chief's heel. His attendants, who seem to be men, look on from behind his cushioned throne. Like all hierarchs, the great Buddhist priests regarded themselves as far above kings, and in their writings kings are constantly represented as taking a humble place in the presence of Buddha and the *Sthaviras* or *Theros*.

The next fragment (fig. 5) is one of those pieces of coping, which are very numerous, that have been split, probably to be used in some later construction, but at what period and how they were employed are unknown. This is the outer side, and represents a Nâga-râjâ, with his snake form coiled under him, worshipping the footmarks of Buddha, and attended by two female *chauri*-bearers. Below is a medallion carved with four *triśula* heads round a central field.

The block represented on Plate xxvi, fig. 6, is the back of that given on Plate xxviii, fig. 1. It is much like all the others on this side: in the first bight of the roll is a plain *dâgaba*, on a base surrounded by the small harpy figures which appear pretty frequently elsewhere as ornaments. The *dâgaba* has a florid canopy of small *chattris* or foliage, and is attended by two worshippers. In the other space is the empty throne with footprints upon it, and behind is the *Chakra* on a pillar, with a worshipper and *chauri*-bearer in attendance.

Next to the sacred tree or *Bodhivṛiksha* and the *dâgaba*, the object that figures most prominently in early Bauddha sculptures as demanding worship is this *Dharmachakra* or Wheel, which must have represented the Law or *Dharma*. Of the lofty pillars that

---

[1] *Notes on the Buddhist Rock Temples at Ajaṇṭâ*, p. 69.

stood at the entrance of the early temples, such as the great rock-cut chaityas of Kârlê and Kanheri, one always supported a *chakra*, borne on the backs of lions. The woodcut (No. 16) is a good example of the worship of this symbol from the very early Stûpa at Bharhut.[1] If compared with the examples in the plates from Amarâvatî, the identity will be at once observed, only the *triśulas*, instead of pointing outwards from the felloe, have their points towards it. Garlands are hung upon it, and one of the male worshippers has a large one to be similarly suspended, and one of the women who kneel at the foot of the pillar has another in a small basket. We have already met with this symbol on the outer rail, but within it occupies a more prominent position, and it occurs frequently both at Buddha Gayâ and at Sâñchi.

16. Worship of the Dharmachakra.

PLATES XXVII, XXVIII.

The stone represented on Plate xxvii, fig. 1, is of considerable interest but difficult to explain. In the background to the right is a male figure in the habit of a Bauddha monk, stretched out, as if dead, upon a bier, and attended by six people male and female. Close to this is a house with an arched roof, from the corner of which a low brick wall runs out in a curve, cutting off the above group. On the left of the scene are other three houses—one of them round—with arched roofs, and a procession of five or six horsemen are coming out from behind them. In the right foreground is a man pulling up a cloth over which another is in the act of running towards some rocks. To the left, and in front of the second house, are two men, one of them bearing a large bundle on his back, and two women, one of them following the others from behind the house. By the side of the small circular house appears something like two vessels one over the other in some sort of stand. The fourth house is very low in the foreground, with a curved wall which runs out to the right, and somewhat resembles the prow of a boat. Over this, on the round of the coping, is the beginning of a single-line inscription, unfortunately only a fragment, but it is interesting as containing the name of a king—possibly one of the Andhras of the first or second century A.D. It reads (Pl. lvi, No. 2)—

Râño Siri-Sivamaka-Sadasa pâniyagharikasa ha . . .

"*The gift* of . . . . . the superintendent of the water establishment (*pânîyaghara*) of king Śrî Sivamaka Sada."[2]

---

[1] From a photograph in Cunningham's *Stûpa of Bharhut*, pl. xxxiv, fig. 4.

[2] Dr. Hultzsch proposes this reading with diffidence, making *pâniyaghara* equivalent to *pânîyaśâlâ*, "a water-shed" or place for the gratuitous distribution of water; otherwise *Dasapâniyagharika* or *Pâniyagharika* might perhaps be taken as an epithet of king Sivamaka or Sivamakasada. Sivamaka might possibly be the same as Simuka of the Nânâghâṭ inscription No. 3 (*Arch. Sur. W. India, Rep.*, vol. v, p. 64). Could *Sada* represent the *Sâta* of Sâtakaṁni and Sâtavâhana?

The fragment represented (Pl. xlix, fig. 1, and Pl. xxvii, fig. 2) was found at the north gate, where, as the inscription tells us, it was part of the coping. The end of another stone has come up against the back of it, and then the carving commenced with one of those quaint dwarfs, or rather obese giants, which alternate with *makaras* at the ends of sections of the roll. His head is decorated with circular ornaments, and a man seems to be adjusting one over his ear and smiling at his work, while two men in front are pushing the end of the roll into the mouth of the grotesque figure behind them; on a bend of the roll are the fore-parts of three elephants who bear a great round platform on which is a goglet or water bottle, perhaps "the precious vase" or vessel of ambrosia—*âmalakarka* or *amarakaraka*—spoken of by the Buddhists.[1] No other example of this symbol has been noticed. It may be noted, however, that in the great Brahmanical temples of the South, a vase of water is daily carried on an elephant, accompanied by a procession round the temple, and when pilgrims bring jars of Ganges water, they are met by a procession, and the water carried on an elephant to the temple.[2] This may represent some similar ceremony.

The inner side of this fragment (Pl. xxvii, fig. 2) is sadly injured. It has been carved with great boldness and considerable artistic power. At the right end, in an inner apartment, sits a chief on a seat well raised, and with a high footstool below it. Three female attendants stand behind with fan and *châmara*. A female sits on a round wickerwork stool to his right, and to his left a man with some long straight object across his knees, and the two seem to be conversing or arguing, while two stout men sit in the foreground, one of them with his hands raised in respect to the chief.

To the left is a brick building, perhaps representing the town wall, at a gateway of which two men are entering. Outside are other three, perhaps talking; and in the back-ground, among rocks, are two men and an elephant. One of the men has hold of the base of the elephant's right tusk with his left hand, while in his right, resting on the trunk half raised, he holds a short straight rod. Whether this is another representation of the Chhadanta elephant story is not quite clear, though it is possible, and the scene to the right may be the interview of the hunter and his companion when he was charged to secure the tusks. The rest of the stone being broken off prevents any better identification.

On the upper part of this stone is a fragment of an inscription (Plate lvi, No. 15) reading[3]—

-kayasa Kalîgâya mahâchetiye utarâyâke unisa dânaṁ.

"The gift of a cope-stone to the Great Chaitya at its northern gate[4] by Kalîgâ (Kaliṅgâ) . . . ."

The next fragment (Pl. xxvii, fig. 3), found near the last, is still less intelligible. An ascetic is seated at the door of his small hermitage, and a woman kneeling down worships him with the lowliest reverence, while two men behind her also make obeisance. Beyond them is what seems a very primitive form of *dâgaba*, on the top of which has been a dog or other animal now destroyed. Other figures are too much injured to be easily recognised. On each side have been scenes in which water-plants occupied the foreground.

---

[1] See Beal's *Bud. Records*, vol. ii, p. 137, 205. [2] *Ind. Ant.*, vol. xii, pp. 319, 324 n.

[3] This appears to have been damaged between the time of its excavation by Mr. R. Sewell and when I first saw it, the first three and part of the fourth *aksharas* having been chipped off. I incline to think the fourth was *ka*. In the facsimile a part of Mr. Sewell's rubbing has been attached.

[4] For *ayaka* or *ayâka*, see pp. 86, 93, 110.

Of the other fragments, we may notice a small one (Pl. xxvii, fig. 4) with an unusually high *dâgaba*, or other object of that description, but without the usual capital, with three broad bands of flowered pattern round it, and with worshippers having unusually large heads. The fragment is a split one, and the round of the top (if it ever had one) has been hewn off; the roll too must have occupied more space vertically than usual. It would seem from this that it probably belonged to a base, or possibly to a different frieze.

The two pieces (Pl. xxvii, fig. 5, and Pl. xxviii, fig. 3) possibly belonged to the same slab. The first has on the back one supporter of the roll and a plain *dâgaba* with two worshippers. The inner face is much crowded with figures in motion. Out of a city gate comes a man on an elephant; in front are two men, one of them with a sword, and before them a man on horseback, attended by a foot-runner just come to a doorway from which two men are coming out. Above and beyond the elephant are four other men—one with a lance or other straight weapon. To the right of the doorway three men are seen huddled together worshipping apparently at the door of a small building; but the stone is broken at this point, and we cannot make out more. The left upper part of the sculpture has an indoor scene, showing a râja on his seat, his wife sitting on his left, and a female looking out from behind over his shoulder. Below this is left only the hind-quarters of an elephant.

On the other fragment (Pl. xxviii, fig. 3) we have, on the right side, a man riding on a horse wearing a plume as in the previous sculpture, two men go before him, one of them with a long lance; beyond him is a man on an elephant which is just behind a doorway like the last, and out of it come several men, one bearing an umbrella and one an offering in a dish; but whom they are about to honour is lost with the continuation of the slab. Above, and cut off by a wall scolloped on the top, are some animals, one being an elephant with a man lying on and looking over its head.

There has been an inscription over this, but the few letters on this portion are much weather-worn.

Another piece (Pl. xxvii, fig. 6) carved with special skill, but unfortunately only a fragment, has on the left an infant amid the foliage of a tree, and a woman holding up her hands towards it, while another bends down behind her. Then two women face to the right, towards some one (quite destroyed) holding the child, and another woman is seated below. Within an apartment beyond is a stout man seated, with a cloth covering his legs, another salutes him, a third makes some offering, and a woman stands behind the latter two. Then come two buildings with their ends to the spectator, with arched roofs, that of the second with four small finials along the ridge resembling those at the Seven Pagodas. Next comes a second apartment, with a man in a chair, and the infant near the right side of it, a woman with her arms crossed beside it, and four attendants behind the man.

This stone has also part of a very clear-cut inscription (Pl. lvi, No. 16) which reads—

. . . rilikâ mahayâya Sujâtaṁya mahâvasibhutaya duhutâya bhikhuniya Rohâya aṭhalokadhaṁmavîtivatâya dana.

"The gift of the nun Rôhâ, who has passed beyond the eight worldly conditions, the daughter of the very venerable Sujâta, of great self-control." [1]

The piece of coping represented in the next figure (Pl. xxviii, fig. 1) is about 4 feet 3 inches by 2 feet 7 inches high and a foot thick, but from the way in which it is broken

---

[1] Dr. Hultzsch reads °*vesi*°, but the word is °*vasibhutaya*. *Zeitsch. der Deut. Morg. Gesellsch.*, vol. xxxvii, p. 553.

only 3 feet 4 inches of the sculpture has been left. The scene to the right is thus mostly destroyed. Two men, probably chiefs, sit on thrones, each with one foot on a square footstool or *morâ*, and the one to the right with a high cane stool close in front, and perhaps something laid upon it. Behind the other are three women, one with a large fan and the other with a *châmara*. On his right in front sits a lady with her foot on a cushion, and an attendant stands behind her. This probably was intended to represent the scene described in the Buddhist legends as taking place in the mansion of Suddhodana just before the conception of Gautama, when Mâyâ requests of her husband to be permitted to give herself for a short time to seclusion and devotions. If so, it must not be confounded with that in the woodcut (No. 17) representing the left section of the coping stone from Amarâvatî, sent to Calcutta by Colonel Mackenzie, and now in the India Museum. This has hitherto been regarded as presenting Suddhodana, in the midst of his court, but it seems more natural to regard it as intended to picture the scene in the Tushita heavens, just before the descent of the Bodhisattva, when he is represented in the splendid palace called Uchchadhvaja, teaching the hundred and eight gates of the law to the assembled gods, who salute him with joined hands and worship him with prostration. This tableau is naturally followed by the next on the same slab, already given at page 35, representing his departure in a heavenly car or *Vimâna*, which is the next episode in the legend. Then comes the next scene as given on this plate.

17. The Bodhisattva instructing the Tushitakâyikas in the Uchchadvaja palace.[1]

On the left end of the stone is a scene that is very frequently represented. It reveals the bedchamber of Mahâmâyâ, the mother of Gautama the Buddha, on the night of his conception, with four female slaves in the foreground.[2] She is represented asleep on her couch, and with four male figures at the corners of it who are the guardian *Devas* of the four quarters—Vaiśrâvaṇa of the north, Virûpâksha of the west, Dhṛitarâshṭra of the east, and Virûḍhaka of the south—whom she saw in her dream take up her couch

[1] From Fergusson's *Tree and Serpent Worship*, pl. lxxiv, to a scale of ⅛th. This illustration has also been given in Foucaux's *Lalita Vistara* (Paris, 1884), p. 42, where it is titled "Le roi Çouddhôdana au milieu de sa cour;" and in E. Arnold's *Light of Asia*, p. 22, it is used to represent the same. For the description of the assembly and the discourse delivered to the gods, see *Lalita Vistara*, ch. iv. The name *Uchchadhvaja* is wrongly defined in M. Williams's *Sansk. Dictionary* as that of "Śâkya-muni as teacher of the gods among the Tushitas."

[2] The *Lalita Vistara* (chap. vi.) names four goddesses—Oastkhulî, Mutkhulî, Dhvajavatî, and Prabhâvatî—who were appointed to the Bodhisattva at his conception.

and bear it to the Himâlayas, where their queens bathed her at the Anavatapta lake.[1] We find this scene also in the Ajaṇṭâ frescoes,[2] where the bathing is the point of time represented. On the Amarâvatî slab now at Calcutta, of which the right-hand section is given in the woodcut No. 18, it is the descent of the Bodhisattva in the form of an elephant after the bath that is pourtrayed.

18. Mahâmâyâ's Dream.[4]

The same scene is represented in the Yuzufzai sculptures in the Lahor Museum, and also in a medallion on one of the pillars from Bharhut now in the Calcutta Museum.[3]

On fig. 2 is represented the outer side of a small fragment of coping showing the worship of a very plain and early type of *dâgaba,* with the large floral crown worshipped by two men.

A still smaller fragment (Pl. xxviii, fig. 4) shows a man forcing a woman down, while a man and woman stand respectfully behind; and in the next compartment the first man is being carried by the woman and followed by another. The carving has been particularly good. On the back (fig. 5), the upper flower border is left, a part of the face of a terminal dwarf, and three capering sprites.

The drawing (Pl. xlix, fig. 2) represents a split fragment, of which only the inner face was found, half of it buried near the west gate, and the other portion lying on the surface. It contains only a portion of some scene. In the upper part are two thatched huts of a village surrounded by a brick wall, and beside the huts two men with infants in their arms. Outside the wall stands a man and two children, and close to them a woman sits with a square fan in her right hand and some dish in her left, while before her is an object like a high stool, behind which a lad sits on the wall. In the foreground on the left two men on horseback with two or three on foot are passing a tree that grows outside the village, and coming to where a figure sits on the ground before an elephant which seems to be sinking in mud, and addresses its rider.

---

1 Spence Hardy, *Manual of Budhism* (2d ed.), pp. 144–45; Bigandet's *Legend*, vol. i, p. 28; Alabaster's *Wheel of the Law*, pp. 97, 98.

2 *Notes on the Buddhist Rock Temples* (Bombay), p. 24.

3 Anderson's *Catalogue and Handbook of the Archæol. Collections in the India Museum*, Pt. i, p. 26; Cunningham's *Stûpa of Bharhut*, p. 83, and pl. xxviii, fig. 2. The sculpture has a short inscription over it, which General Cunningham read "*Bhagavato rûkdanta*" and "*rukdanti*" (p. 138), and translated by "Bhagavato as Rukdanti," or "Buddha as the sounding elephant;" but the inscription plainly reads on his photograph—*Bhagavato okraṁti* (Pali, *okkanti*), that is, "The descent of the Bhagavat."

4 This woodcut is from Arnold's *Light of Asia,* and has been produced from Pl. lxxiv of *Tree and Serpent Worship*, but not with perfect fidelity—the right edge of the slab being broken, has been restored by the engraver. The scale is about one-eighth of the original. The figure on page 35 is the middle section of the same slab from Dr. Fergusson's plate, but to the scale of the other illustrations in this volume, *i.e.*, one-tenth of the originals.

CHAPTER VII.

EARLIER SCULPTURES.

We come now to a group of stones which are somewhat puzzling. They evidently belong to a much earlier period of art than what we have hitherto been noticing, and are on that account all the more interesting, as the comparison enables us to trace the development of the style. Other stones will be noticed later on; meantime there are a number similar in general character to those we have been describing, of which certain were undoubtedly coping-stones of a rail. They are 26 inches high, and, like the more modern ones, vary from 12 to 13½ inches in thickness, and are rounded on the top. All bear the roll—upheld, not by tall men of the usual proportions, as in those already described, but by very fat dwarfs or monsters, and including the bands of leaf and rosette patterns above and below, the sculpture does not cover more than 20 inches in height, leaving 6 for the crown of the stone. The carving is quite surface-work, not at all so deep as in the later style, and is characterised by a larger scale and a stiffer treatment of the human figure, but the animals are drawn with much power and knowledge.

We have four good specimens of this type; the first, and most injured (Pl. xxx, fig. 1), is 5 feet 9 inches long, and about 6 inches thick, the back having been split off, probably to apply it to some other purpose in some reconstruction. The roll is very carefully carved in stripes of varied patterns, and is upheld by a droll-looking fat dwarf with the head of an elephant *minus* proboscis and tusks, and by an obese female with short drawers, crushed down apparently by the weight of the roll, but her face is rubbed out. The only band about the roll is at its lowest point, but in this case it has been rubbed so that the carving on it can hardly be made out. Over the rolls in the intervals are half-discs, carved in a pattern which exactly resembles in all details the pattern of a large number of cross-bars of smaller size than usual—the discs measuring 26 to 28 inches in diameter with proportionately large tenons.

The band or border over this sculpture is neat and worth attention. The upper member is a twisted cord, and the lower broad leaves and bells alternately, dependent from it. The band below is divided into square compartments, each containing one X shaped flower.

The second of these, represented on Plate xxviii, fig. 6, was found a little to the west of the south gate. Its extreme length is 5′ 9″ by 2′ 2″ high and 7½ inches thick, the back being split off. The right end has terminated with a large *makara* from the mouth of which a female, with three very heavy rings on each ankle, unusually large breasts and eyes, striped drawers, and a star or rosette on her forehead, is pulling out the long roll, which, as on the outside of other coping-stones, runs along these. This roll is carefully carved, and has a half rosette over the first downward bend, similar to those at the tops of the rail pillars. Then a fat dwarf supports it on his shoulder. He has very large features, moustache, wrinkled brow, and a close-fitting cap with two tails sticking out of it, and his head is turned clean over his shoulder. Below the roll, the margin of the stone is carved with a band of rosettes; and above is a leaf-and-bell pattern. On the round of the stone is part of an inscription in early square characters (Pl. lxi, No. 52); the beginning is broken away and at the end of it is a *svastika* mark. What is left reads—

. . (duhu)tukâya sanatukâya unisa dâna.

"A coping-stone[1] the gift of . . . (with her daugh)ters with her grandsons."

The fact that this stone is called *uṇîsa,* a frieze or coping-stone, shows that originally these slabs did form the plinth over a rail, possibly replaced by the more elaborate one of which we have already examined the remains.

The third example (Pl. xxix, fig. 1) is 6 feet 3 inches long and a foot thick; but if there ever was any carving on one side, it has been entirely obliterated by the vulgar uses to which that side of the stone has been put. The carving on the other side is in good preservation, and contains three of the fat supporters, each in a different attitude, one with curly hair, sitting. The two bands round the roll are formed of foliage with two birds in each. The other details are as in the preceding example.

A fourth stone (fig. 3), found close to the last, near the north gate, is 4 feet 9 inches long and 13½ inches thick, but quite plain on one side. This has been used at an angle or corner, for here we have the terminal *gaṇa* or spirit in short striped drawers, with a heavy bead or small round box hung by a string round his neck, and either swallowing or vomiting the core of the roll. The second figure has also a large cylindrical bead hung round his neck, short drawers, and a jaunty little cap. The band round the roll is carved with foliage, out of which rises a cobra's hood, on each side of which stands a bird with some sort of scroll in its beak. The band below is formed of rosettes of ten petals, otherwise the sculpture does not differ from the two preceding. There is only one specimen of this style of coping-stone among the Elliot marbles in the British Museum—that represented in *Tree and Serpent Worship,* Plate xcii, fig. 5.

On Plate xxxi, fig. 3, is given a small fragment of yet another of these coping-stones, with a peculiarly ugly dwarf or *yaksha* bearing up the roll, and on the brow of the stone a fragment of an inscription in early characters reading—

(Ma)hâtherasa Mahâdhaṁmakasa ka. . .

"Of the great sthavira Mahâ Dharmaka. . . . . . ."

The other group of this early style of frieze consists of stones, the entire examples of which are each about 23 inches high, thin, and sculptured only on one side. At first sight many of them look like the inner side of coping-stones of the class just described, split and the crown hewn off. But the fact that all these are split, and that the sculpture is 3 inches broader than on the preceding, while in no case have we found one with any portion of the round above, seems to justify Mr. J. Fergusson's conclusion that they probably formed part of a base course; and though of older date than the great rail, they may have been used also for the outer side of it.

---

[1] In another inscription, No. 31, this word *unisa* is spelt *uṁnisa*: it is the Pâli *uṇhîsa* and Sanskrit *ushṇîsha.* The translation of it in the text can hardly be questioned. It occurs also in one of the inscriptions from Amarâvatî in Fergusson's *Tree and Serpent Worship,* p. 262, No. xvi, and pl. xcii, fig. 1. Hultzsch, *Zeit. D. M. Gesel.,* Bd. xxxvii, S. 550.

It is unfortunate that the specimens of these sculptures are so fragmentary and broken. Mr. Fergusson has given four examples in *Tree and Serpent Worship*, Pl. lvii, p. 188, and those now added only prove the uniformity of their style and subjects—men or boys with short drawers, holding or driving bulls, winged lions and deer, elephants, &c., by their tails, a cord, the leg, or a tusk. The native bull and elephant are generally excellent representations of the animals, free and animated; but the mythological animals are wanting in artistic ability.

The upper face of the stone is covered to a depth of 6 inches, part of which has in several cases been afterwards hewn away, with foliage of a very mixed kind, the central stem winding from side to side with very angular bends, as in some of the friezes at Nâsik, and within each bend there is frequently a different type of leaves or flowers; occasionally, too, human figures or dwarfs and birds give variety to the ornament. The lower margin is about 2 inches broad, and is carved with long lentil-shaped beads, divided by very small ones. Sometimes half-rosettes are projected from either border into open spaces of the frieze between.

Pl. xxix, fig. 2, represents a stone 5 feet 2 inches long, 23 inches high, and 10 inches thick, plain on the back, and well illustrating the somewhat crude attempts made to give variety to the upper borders of these slabs. The field is occupied by a humpbacked Indian bull in full career, with a rope round its right horn, the holder of which has been on a slab now lost. In front of it is a man seizing a winged deer by the hind-leg.

At the same place in the north-west of the circle was found the piece given in Pl. xxxi, fig. 4, of the same height as the others, but only 6½ inches thick. It represents a young man seizing a rather mild-looking winged lion by the ear, and having a rope in his left hand to bind it with.

On the next example (Pl. xxx, fig. 2) is a bull galloping, somewhat weather-worn, but not specially notable. The next two pieces (figs. 3 and 5) show a bird-headed quadruped, such as we meet with also on the capitals of the Gautamîputra Cave (No. III.) at Nâsik, and also at Sânchi,[1] but here the body is entirely destroyed; before it is a man with striped drawers, holding the end of a cord which was fastened to the horn of the bull he is driving, but of which the head has been broken away. The smaller fragment shows a similar figure driving by its long tail what, when entire, was probably a winged lion.

The next (fig. 4) is a very similar fragment, in which, however, the wing of the animal is left, and is so like those on the capitals at Pitalkhôra, and in the small vihâra cave at Bhâjâ, that we can hardly fail to connect them.

Another fragment (not given in the plates) had borne an elephant, very well represented, and again the man with short drawers, and the feet of another lion.

There is one much-worn piece of a split coping-stone (Pl. xxxi, fig. 1), 1 foot 3 inches high and 6½ inches thick, which must belong to the same early date as these last, but which must have belonged to a different rail, or even building. Possibly it formed part of the first inner rail. It has four lines of mediæval Nâgari characters faintly carved across the back near one end of it.[2]

A fragment (fig. 2) 2 feet 4 inches by 11½ inches broad and 5 inches thick, found at the south gate, has a curve on the plane of its face showing that it must have formed part

---

[1] *Tree and Serp. Wor.*, Pl. xv, fig. 3.

[2] See *Zeitsch. d. D. Morg. Gesell.*, Bd. xxxvii, S. 552, No. 11.

of a circle about 11 feet in diameter. Though much worn, the style of the carving can be so far made out as to assimilate it with these earlier sculptures. The animals are not well drawn, and the motion is constrained.

The stone, fig. 5, was found as a step in a doorway of the small brick structure at the west gate; but it may have been carved as a frieze or a division between pieces of sculpture, such as is represented in the frieze over the *dâgaba* in the next plate.

19. Border Ornament from a Pillar of the Outer Rail (Fergusson's *Tree and Serpent Worship*, plate lxvi, fig. 1).

CHAPTER VIII.

THE INNER RAIL: CHAITYA SLABS AND CHAKRA PILLARS.

THE inner rail was shown by Mr. J. Fergusson to have been only about six feet in height from the pavement, and, though with some doubt, he gave a reconstruction of a section of it, making it to consist of the large chaitya slabs with a slender stele at each side, then a *chakra* pillar, and again the stele and *dâgaba*—the *chaitya* or *dâgaba* slabs (on his plate lxxv) stand 4 feet 10 inches apart between centres. Whether the *chakra* pillars and the steles terminating in small *dâgabas* were placed quite in this way he was uncertain; but now that we have secured a *dâgaba* slab with the *chakra* pillars attached, we know pretty surely that the order was one of these latter on each side the *dâgaba* slabs, and a stele between, rather than Mr. Fergusson's arrangement; and this would separate the slabs by about 4 inches more, supposing they were otherwise disposed, as Mr. Fergusson indicated—and we know nothing for certain to the contrary. But as the slabs vary considerably in breadth, the distances from centre to centre may have varied from about 5 feet to 6 feet 3 inches, and it is possible that others may have been interposed.

The slabs now in the British Museum representing *dâgabas* have been published in *Tree and Serpent Worship*, and we have only one more of these slabs entire to describe, though there are a considerable number of drawings of them among Colonel Mackenzie's, of which not a fragment is now known to exist.

The slab represented in Plate I. was at Masulipatam till 1881, and, except the inscription which ran along the lower line of the frieze, most of which has been broken off, it is in a fine state of preservation. It represents a *stûpa, chaitya* or *dâgaba*, such as that of Amarâvatî may have been, framed as it were by the *chakra* pillars at the sides and the sculptured frieze above. The slab stood 5′ 8″ above the pavement and about 5′ 10″ broad, and in this the *chaitya* occupies an area 4′ 0″ wide by 4′ 1½″ high. The *stûpa* is surrounded by a high outer rail with four cross-bars between its pillars, surmounted by a plinth carved on the outer side with men carrying the roll ornament. The sides of the entrance are shown in a rude sort of perspective as coming outwards, and terminating in neat pillars with bases and capitals, crowned by figures of lions; at the angles too, above the roll, on each side is a lion. And at the sides of the *dâgaba* we have views of other two gates. Inside we see the *stûpa* itself, and facing the gateway is the throne with the sacred footmarks, and the *dharma chakra* with attendants and worshippers; and above in a separate sculpture is Gautama seated teaching, with attendant disciples.

This central portion differs largely on the various slabs. The principal sculpture on it is sometimes the polycephalous snake; sometimes Buddha standing among his hearers; sometimes the same sitting like Pârśvanâtha Śeshphani, his head surrounded by the hoods of the snake; sometimes the Nâgarâja worshipping the footmarks, sometimes the Bôdhi tree and footmarks, or a throne with a relic casket, Buddha and a horse, the elephant kneeling to Buddha, &c., and sometimes it consists of two medallions containing sculptures.

Over the outer railing we can see that the base of the *stûpa* is surrounded by carved slabs of the *chakra*, the great *Nâga* or snake, the Bôdhi tree, and in some the *dâgaba*; and this is surmounted by a richly sculptured frieze.

Above the front slab, which slightly projects from the base of the *dâgaba*, rise five tall stelæ, the bases square and sometimes ornamented with carvings of the *chakra*, *bôdhi* tree, and *dâgaba;* the shafts are octagon, and they have square carved capitals. That such actually existed on the great *stûpa* is supported by the discovery of a number of these pillars at the Jaggayyapeṭa stûpa, where, in an inscription, they are called *âyaka khaṁbhe*.

Round the base of the dome behind these is a broad belt of very rich figure-sculpture, in which are easily recognised some of the scenes we have already met with on the outer rail. Still higher round the dome are hung placques square and round containing also carvings, with some at least of which we are familiar. Below is a sort of fringe in which the *triśula* forms an element. On the top is the usual square box-like capital, surmounted by two small umbrellas and what closely resembles the top of one of the stelæ. To this the *devas, Nâgas*, and *Yakshas* are flying and capering through the air, with offerings and music.

The *chakra* or wheel pillars by the sides are very remarkable objects. At the base of each is a chair or throne, with two round cushions, and the footprints on the footstool. Two attendants stand by with *châmaras*, and two chiefs or *devas* sit and worship by the sides of it. The shaft which rises from behind the chair is divided into sections by tori, most of them toothed, and four of the sections are ornamented with the foreparts of three animals, such as we have already met with on the rail sculptures; one has three human busts, and the uppermost has three dwarfs or *yakshas*. The abacus consists of three flat members and supports three lions, on which rests the *chakra* or wheel,—the edge ornamented with fourteen *triśulas*, and the central part rayed. On each side the shaft are five figures riding on different animals, one being a horse, another having a human face. Above the uppermost of these a female is represented dancing excitedly on a cushion; and above her and just under the wheel is a *yaksha*. Over the wheel are *gandharvas* and other *devatas*, making music and jollity.

Over the whole runs the frieze, the lower member of which or architrave has been ornamented, between two *teniæ* projecting members, with figures of the bust of a nondescript bird or animal. On the upper tenia is a line of animals, and on the lower the inscription. Above this is a broad band, divided into three larger and two smaller compartments by small projecting discs representing rail or bolt heads, and through one of them an iron bolt has passed to secure the slab to some wall or other support behind. The larger compartment in the centre contains a figure of the Buddha seated cross-legged, holding up his right hand in the attitude of blessing. Dwarf figures are represented in front of his seat in various attitudes; on his right stands a tall figure with his head on a dwarf, and behind are more dwarf figures represented as assailing the Buddha, while the temptresses at Buddha's left leave little doubt that the scene intended is the temptation by Mâra or Namuchi. On each side this a vertical line of three bolt-heads separates it from a figure of a Nâgarâja and his wife worshipping the Buddha. To the right again, beyond another division formed by three bolt-heads, is a scene in which the empty seat of the Buddha is surrounded by about fourteen figures, perhaps all females, seated or lying in various attitudes, apparently asleep. On the left is the throne again, with the *triśula* on the back of it and behind it the sacred tree. A number of men stand to the right of it, one of whom appears to lay some object on the throne, and in front and to the left are numerous women in various attitudes worshipping.

The inscription, No. 17, is largely destroyed, but is cut in characters of the type employed in the time of the later Andhra kings. It reads—

[Sid]haṁ. Cheṁpukiraṭhe Adhiṭhâṇa . . . vathavasa Haṁghagahapatiputrasa vâniyasa Samudasa gharaniya cha koḍichaṁ digaha(?pa) . . . . [naṁ cha] savasa cha lokasa hitasukhaṭhatâya bhagavato mahâ[cheti]ye sa u[ni]s[e] [sapa]. . . . .

"Hail! A *Kodicha digapa*, (the gift) of the merchant Samuda, the son of the householder Haṁgha . . . . . of Adhiṭhâna,[1] in the province of Chempuka, for the welfare and happiness of . . . and of . . . and of the whole world; to the great Chaitya of the honourable, furnished with a coping (*or* frieze—*unisu*). . . ."

If slabs of this kind with the *chakra* pillars and steles alone formed the inner rail, then as each quadrant of it, exclusive of the entrance, must have measured from 95 feet to 100 feet, there must have been from 16 to 19 of these richly carved *dâgabas* in each quadrant. If we suppose only twelve were used in each, then we must suppose eleven narrower slabs interposed; and this is not at all improbable. We have some tall narrow slabs which belong apparently to this rail, and which, if so interposed, must have added considerably to its artistic effect.

In the Elliot and Mackenzie collections we have thirty different representations of these *dâgabas*, to which must now be added at least three more, indicating how frequently they must have recurred round the circle.

Of the broken specimens of these chaitya slabs recovered, that given in Plate xxxi, fig. 6, had been for some time at Bejwâḍâ. It may possibly have been removed from Amarâvatî by Colonel Mackenzie, and if so, was probably in much better condition when he took it away. It now measures about 3 feet each way, the edges and the whole upper part of the dome being destroyed. Outside the entrance on each side a woman is seated with a cloth thrown across her shoulders, and a man holding, probably, a bunch of flowers stands besides her, one on the right being perhaps a mendicant. Just by the gate is the figure of a dwarf on each side, with a tray or bason on his head. These small figures occur so constantly at all the gates, that one is tempted to suppose they represent statues bearing trays to receive the offerings of visitors. No example of them has been found, and the only analogue I know of is a similar small figure bearing a bason by the door jamb of the cave at Lonâḍ in the Thâṇâ district near Kâlyaṇ.[2] The plinth of the outer rail is carved, after the older pattern, with animals and men, not with the flower roll, and the lions on the gateway are of the usual pattern. Inside the rail are seen two slender pillars with capitals, that at once remind us of those of the Aśoka Lâts in Northern India and the iron pillar at Dehli. Each supports a small *chaitya*, which may have been the emblem of the Chaityika School. The dome of the stûpa has been elaborately carved in panels, with scenes similar to those on the outer rail, and among them may be noticed the Chakra and Buddha teaching.

On the front are the usual five steles, and on the base supporting them a sculpture of Buddha seated, with a nimbus round his head and worshippers approaching him. On the frontispiece, below this, is another representation of him in the teaching *mûdra*, with figures

---

[1] Adhishṭhâna is mentioned in the *Amarakôsha*, iii, 4, 128; Hemachandra's *Apêkârthasaṁgraha*, iv, 156; and *Medinîkôsha*, n. 163; but as it means merely "the capital," it may stand here for 'the chief city of the province of Chempuka.' If this latter is meant for Champaka (*Vyutpatti*, ed. Schiefner, 102), its capital was Champakâ, in Magadha; *Hitopadêśa*, 27, 10; conf. *Vâtâpy-adhishthane*, in *Ind. Ant.*, vol. x, p. 60.

[2] *Arch. Sur. W. Ind. Report*, vol. v, pl. xlv, fig. 2.

on elephants approaching on each side. The throne on which he sits is surrounded below by a crowd of dwarfs or *yakshas* raised on a ledge, and below all are two worshippers.

Another example of the same sort, and almost of the same size, is given in fig. 7 (Pl. xxxi), but more of the dome of the *dâgaba* is destroyed. The dwarfs at the entrance stand on small pedestals, and one of the approaching worshippers on each side seems to be about to deposit his offering in the receptacle borne by the dwarf. In this and in most other cases, a flower vase stands on each side the entrance, but in this one the jambs of the entrance, instead of being carved with discs, like the cross-bars of the rail, bear a tall figure of a man as if rushing in with his hands joined over his head. The Buddha on the frontispiece is attended by two *chauri*-bearers, and his throne consists of the body of a great snake, whose seven hoods appear round the aureole behind his head, while two Nâginîs worship in front of it, and two mortals below, with perhaps an offering lying between them. Here there is a close combination of Buddhism and Nâga-worship which we meet with in so many other forms in these sculptures.

Plates XXXII–XXXIX.

Of the Plates xxxii–xxxix taken from the Mackenzie drawings little need be said; their publication will convey as good an idea as it is now possible to form of these sculptures. All of them represent the chaityas as surrounded by a rail of four discs or cross-bars in height, whereas the great rail has only three. The rail in these representations is surmounted by a frieze, sometimes of animals and sometimes of the great rolls which are so marked a characteristic of the rail of the stûpa, and in the majority of them a separate pillar is represented inside the rail, on each side of the entrance, crowned by a small chaitya, sometimes with quite a multitude of umbrellas over it.

Outside the entrance on each side, a man or woman is always represented either as purchasing offerings from persons who are seated selling them, or are bringing offerings borne on the heads of dwarfs. And a vase or pot with flowers is always placed at the entrance.

That represented on Plate xxxii, fig. 5, is not of the usual type, but may be compared with the stone in Plate xli, fig. 2, which was found in the south-west quadrant, apparently in the line of the inner rail. The multitude of umbrellas over the capital is here well illustrated. The five-hooded cobra figures on front of the *dâgaba*, a very rich belt of carving surrounds the upper part of the dome, and two Vidyâdharas bring offerings, whilst a worshipper on each side salutes it reverentially.

Plate xxxiii presents drawings of two of the larger slabs and of a Chakra pillar. Though the upper portions of the slabs had been injured before they were drawn, they are sufficiently complete to show how very richly carved these slabs were.[1] In that given in fig. 1, the central stele of the front and the two pillars within the rail bear small *dâgabas* crowned with a crowd of umbrellas, while *dâgabas* are also carved on the shafts of the steles. On the plinth below them is sculptured the worship of the wheel. Over the rail we can just see on the base of the dome the tops of two wheels and of a tree, and this helps us to allocate the larger slabs bearing these symbols. On the front of the Chaitya the chief representation is that of the favourite legend, told in all the lives of Buddha, of the intoxicated elephant

[1] It is to be remembered that all these drawings have been reduced to the same scale as the other plates, namely, 1-10th, or 10 feet to 1 foot.

Nâḷâgiri, let loose by Devadatta, the cousin of Śâkya-Muni, in Râjagṛiha, to destroy him. "Followed by guardian Nâga spirits," says the story, "he slowly approached the maddened elephant. The Bhikshus all deserted him; Ânanda only remained by his side. The drunken elephant, savage and spiteful, beholding Buddha, came to himself at once, and bending, worshipped at his feet, just as a mighty mountain falls to earth. With lotus hand the Master pats his head, even as the moon lights up a flying cloud." Then Buddha preaches to him and converts him to his doctrine.[1] This same scene is represented in the annexed woodcut (No. 20), from a fresco in Cave XVII at Ajaṇṭa. The same is represented also on a slab from the frieze of the inner rail.[2]

20. Buddha and the Elephant.

The domes of both Chaityas are carved with the utmost elaboration, and with a spirit that may yet enable students of Bauddha legends to identify the scenes. In fig. 3, the frieze of the rail, it will be observed, is carved on the outside with the great flower roll or *toraṇa*, borne by men, as in the slabs of the actual rail. The shafts of the five steles are carved with a *dâgaba*, two *chakras*, and two sacred trees—the three principal sacred emblems. The frontispiece below contains two circular panels: in the upper one is the horse Kaṇṭhaka, its feet supported by the *Yakshas*, and attended by the umbrella-bearer, but without any visible rider; and in the lower panel is the worship of Buddha, perhaps in the Tushita heavens.

The Chakra pillar (fig. 2) has two deer at the foot of the empty throne, and the *Srîpâda* or sacred footprints on the footstool. The shaft is more richly carved than in the example on Plate xli, fig. 3; but otherwise they are alike.

The Chaitya slab given in fig. 1 of Plate xxxiv has been scarcely at all damaged when it was drawn, and it was equally rich with the others, with Vidyâdharas or other spirits flying round the capital, some of them bearing offerings. The front bears a representation of Buddha followed by four women bearing water-vessels on their heads, and worshipped by Nâga figures. Fig. 2 represents another, somewhat broken above, and having on the frontal slab a sculpture of a Nâga râja, with his companions and their wives, worshipping the sacred footprints or *S'rîpâdas.*

The object of adoration on the Chaitya given in fig. 1, Pl. xxxv, is the Buddha, who is attended by two *chauri*-bearers; but in front stands a horse and two men, while a third kneels apparently to the horse. On the side of the Chaitya to the right the legend of the Nâḷâgiri elephant is told, with the addition, in the second panel to the right, of the mischief caused by it before Buddha met it and subdued it. In fig. 2, the scene in the front is quite unusual. A Nâga râja and another are seen seated discussing some topic, and to the left perhaps the same pair are walking together, but the action of the other figures in the picture is not clear.[3]

Plate xxxvi, figs. 1 and 2, represent two *dâgabas* with the five-hooded snake only on

[1] Beal's *Fo-sho-hing-tsan-king*, p. 247; see also Bigandet's *Legend of Gaudama*, 2nd ed., p. 250; S. Hardy's *Manual of Budhism*, p. 331; Beal's *Buddh. Rec. of the West. World*, vol. ii, p. 150.

[2] *Tree and Serpent Wor.*, pl. lxxxii, fig. 2; conf. *Cave Temples*, p. 311.

[3] This should be compared with a scene painted in one of the Ajaṇṭa caves,—*Cave Temples*, pl. xliii.

the frontispiece, without any human worshippers,—only Vidyâdharas flying round the capitals, which are supposed to contain the relic. Fig. 2 is one of the most richly decorated of this sort, of which others are described below.

Figs. 3 and 4 are drawings of large fragments of two other slabs, the first representing Buddha on the frontispiece, upborne by *Yakshas,* with two worshippers below; and the second resembles very closely that given in Plate xxxiii, fig. 3. In this example the *S'rîpâda* or sacred footprints figure conspicuously on each side of the dome of the stûpa, with the *chhattra* over them and worshippers.

The two dâgabas drawn on Plate xxxvii are equally elaborate with the rest. In Fig. 1 Buddha is represented as in Pl. xxxix, fig. 3, and elsewhere, seated on the coils of the great Nâga Muchilinda, with Nâgas and their wives, in their human form, worshipping him. On the body of the stûpa, to the right, is represented a man throwing a dead horse from him, and a struggle among the people crowded round. In the next compartment men and women in pairs are struggling or caressing. In Fig. 2, Buddha is preaching to the Nâga women and one chief, while behind him four females appear with vessels on their heads, and birds are seen flying past.

In Plate xxxviii, fig. 2, is a drawing of a somewhat plainer and smaller Chaitya slab, only 3 feet wide. There are no dwarfs nor flower vases, nor people at the entrance, and the sculptures on the dome are restricted to the Chakra, the pillar supporting the double *triśula,* the *bodhî* tree, and the five-hooded snake which figures so prominently on the front, but even there without worshipper. Under the steles, is a sculpture of an elephant and four men worshipping the flaming pillar with the *S'rîpâda* at its base. Curious looking sprites float round the dome. Figs. 1 and 7 represent a Chakra pillar and part of another, differing from the others chiefly in the figures up the sides of the shafts.

On Plate xxxix, fig. 3, is also a snake-chaitya, even plainer than the last. Those in figs. 1 and 2 are of the usual richly sculptured type, and in the first, as in some other instances, the course of animals at the very base strengthens the probability of Mr. Fergusson's conjecture, that the great rail had actually such an adjunct on the outside. In the first of these slabs, Buddha is attended and worshipped by women as well as men; and in the second, he is seated, Vishṇu-like, on the coiled-up body of the great snake Mahâ-muchilinda, whose seven hoods overshadow him.

These Chaitya slabs are very interesting, as showing how the great Buddhist *dâgabas* were ornamented at the time when this inner rail was erected. It is probably later than the outer rail, and, as Mr. Fergusson has remarked, "If we compare the very plain rail at Sânchi with the very elaborate sculptured enclosure at Amarâvatî, we ought to expect the same progress towards elaboration in the *dâgabas* themselves. Even if we assume that the older Dâgaba was as little ornamented as it now appears, or as plain as those sculptured on its gateways represent" the Dâgabas of that period to have been, "it seems natural to expect from comparison with the Rails, that" three centuries later "the Dâgabas may have been as richly sculptured as these representations would lead us to expect they were. The progress, however, is so great that it seems impossible it could have been effected in less than three centuries of time."[1]

"All this," as Mr. Fergusson remarks, "is practically new to Indian antiquaries. Hitherto our ideas regarding structural Dâgabas have been derived from the present appear-

[1] *Tree and Serp. Wor.*, p. 217.

ance of those at Sânchi or Manikyâla, or from the very imperfect representations we possess of those in Afghanistân, and these are all, now at least, plain or nearly so. The one which it seems was intended to have been as richly ornamented as these was that at Sârnâth; but it was left incomplete, probably at the great revolution which took place in the middle of the eighth century. Had it been completed it would have been even more elaborately decorated than those at Amarâvatî. The Dâgabas in Caves hardly help us in this respect; they probably were painted, and the colours having perished, there is nothing left from which to form an opinion. Those in Ceylon, too, are in much too ruinous a state to aid in this inquiry, so that these representations on the inner Rail are really the only authentic documents we have, and they thus become in this respect invaluable."[1]

Plates XL, XLI, XLII.

Among the fragments found at the temple of Amarêśvara were two portions of one of these chaitya slabs (Pl. xl, fig. 1), the central figure on which is the five-hooded Nâga; but, as in the examples previously known, no human or other figures are represented as worshipping it, as is the case when the *chakra*, the *Bodhi* tree, or Buddha occupy this position; nor are any votaries at the entrance buying or selling offerings, nor the flower vase. Was the Dragon then the forsaken god of a previous cult, only kept in pictorial remembrance, or only reverenced once a year on the *Nâgapañchami* festival?

The rail is represented as carved outside with the roll, borne by fat dwarfs, and the frieze round the chaitya is of an unusually simple pattern.

Mr. Fergusson has called particular attention to one of these chaitya or Dâgaba slabs,[2] which has been carved on the back of a slab bearing a much earlier sculpture. In Pl. xl, fig. 3, and Pl. xli, fig. 1, occurs a beautifully sculptured slab of the inner rail frieze carved on the back of part of a chaitya slab. It has also been one in which the Nâga, without worshippers, was the central figure. The dome in this case has been quite plain, and the band round the base of it, carved only with the early pattern of the Buddhist rail. This, therefore, may, like the sculpture on the back of Mr. Fergusson's slab, belong to the earlier period of the stûpa. Another Nâga slab is still worshipped at the east end of the village.

A very similar fragment, with the sculpture chipped off (Pl. xl, fig. 4), was also found to the east of the north gate. It had evidently also been utilised at a later date, but the other face had been entirely split off.

There is among the stones so long at Masulipatam a fragment of a small dâgaba slab of somewhat archaic style (fig. 2). The dome has two five-hooded[3] cobras twisted and knotted round it; but the rest is too much destroyed to allow of any restoration.

---

[1] *Tree and Serp. Wor.*, p. 218.

[2] *Tree and Serp. Wor.*, pl. lxxviii, figs. 2, 3, p. 219.

[3] Mr. Fergusson notes the frequency of 'fives' in the Bauddha sculptures; may it not be connected in some way with the five fingers? The word *pañchan*, 'five,' primarily means 'the spreading out of the hand.' Groups of five are very numerous in Indian literature, *e.g.*, five classes of beings; five classes of men; five elements; five members; five vital airs; five great sins; five sacrifices; five kinds of knowledge; five animals to be eaten; five products of the cow; five spices; five jewels; five metals; five kinds of fig trees; five kinds of salt; five gestures in making an offering; five modes of medical treatment; five marks of decay; five sheaths of the soul, &c., &c. See the compounds of *pañcha* in the Dictionaries. Compare the fragment referred to above with one on a slab, drawn by Colonel Mackenzie's men and published in *Tree and Serpent Worship*, pl. xcviii, fig. 2.

A fragment of one of the richly carved chaitya slabs (Pl. xlii, fig. 3) was recovered from the walls of a large well about a furlong to the west of the stûpa. Only sufficient is left to show how richly carved it must have been, and to prove how little these beautiful sculptures are regarded by the modern Hindus.

In the line of the inner rail were found some narrow slabs which in all probability formed part of it and gave additional variety to its sculptures. The first of these (fig. 5) is only 8 inches broad, and the upper section is wanting, while the remainder is broken into three. It seems probable that the edges of this stone have been pared off at some time or other. Of the remaining three sculptures on it, the uppermost represents a prince with a high square-topped cap on his throne, with his queen beside him and attendants behind. A woman kneels at his right, and another perhaps supports her—but this is not clear. On a wall or high bench behind, two women are seated to the right looking on; and to the left is Buddha or some Buddhist saint with an aureole behind his head instructing a disciple.

It will be remarked that in almost all these indoor scenes the women are represented naked to the waist; and this was probably the universal custom in the Telugu country, as in private it is to some extent still; but it is also to be remembered that it was an ancient custom in some districts for every woman in entering the presence of a chief or person of rank to bare her breast.

The sculpture next below this represents Buddha with an aureole behind his head seated on a throne, with eight people—one or two of them monks—worshipping him or listening to his discourse. A man of higher rank sits in front, with his right shoulder turned to the throne.

The third sculpture seems to represent two scenes. On the left a man seated beside a woman on a high couch puts his hands on her head or eye, and a woman is entering rapidly with some long object on her shoulder. To the right is apparently the same man holding up an almsbowl to the Buddha.

Another slab of this kind (fig. 6) was found in the same line broken in two. It is about 14 inches broad, and stood 4 feet above the platform level. It has four separate sculptures. The lowest contains a very favourite representation—that of the Siddhartha leaving Kapilavasta to become an ascetic. The feet of his horse Kaṇṭhaka are borne up by Yakshas; the Devas attend him, and Chhandaka precedes him, dressed in a kilt and with some long weapon in his left hand.

The second sculpture above this is another favourite scene, the temptation by the daughters of Mâra Pâpiyân, while his demon troop surround the sage. One point is unusual. In other representations of the Buddhas of later date he sits in the Bhūmisparśamûdra, cross-legged, with the right hand over the knee and pointing downwards. Here the right hand is uplifted as if in the act of addressing his enemy.

In the third scene the position of Buddha is exactly the same; two deer are couched as his cognizance below the seat, and admiring listeners attend his discourse. In the fourth and uppermost scene is a *dâgaba*, with Buddha standing in front of it, within the entrance, having his right hand raised exactly as in the two lower scenes; Devas float above worshipping it, and a tall female guardian stands in a doorway saluting it. The dâgaba must here represent the *Nirvâṇa*, or perhaps the *Dharma* or religion of the Buddha.

On the upper edge of this stone is an inscription (Pl. lvii, No. 19)—

. . . Bhagavato Kevurure vathaviyâ pavajitikayâ (Vasa)yâ tha-
. . . yâ Haṁgiyâ bhây(aṁ)tiyâ Bodhiyâ utayâ imaṁ peṁḍaka patiṭhaṁ(pi)-
ta

"(Adoration) to the Blessed one! this *peṇḍikâ* (slab)[1] was set up by Haṁgî (Saṅgî) the daughter of the venerable Bodhî . . . . . of the female ascetic Vasâ (Vaśâ) resident in Kevurura."

Found with the last was a small *dâgaba* slab (Pl. xli, fig. 2), 2 feet 6 inches broad and 5 inches thick, which stood 4 feet above the pavement. Round the dome three five-hooded snakes are knotted; on the drum are other three in as many separate panels; over the capital is an immense bunch of small *chhatris*, and a flying Nâga râja on each side bears an offering. By the sides stand two tall Nâga chiefs, the one on the right having a specially large and splendid head-dress, with curled hair, and holding in his right hand a flower, on which a bee is feeding. At the feet of each chief his wife kneels in worship.

In Plate xvi, figs. 3 and 4, we have two more of these narrow slabs, drawn by Colonel Mackenzie's draftsmen, one of them only 8 inches broad, and the other 1 foot 2·2 inches, both of them very closely resembling that on Plate xl, fig. 6. The lower parts of others are drawn in Pl. xxxii, fig. 4, and Pl. xxxviii, figs. 5 and 6,—the last, however, differing so much in scale and subjects of sculpture as to suggest that it probably belonged to the central Chaitya.

From the temple of Amareśvara a portion perhaps of one of the pillar slabs of the inner rail (Pl. xlii, fig. 1) was obtained. It is much rubbed, but represents a figure seated cross-legged with a nimbus behind the head and foliage beyond that; he wears heavy bracelets and heavy earrings, with a Brahmanical thread, otherwise we might suppose it to be the Buddha. On his left are women, and on his right a man speaks to or reverences him, while others appear behind.

One of the *chakra* pillar slabs which stood on each side the larger Dâgaba slabs is shown in Pl. xli, fig. 3. It is 13 inches broad, and 4 feet 5 inches long, exclusive of the rough part that has been sunk in the earth. At the bottom is the chair with the footprints below, and at each side two seated worshippers and two attendants standing behind them, two of them waving *chauris.* Above these again on each side of the shaft are three pairs of figures floating in the air; and just under the abacus of the capital a rider on a mythical steed. The shaft is divided by five broad bands into short sections, each of which is wrought in a different pattern complicated fret engraving. Three of the bands consist each of a thick torus richly carved, between two astragals carved with beads. The second band is carved with three dwarfs supporting a fillet, and the fourth with three half-mythic animals. Over the fifth also stand three fat dwarfs supporting the capital, the principal member of which is a thick torus strongly ribbed, and over it an abacus of three fillets, each of them minutely carved. On the abacus sit two lions, and between them a short rounded knob to hold the edge of the wheel or *chakra*, the favourite emblem of the Bauddha doctrine, derived perhaps from the endless circle of transmigration from which Buddha undertook to set men free; but

---

[1] Compare the Sanskrit *piṇḍikâ*, "a plinth."—E. H. But probably the word means rather a jamb or upright slab.—J. B.

the *chakra* was also the symbol of a Chakravartin or Universal Monarch, to whom the Buddhist writers are ever and anon comparing their great teacher, and this may have led to, or influenced the introduction of the symbol as that of the Buddha who turns the *Dharma-chakra* or wheel of doctrine, and conquers, as they represent, every world by his teaching, of which it is the emblem. This "thousand-rayed" wheel is always one of the principal marks on the soles of Buddha's feet.[1] Round its edge are fifteen *triśulas*, alternating with broad flat teeth, and at each corner is a flying sprite or *devata*.

In fig. 4 is represented the upper part of a much smaller *chakra* pillar. Unfortunately the lower half is destroyed, and what is left measures only 1 foot 10 inches by 7 inches.[2] A similar slab, but entire, was excavated by Sir Walter Elliot, and is now in the British Museum.[3] It is hard to say where these small pillars were arranged, unless it were on the stûpa itself.

The top of this inner rail was crowned with a zoophorus or frieze about 15 inches deep, elaborately carved in a high style of art. Only a few fragments of it have been preserved. Those in the British Museum are represented in *Tree and Serpent Worship*, Pl. lxxxiii, and four drawings by Mackenzie on Plates lxxxiii and lxxxiv. Two larger fragments and two smaller were discovered during the last excavations. The two larger are about 4½ feet long each, and contain about ninety figures; and if this be taken as an average for the whole frieze, it must have contained about 5000 figures of men, *dêvas*, and horses, forming a panorama of Bauddha legend, and perhaps of local customs and tradition. Of all this only the few fragmentary scraps just mentioned are left us.

The first of these slabs (Pl. xli, fig. 1) I discovered on the south-west of the circle, and some days later the fragment broken off the left end of it.[4] It is 4′ 6″ long and 15½″ in height, and about 4″ thick, having been carved on the back of a portion of an early dâgaba slab (Pl. xl, fig. 3). The lower margin is a sunk band about 2½ inches high, with projecting heads of those nondescript sphinx-like animals that recur so often here, placed at intervals of 4 inches. These support the zoophorus, which is 11 inches deep inside the fillets, and on this slab is divided into four compartments, which, as in other instances here, seem to read from right to left. The first, 5½ inches wide, is probably only a terminal representing a man and woman who possibly act as guards or the watch outside the royal apartments. In a sculpture of the following scene from Jamâlgarhi in the Yusufzai or ancient Gândhâra country, represented in the accompanying woodcut (No. 21), we have also similar guards repeated on each side of the apartment.

The next compartment pictures the prince Siddhartha sitting in meditation among the sleeping women of his harîm, who are lying about in all attitudes as described in the legend. Behind him is an aged female whose face is admirably delineated, and is perhaps intended for Mahâprajâpatî, his foster-mother. It is difficult to say whether the two on the left are Dêvas or human beings. In the Gândhâra sculpture, now in the Lahor Museum, as will be observed in the woodcut,[5] Gautama sits on the couch of Yaśodharâ, who is asleep, as are

---

[1] Alabaster, *Wheel of the Law*, p. 286.

[2] This and the preceding were among the slabs excavated by Mr. R. Sewell in 1877. See his *Report*, p. 51.

[3] Presented by Sir W. Elliot after the other marbles had been placed in the Museum, and not figured in *Tree and Serpent Worship*.

[4] Nos. 23B and 24B in *Notes on the Amarâvatî Stûpa*.

[5] Engraved from a photograph lent by the late James Fergusson, C.I.E., D.C.L., LL.D., and published in E. Arnold's *Light of Asia*.

also two musicians resting on their drums in front of the bed, while two behind, perhaps Devas, watch the sleeping wife.

21. Sculpture of Siddhartha about to leave his home, from Jamâlgarhi.

The next scene is the departure of Gautama from the Vyâla gate on the horse Kaṇṭhaka, attended by all the supernal hosts, and Chhandaka with his loins girt up running in front. It is to be regretted that the faces of so many of the figures here have been destroyed. In another Amarâvatî sculpture of this same scene (No. 22), on the central panel of an outer rail pillar,[1] now in the British Museum, and which may be here introduced to fill up the picture, the prince is depicted as mounted and on his journey. There as here he is surrounded by Sakra and the hosts of the heavens, while Patrapada and the Yakshas bear up the feet of his horse lest their sound should awake any of his family and so prevent his escape.

22. Siddhartha leaving Kapilavastu.

Among the Gândhâra Buddhist sculptures also we find the same scene represented in a very different way, as shown in the woodcut No. 23, and if hardly so realistically at least

[1] *Tree and Serp. Wor.*, pl. lix, fig. 1; also in *Light of Asia*, p. 88.

more naturally. The Yakshas are absent, but the chhatra is held over Gautama's head by a Dêva, and the Guhyaka bears the torch [1] in front to show the way. The housing of the horse in both sculptures is the same.

23. Siddhartha leaving home, from a Gândhâra sculpture.[2]

The fourth scene represents the Buddha enthroned and worshipped, with the rather unusual adjunct of a horse among his hearers. As is commonly the case here, while it is so rare at Ajaṇṭâ, his right hand is raised, but the left foot is down and rests on a small footstool: this is the position known as the *Lalita-mûdra*.

The second of these slabs was found to the west of the north gate, and though a piece is broken off from the right end, the rest is in good preservation (Pl. xlii, fig. 4).[3] It is 16½ inches high and about 4 feet 8 inches in length. On the lowest member is an inscription, considerably injured, but in an alphabet of the time of Śrî Puḷumâvi, or very soon afterwards. On the sunk band are the usual animal busts, and the tænia above is carved with men and animals—lion, elephant, bull, deer, &c.

The right-hand scene has been mostly destroyed, but from the attitudes and excitement among the figures left of it we may suppose it was another representation of the translation of the *pâtra* or begging-dish.[4] One of the *dêvas* has over his shoulders what may perhaps be a snake. The division between the scenes on this slab is made by three knobs or rivet-heads, neatly carved, and the middle one in each case carved with small figures.

The second scene is Buddha seated with a worshipper behind each shoulder and a Nâga râja and his Nâgini rising out of the ground and worshipping him. Three more nail-heads separate this from the next scene, the middle one carved with very small figures.

The third scene presents a man and his wife seated, with two female attendants behind the lady and five in front, four seated, playing on musical instruments, and one rising with a sheathed sword over her shoulder. Six men are on his right, one with his waist tied up seizes the chief figure and pulls him by a cloth or cord round his waist; other three similarly girt, two of them with spears, appear behind, one of them just entering by a gateway. In front are two men, one resting his right hand on the hilt of a sheathed sword, and lifting the left as if speaking: the other with a spear, and what may perhaps be a shield at his foot. Three nail-heads as before divide this from the next, in which are only two tall figures, sculptured with no mean art, the man with a loose cloth round his loins and hanging over his left arm, and a long spear in his left hand, addressing the woman, who holds a small drinking vessel in her right hand. She too is dressed in a loose cloth, but appears to have drawers below it, and at her feet stands a vase or vessel. Then again is the division of three knobs or nail-heads.

---

[1] Foucaux's *Lalita Vistara*, p. 193.

[2] From *The Light of Asia*, p. 86.

[3] Excavated by Mr. R. Sewell in 1877; see his *Report*, p. 48, No. 52.

[4] *Ante*, p. 46.

The last scene to the right represents apparently the same chief as in the third. He holds up the cord with which it had been attempted to drag him in his hands, and appears to speak to the tall man to the left. His wife sits facing him, with her two attendants beyond. In front a woman seated presents some conical object to him on a round tray; the woman, with a sword now hung at her left thigh, kneels before a lady seated at the chief's right, resting her cheek on her hand, and with an attendant seated at her left. Another woman seated above respectfully addresses the chief, and a tall man with a high turban and attended by a dwarf is retiring on the left, while a short female addresses or clings to him, and behind is an onlooker.

The inscription (No. 28, Pl. lviii) reads—

. . . . . [savasa] tutamasa Naravasabhasaṁmasaṁbhudâdichasa ‖ Upâsakasa Nârasalasa vâniyasa Nâgatisasa gharaṇiya Nâkhâya sahâ apano putehi heraṇikena Budhinâ Mûlena . . . .

"[*Adoration*] to the sun, the truly enlightened one, the chief of men, the best (*of all beings*)! *The gift* of Nâkhâ, the wife of the lay worshipper, the Nârasala, the merchant Nâgatisa (Nâgatishya) with her own sons, the goldsmith Budhi, Mûla . . . ."

The other two pieces of this frieze are fragments 24 and 22 inches in length, but they show the same remarkably careful and minute style of sculpture. The one (Pl. xlii, fig. 6) represents Buddha standing under a tree with some disciples to the right, and one figure rushing forward towards him. Over their heads, from three openings, are five figures looking out. In front of Buddha to the left two women are dancing, their hair apparently flying in a cloud behind their heads; one sits between them, another kneels at his feet, and others are behind, with perhaps two male figures.

The other fragment (fig. 5) has a guard[1] in the right end compartment, divided off from the next by a pillar. To the right Buddha stands with uplifted hand teaching, two women kneel before him, and a man and perhaps another woman stand behind. To the right a woman is pushing a boy up towards Buddha; another woman behind her stands with another boy; and beyond them are four more women paying respect to the sage. If in the legends Buddha is represented as disparaging women,[2] they are certainly represented in these sculptures as among his most ardent votaries.

Near the west gate was found a large fragment (Pl. xlii, fig. 7), apparently split off from an octagonal pillar, perhaps one of those that stood inside the entrances; but it is possible it may only have been a portion of a pilaster. At the bottom are three standing figures of Buddha, with *nimbi*, and the right hands uplifted. On a band 7 inches broad between them and the next row of similar figures is carved in early characters the inscription (No. 18, Pl. lvii)—

Aya-Retiyâ atevâsiniya aya-Dhamâya dânaṁ.

"The gift of the worthy Dhamâ, the female disciple of the worthy Rêtî (Rêvatî)."

Above this, to the right, in more modern characters, is scratched the syllables—

Sri viprajâtapriyaṁ.

It would be difficult to say from what part of the building the fragment given in Plate xlii, fig. 8, has come. Nothing else of the kind has been found at Amarâvatî. It is much

---

[1] Similar figures appear in the representation in woodcut No. 21, p. 80.

[2] *Mâtu gâmo nâmo pâpo*, 'that which is named woman is sin.'

more like the style of the façades of the earliest Cave Temples, at Pitalkhorâ, Bhâjâ, the Chaitya at Nâsik, and Cave IX at Ajaṇṭâ, than anything of later date; and it may have formed part of some very early structure here. The few characters upon it are of an early type.

On the line of the inner rail or near it was found, but probably not *in situ* (Pl. xlix, fig. 3), the lower portion[1] of a large slab representing four women in the scanty costume of Eastern India in that early time, worshipping the footprints of Buddha, which are placed on an ornamental stool (*padâsana*) or *pâdapîṭha* in front of a throne or seat. Probably the tree rose behind it. These worshippers are not Nâgas; but the frequent combination of the throne and tree in these sculptures is connected with the legend given in the *Samantakûṭa-warnnanâwa*, that in the fifth year of the Buddhahood there arose a dispute in Nâgadvîpa between two Nâga kings, Chûlôdana and Mahôdana, about the gem throne, and which led to a war. Buddha resolved to go and reconcile them, and the Dêva Samidhi-sumana[2] taking up a *kiripala* or fig tree that grew near the door, held it over his head as a canopy whilst he passed through the air. On seeing him, each of them, attended by a female, brought offerings to Buddha, and he sat on the gem throne and taught them. "For the increase of their merit, he appointed as objects of worship the throne upon which he sat, and the tree that had been brought through the air by the Dêva."[3] This would seem to help us to understand the combination of these symbols so frequently here. The *S'rîpâdas* or sacred footprints[4] are each marked with a lotus or a wheel.

---

[1] No. 53 in *Notes on Amarâvatî Stûpa*, p. 17.

[2] *Samṛiddhi-sumana* = 'happy success.'

[3] Sp. Hardy, *Man. Budh.*, p. 214.

[4] *Pada-chihṇa* or *Pâdachihṇa*, 'footmark;' also *Padasthâna*, *Padâṅka*, *Pâdamudrâ*.

24. Frieze from a Gândhâra Sculpture.

CHAPTER IX.

SMALL FRIEZE AND OLD SCULPTURES.

We now come to a class of stones from 8½ to 11½ inches in height, whose place in the structure is not very easily determined; indeed they appear to belong to two or three different periods, and may have belonged to different parts of the central building. All have been friezes of some sort, and the deepest (11½ inches) is carved in very low relief and in a very early style (Pl. xliii, fig. 12). It is 2 feet 6 inches long, and has at the bottom a quadrantal moulding, above which is a sunk plain fascia, where on the inner frieze are the Harpy figures, with four upright oblong holes in it, as if for attaching some objects to it. Over this is a narrow curved moulding which has been carved with animals after the style of the Nâsik friezes, and one of the inner rail, already described. Above this the face, 6½ inches deep, is ornamented with one grooved rail pillar at the left end, and towards the right three, with two cross-bars between each pair, leaving a panel 14 inches wide in which five Dêvas are dancing with the begging-dish, as on the disc already described. The rail pillars are represented with half-discs above and below, connected by three flutes. The upper cross-bar of the one pair is carved with a figure beating a drum, the lower one of the other pair bears an elephant, and the remaining two bear rosettes. On the extreme right is a tree. Two holes through the stone show that it has been attached by iron rods to the building.

Another piece (Pl. xliii, fig. 1), 2 feet 8 inches by 8½ high and 6½ inches thick, has been built in with lime. It is covered with figures, among which are three at about equal distances seated, and forming the centre of groups; and at the right-hand end of the slab is a Dâgaba with a cloth knotted crosswise over the dome, and which has had flower-like *chhatras*. To the left the first seated figure, with a high footstool, is some prince with a high turban, *chauri*-bearers stand behind, a Nâga râja and his wife sit respectfully to his right; other two men are on his right, and spectators stand behind while he seems speaking. The second has one foot drawn up on the seat, and is surrounded by men and dêvas; one kneels at his right as if supplicating him. The surroundings of the third figure are more broken, but it seems to represent Buddha seated, and, as almost always in the Amarâvatî representations, with his right hand upraised.

Another slab (fig. 2), 3 feet 6 inches long by 8½ high and 6 inches thick, is carved in similar style. There is a plain Dâgaba at the left end of it, with a tree on each side but no umbrella, and the remainder is divided into three panels. In the first a scene is represented in a forest, indicated by trees in the background. An ox-cart has arrived from the right, and in front of it a man is apparently meeting another and welcoming him; behind the first is a female, while nearer the Dâgaba is a man and woman, each bearing a child on their shoulders. In the centre panel is a man lounging on a seat, whom two others from the right approach with salutations, and other five look on.

In the third or right-hand panel, an elephant, whose head and forelegs only appear, is entering from the right; two men in front of it, with a dwarf carrying something on his head, are meeting five others, clad apparently as Śramaṇas or Buddhist devotees.

The other slabs of this class are mostly carved with figures of Buddha seated alternately with Dâgabas, sometimes separated by partitions or pilasters, and at others not. The Buddha is always represented as holding up the right hand, and with the left he holds part of the cloth coming over his left shoulder.

Several of these have inscriptions, all donative, and only partially legible; thus we read on one (Pl. lvii, No. 22)—

Sidhaṁ | Namo Bhagavato Savasatutamasa Budhasa Maṁdaravathavasa pavaïtosiuṁ tasa bhaginiya . . . . . .

"Hail! Adoration to the holy Buddha, the best of all beings, [the gift of . . . .] sister of the ascetic Isiuṁta [Ṛishigupta] residing at Mandara."

On another (Pl. lvii, No. 23) is—

. . . [ante]vasikâsa Maheṁkhânâjakâsa bhâyaṁtâ-Nâdhasirisa si[so]bhâyaṁtâ Bu . . . .

". . . the venerable Bu . . . [the disciple] of the venerable Nâdhasiri (Nâthaśrî) the Maheṁkhânâjakâ, [the disciples of] . . . . ."

On a third, shown in fig. 3 of Plate xliii, across the bases of the dâgabas is a scarcely legible inscription (Pl. lviii, No. 29) beginning with—

. . . . . vâniyiniya Nâkachâpakâya, &c.

". . of the merchant's wife Nâkachâpakâ," &c.

On a fourth (Pl. xliii, fig. 8) we read (No. 30)—

Sidhaṁ—Namo Bhagavato—Vijaya[pu]ravathavasa Chhada[sa bâlikâya]—vaṇiyiṇiya—Sidhiya—[uni]sa patiṭhavitaṁ.

"Success! Reverence to the Exalted one! A plinth was set up by the merchant's wife Sidhi [*the daughter*] of Chhada (Chhanda) residing in Vijayapura."

On a fifth (fig. 9), in rounded letters of quite unusual type (Pl. lviii, No. 31), is the inscription—

Sidhaṁ hayaḍaya kaṁdaḍaya saṁghaḍaya . . . . . [i]ma u(ṁ)nisa [1] pat[i]ṭhavit[a] ti.

"Success! This coping-stone was erected . . . . . ."

On a sixth we read—

Bhavâta—Dhaṁmasiriayâ—Pasamayâ—Ha[gi]s[i]riṁ—Chapâṁ Ravisiriuvasakaṁ—ima patiṭhavi[ta].

"Erected by reverend Dhaṁmasiriâ (Dharmaśrîkâ) *and* Pasamâ (Praśamâ) [*with*] Ha[gi]siri (Agniśrî), Chapâ (Champâ), [*and*] the laic Ravisiri (Raviśrî)."

Plates XLIV, XLV.

None of the pillars which must have stood at the gates have been left; fragments, however, of some of them have been found. One (Pl. xliv, fig. 2) that I dug up at the east gate, 9½ feet in length, had been sunk 4 feet below the pavement. It had been split vertically, and the fragment was 20 inches broad by about a foot. The lower portion of the

[1] Possibly the *ṁ* is only an injury in the stone.

shaft, about 2 feet 9 inches in height, had been squared, and on the face of this was carved in low relief a dâgaba with a five-hooded snake on the front between two pilasters of early pattern. The drum had a moulded base and cornice, the latter carved with a simple rail pattern: the dome is quite plain, the capital has a double coffer, and is crowned by an abacus of four slabs. Over this are twenty-one small umbrella-like flowers. The shaft above this changes to an octagon, the corners of the square being rounded off. Just where this is fractured has been a Pâli inscription (No. 32), very clearly cut, of which we can read the syllables—

Adhah[a] bh[a] . . . .
tukasâ dâna ma . . . .
pasanikamâtulena d . . . .

The characters are of the same age as in the inscription on the fragment of a smaller pillar (Pl. lix, No. 38) found at the south gate.

Below the level of the pavement, along with many other stones, was found a large piece of a *chakra* pillar of more than usual size, 9 feet 10 inches long, of which about 6 feet was above ground, and this does not reach to the capital (Plate xliv, fig. 1).

It is 17 inches broad, and a good deal injured, but of the usual style. The throne, with the Śrîpâda on the footstool, is worshipped by two figures with high turbans, one above the other; on each side and above them are the *chauri*-bearers. The first section of the shaft consists of the foreparts of three elephants, each bearing a râja, with his hands joined in reverence. Above are curious animal busts, five in each of two groups, and still higher three dwarfs. Along the edges are figures mounted on lions and other steeds, and a fat grinning figure above each—in some cases with a club.

Near the south gate[1] was found, buried below the pavement level, the portion of a pillar given in fig. 3; it is much injured, but has borne an inscription in six or more lines in very early characters. Fragments of smaller pillars are given in figs 6 and 7.

Near the east gate was found a short octagonal pillar (Pl. xliv, fig. 4); the base is about a foot high and 18 inches diameter, carved with plain rail pattern. Above this is a short tapering shaft, crowned by a flat top, about 4 inches thick and 20 inches in diameter. Apparently it has formed at one time a large carved block, for on the part sunk under the level of the pavement there are several portions of sculpture representing both human and animal figures.

At the south gate, however, was found the finest fragment of a pillar recovered (Pl. xlv, figs. 1–4). It measures 13½ inches by 11, and about 4 feet 3 inches in length, and is carved on all four sides in low relief, with four of the principal emblems of Buddhism. The front has the Dâgaba, 23 inches high, inclusive of the *chhatras*, with a carved base, a very simple rail-pattern frieze, some festoons and medallions round the top of the dome, and the usual cloud of umbrella-like flowers over the capital. Above this is a half-disc over which the corners were chamfered off the pillar and it becomes octagonal. Below the chaitya, in clearly cut letters, is the inscription (Pl. lx, No. 47)—

Sidham Vâniyasa Kuṭasa sa
bheriyasa saputakasa saduhu-
tukasa sanatukasa dakhinâyâ-
ka chetiyakhabho sadhâduko dânaṁ.

"Prosperity! A chaitya pillar with a relic, at the south entrance—the gift of the Vania (dealer) Kuṭa with his wife, with his sons, with his daughters, with his grandsons."

[1] In front of Nos. 10, 11, on Plate iv.

The right side has a pippal tree 16 inches high, with the low *âsana* or seat at the foot of it, on which lies a round cushion, and the *Buddhapâda* in front. The tree is carved in a very conventional and archaic style.

The third side is carved with a relic chaitya, or small circular temple or pavilion supported on pillars. The frieze is ornamented with the chaitya window, and the dome above it with the same. The base is surrounded by a small parapet of rail pattern, and inside on a square pedestal is represented the relic-casket, crowned by a small umbrella, which is attached to some canopy above.

The fourth side has the *Chakra* or sacred wheel on a low pillar behind an *âsana*, against the back of which is a round cushion marked with a curvilinear *svastika*. The Buddhapâda are below as usual. Lotus flowers spring by the sides of the pillar, and over the Dharma-chakra is a *chhatra* or umbrella with streamers, &c.

Near the west gate was found an octagonal block, 15¼ inches in diameter, with a 'chaitya-window' ornament on four sides and a female bust in each (Pl. xliv, fig. 5). This must have been the finial of one of the pillars that, from the representations on the Dâgaba slabs, we believe must have stood near the gates.

Among the smaller stones are some blocks carved with figures of capering dwarfs (Pl. xlv, fig. 5). It is not easy to assign the place of these in the structure; indeed it is probable that they were employed in more than one position. One is carved in a panel, and has been built into some wall or facing; another is larger, and on a thick block which may perhaps have formed a support to some vase or other object near one of the gates.

Plate xlv, fig. 6, represents a stone found near the west gate, along with three others similar to it, three of them being 14 inches in diameter, each carved with a thick torus between two fillets, and with holes in one side as if to secure them on the pillars, of which they probably formed part of the caps. The fourth one, shown in the accompanying illustration (No. 25), is 16 inches in diameter and 10 inches thick, and is carefully carved, as if for a base, with a square hole right through it.

25. Base of a Pillar.

Under another stone was found a flat thin slab, 25 inches in diameter, with a raised ledge 2 inches broad (Pl. xlv, fig. 7), on which is an inscription. In the centre is a hole about 2¼ inches square in a raised circle 9½ inches diameter, carved with leaves. The interval between this and the ledge is scored with rays as in the *chakras*. This has been a *chhatra* or umbrella, perhaps over some small stûpa. The inscription is perfectly distinct (Pl. lx, No. 45), and reads—

Uvâsikâya Chadaya Budhiṇo mâtaya saputikâya saduhikâya aïrânaṁ Utayipabhâhînaṁ chediyasa chhata deyadhamaṁ.

"A parasol (*chhatra*), the meritorious gift of the laic Chadâ (Chandrâ), the mother of Budhi, together with her sons, together with her daughters of the venerable Utayipabhâhis[1] (?) and to the chaitya."

Of the lions that stood on the gate-posts, one, very much injured, and one foot perhaps

[1] May this not be synonymous with Uttaraparvatas, or Uttaraśelas?

of the same, with the forefeet of a couchant one, were found near the west gate (Pl. xlv, figs. 8, 9).

A small fragment, perhaps part of an early pilaster, carved in a very archaic style, is given in Plate xiv, fig. 6. It contains a *chaitya*, with a *bodhi* tree growing out of the capital, ornamented by three similar *chaityas* carved on the drum.

One stone, or rather fragment (Pl. liv, fig. 1), 22½ inches wide and about 4½ feet high, is carved on one side similarly to the outer rail pillars, and on the other it has had a fat dwarf at the bottom, similar to those on the basement of Cave III at Nasik, with five round discs on his hair, holding up one of the flower vases out of which flowers grow, and one large tendril forms a sort of oval compartment above, in which are two wingless gryphons. Above was the throne and perhaps the *chakra* with worshippers.

26. Roll Ornament from Gândhâra.

CHAPTER X.

SLABS, &c., FROM THE CENTRAL STUPA.

WE come next to a series of broad slabs, which we naturally conclude formed part of the casing of the central Dâgaba or Stûpa itself. They are found scattered about in broken fragments everywhere, and are generally about 2 feet 10 inches broad, with a division or pilaster up one side and divided into two panels, containing the usual Bauddha sacred objects, the Buddha in different scenes, the dâgaba, the chakra, and the sacred tree. Few of them, however, are entire.

From the varying heights of different slabs, it would seem that the casing to which they belonged was about 10½ feet high, and consisted generally of two slabs set one over the other. The lower usually contained two panels, and the upper a third, with a broad frieze carved with a line of animals and over them a crown of double *triśulas*. But in some cases at least, the frieze was formed of a separate piece, and the slab below contained three panels, as in the example in the woodcut (No. 27), and in two other very similar slabs, each about 8 feet high, in the British Museum.[1] All three show the same three objects of Buddhist worship at once, and in other slabs we have the two lower together, and the upper one and frieze on a separate stone,—the *dâgaba*, however, is not usually represented as it is here, with the rail round it. The five-hooded snake or Nâga appears in front of the *dâgaba*, either as an object of reverence or perhaps as the guardian of Buddhism. In the central compartment is the *Dharmachakra* or sacred wheel, the second member of the Bauddha Triad; and below that is the *Bodhidruma* or tree, possibly representative of the *Saṅgha* or Congregation, but also the venerated symbol of Buddha's triumph over Mâra and his evil host.[2]

27. Slab from the Stûpa.

At the foot of the tree stands the empty throne of the vanquisher, on which is placed what Mr. Fergusson has supposed to be a relic, but which may only be a cushion;[3] while on the

---

1 The woodcut is from Fergusson's ***Ind. and East. Architecture***, p. 101, and was first published in the *Jour. R. As. Soc.*, N.S., vol. iii, p. 160. It appears in ***Tree and Serpent Worship***, plate lxxv, as the middle slab in a reconstructed section of the inner rail; but there can be no doubt this was an oversight, as the two slabs referred to above, which appear in plates xciii and xciv, fig. 3, of the same work, are repetitions of the same sculptures and belong to the class we are now describing.

2 The war between Buddha and the angels of Vasavattimâra is called the ***Mârayuddha***, and Buddha as conqueror is called Mârajit and Mârâbhibhu.

3 We have a representation of a relic casket set upon a throne and worshipped in ***Tree and Serpent Worship***, pl. lxii, fig. 1.

footstool are the *Srîpâda* or footprints of the Teacher. All three objects have their attendant worshippers.

"This combination," as Mr. Fergusson has justly remarked, "is repeated again and again in these sculptures, and may be almost designated as the Shorter Buddhist Catechism, or rather the Confession of Faith, Buddha, Dharma, Saṅgha."[1]

PLATES XLVI–XLVIII.

An entire slab (Pl. xlvi, fig. 1), measuring 3 feet 2 inches broad by 5 feet 7 inches high, represents Buddha seated in the lower panel with his feet drawn up, and, curiously enough, the Śrîpâda on a footstool below. Behind the nimbus round his head is the foliage of the pippal tree. On each side are seated two male worshippers, princes or gods worshipping him, and above are two genii bringing offerings. Buddha's right hand is raised—the prevailing *mudrâ* here—and his left lies in his lap, with a corner of the robe over the wrist. The prevalence of this attitude at Amarâvatî and of the *dharmachakra* mudrâ at Ajaṇṭâ must have some connection with the difference of the schools located at the two places.

Under this panel is the inscription (Pl. lxi, No. 53)—

Sidhaṁ | Namo Bhagapato Logâtichasa Dhaṁñakaṭakâsa upâsakasa
Goṁḍiputasa Budharakhitasa gharaniyâ cha Padumâya pusa[2] cha Haṁghasa Budhi-
. . . . . . Bodhi . . . Budharakhitasa savaka(sa) . . . (u)dhapaṭâ (vasa)

"Success! Adoration to the blessed one, the Sun of the world. *Ûrdhvapaṭṭas*[3] (*the gift*) of the lay worshipper Budharakhita of Dhaṁñakaṭaka, the son of Goṁḍî and of his wife Padumâ (Padmâ) and of (*their*) son Haṁgha . . . . of the pious disciple Budharakhita. . . ."[4]

This inscription contains the name of Dhaṁñakaṭaka, or Dhanyakaṭaka, the old name of Dharaṇikôṭṭa,[5] and which in the seventh century gave name to the kingdom otherwise known as Mahâ-Andhra.

The upper panel represents the worship of the Dharmachakra behind the throne with the footprints below, by two persons of note on each side and by two Dêvas above.

Another broken slab (Pl. xlvi, fig. 2), of which the lower panel is nearly entire, represents Buddha seated under a tree on what may be intended as a stone seat, with his hand raised as if forbidding some one or refusing some proposal. Two Dêvas above bring offerings, but an imp at his right hand brandishes a sword at him, and the female on his left is in no attitude of worship. This is probably a 'brief account' in sculpture of the temptation.

In the upper panel we have the throne with a deer on each side, the cognizance of Śâkyamuni, and a worshipper. Probably the *Dharmachakra* was represented above, but it is broken off.

A faint and much-worn inscription is cut on the middle bar, of which the following is the reading as far as can be made out (Pl. lx, No. 50)—

Sidhaṁ Kutaparavane vathavaya pavajitikaya Sagharakhitâya bâ(li)kaya ja
pavajitikâya Hi(ḷa)ya kumârikâya ja (Se)vaya dâ(na) deyadhaṁ(mâ) upaṭâ.[6]

"Success! Ûrdhvapaṭṭas meritorious gifts of the female ascetic Sagharakhitâ, residing

---

[1] *Ind. and East. Arch.*, p. 102. [2] Read *putasa*. [3] Upright slabs.
[4] Translated by Dr. E. Hultzsch, *Zeitsch. der Deut. Morg. Gesellsch.*, Bd. xxxvii, S. 557.
[5] *Ind. Ant.*, vol. xi, p. 97. [6] Read *udhapaṭâ*.

in Kutaparavana,[1] and of (*her*) daughter, the female ascetic Hi(lâ ?) and of (her) daughter (Se)vâ."[2]

Another lower fragment (Pl. xlvi, fig. 3) shows the worship of the Dâgaba by two men, with two dêvatas above. And still another (fig. 4) shows the worship of the tree by two couples, who are each bringing offerings in *lôtas* or jars, and the man in one case is pouring out the contents of his vessel behind the throne, which always stands in front of the stem of the tree. Two flower garlands hang from the foliage, and two Vidyâdharas or other dêvatâs are bringing offerings to it. From what is left of the upper panel in this case we learn that it was the Chakra worshipped by a standing and seated figure on each side.

Still another (Pl. xlvii, fig. 3) shows the tree and throne; a man on each side holds a long rod, that on the right having two small parasols upon it; the other perhaps bore a small pennant, now hardly traceable. Behind each is a woman, and above are the usual pair of flying genii. On the upper panel has been the Chakra again.

On the lower bar of this slab are two lines of inscription (Pl. lviii, No. 35), which reads—

Sidhaṁ Saṁyutakabhatukânaṁ Pusa(kavanava)sâna mahath(e)rânaṁ Paravanutânaṁ charanagata at(e)vâsikasa peṁḍapâtikasa Mahavanasalavathavasa Pasamasa Haṁghasa cha deyadhaṁma ima udhapa(ṭo).

"Success! This *Ûrdhvapaṭṭa* is the meritorious gift of the mendicant monk[3] Pasama (Praśama), residing in the Mahâvanaśâlâ, the devoted disciple of the great Sthavira . . . . . . who dwells in Pusa[kavana] (the Pushyaka-wood), the brother of Saṁyutaka, and (*the gift*) of Haṁgha (Saṁgha)."

The division across this slab was ornamented with animal figures—horse, lion, &c., and through it passed three iron rods, probably to attach it to the wall or building against which it was placed.

Numerous fragments of slabs have been found which have been carved with representations of vases richly ornamented, from the mouths of which spring water-lilies. One of these (Pl. xlvii, fig. 1), pretty entire, is 4 feet 7 inches high and 2 feet 10 inches broad; and another (fig. 2) measures 4 feet 2 inches by 3 feet. Each has a divisional margin up the left side.

The second has an inscription along the lower margin (Pl. lviii, No. 36), which reads—

Sidhaṁ | Chaṁmakârasa Nâgagharu[tapa]putasa Vidhikasa samatukasa sabhayakasa sabhatukasa putasa cha Nagasa sama(dhu)tukasa[4] sanâtimitabaṁdhavasa deyadhaṁma
punaghaḍakapaṭo.

"Success! A tablet with a filled vase, the meritorious gift of the leather-worker (?)[5] Vidhika, the son of Nâgagharu(tapa), with his mother, with his wife, with his brothers, and of his son Nâga, with his daughters, with his relatives, friends, and connections."

---

[1] For *Kuta°*, however, we might read *Deva°* or *Jêta°*.

[2] Dr. Hultzsch in *Zeitsch. d. Deut. Morg. Gesel.*, Bd. xxxvii, S. 557.

[3] The *Piṇḍapâtika* or *Peṇḍapâtika* is a priest who must obtain his food by going personally to the houses of the faithful and having it placed in his bowl. See Burnouf, *Introd.* (2d ed.), pp. 273–74; Spence Hardy, *E. Monach.*, p. 97; Remusat, *Foe-koue-ki* (Laidlay's ed.), p. 59.

[4] The *dhu* has been omitted, and then inserted below the line.

[5] Childers remarks that the word *Chammakâro* appears to mean a blacksmith or carpenter.

The *puṇṇaghaṭa*, we learn from the *Mahâwanso*, was a favourite symbol of good luck. When Duthagamini was about to lay out the dimensions of the great Ruanwelli Dâgaba (cir. B.C. 160), a *puṇṇaghaṭo* or 'filled chalice' was deposited in the centre with all honours. In the relic-casket he placed a *bodhi*-tree of gold, and at the foot of it were arranged "rows of vases, filled (*puṇṇâ-puṇṇaghaṭa*) with the various flowers represented in jewellery, and with the four kinds of perfumed waters." And among the sculptured decorations we read of "the four great kings, thirty *dêvas* and thirty-two princes, twenty-eight chiefs of *yakshas;* above these again *dêvas* bowing down with clasped hands raised over their heads; still higher (others bearing) vases of flowers (*pupphapuṇṇaghaṭâ*), dancing dêvas and chanting dêvas,"[1] &c.

Another slab (Pl. xlviii, fig. 2) is a fragment of one of these, forming part of the lower panel. It represents Buddha in an ample robe with his left hand in his lap and the right uplifted teaching the Nâgas; on his left one Nâga-râja and his queen are worshipping him, and the same was on the other side but is mostly broken off. Above is a Gandharva or other dêvatâ flying with an offering. At the right edge is a border with three flutes and rosettes 11 inches apart.

Another of the slabs first described (Pl. xlviii, fig. 1), fractured at the top, has the *Chakra* and worshippers in the upper panel, and the tree, with two male worshippers on each side bringing vases as offerings, or perhaps containing perfumed water to be offered. Below is an inscription in two lines, but not very clear.

Other slabs (Pll. xlvii, 3, and xlviii, 2) are surmounted by a band of *triśulas*, which are perforated in the centres for iron bolts, that passed through them and secured them to the building. The lower half is occupied by a representation of the *dâgaba* and worshippers, and over this is a belt carved with animals, all galloping to the left. From the irregular way these slabs terminate below, the side division at one edge of the lower panel, and the way in which the slabs previously described break off at the top, it seems pretty certain that those now under notice formed the upper portions of the others, and it confirms this that three slabs in the British Museum, as already noticed, contain three panels—the tree, the *chakra*, and the *dâgaba*, and measure fully 7½ feet; and if on this be placed the height of the *triśulas* and bands over the *dâgaba* the whole is about 10½ feet; so also one of the *dâgaba* and triśula slabs placed over the two-panelled slabs first described gives a height of about 10 feet 4 inches. And as these belonged to the stûpa itself, they may have ornamented either the basement or the first and perpendicular portion just above the base: to the one or other they must be assigned. They are no way remarkable in sculpture, but a good deal weatherworn, and have been found in the débris surrounding the outer rail, often lying flat, as if they had at some time been in process of removal for building purposes or to be burnt to lime.

Broken fragments of these slabs are numerous.

Among the sculptures of this class in the British Museum is a fragment of one that has evidently been cut down, for it is now only twenty inches wide; but it probably formed the lower panel of one of these slabs, and is represented in the accompanying woodcut (No. 28). As is the case in many other examples, the Dâgaba is divided into compartments by pilasters with two lions on the capitals, which are of a curious Persepolitan type, but altogether of considerable elegance, and found also in the early caves at Pitalkhorâ, and in other sculptures here and on the casing of the Jaggayyapeṭa stûpa, in which

---

[1] *Mahaw.*, pp. 172, 180, 182.

too the shafts are of the same form, and, like the pillars of the outer rail, have one central circular disc, and two half circles at top and bottom. Between them, as if in the place of honour, is placed the five-headed cobra or Nâga, on the right the sacred wheel, and on the left the tree. The peculiar arrangement of numerous umbrellas over the capital is also met with in Cave III, or that containing the inscription of Sâtakarṇi Gautamîputra, at Nâsik; and in later examples here these appendages appear in great clusters like thick foliage. As representing a relic shrine, of which the great stûpa itself was an example, these sculptured *chaityas* or *dâgabas* were probably objects of veneration, and with the *chakra* and the Sacred Tree were distinctly Bauddha symbols; while the snake may represent the aboriginal cult with which Buddhism allied itself in the Andhra country, as it did with other forms of demonology in Ceylon and Nepâl.

28. Representation of a Dâgaba with emblems.[1]

A few stones, mostly broken, were found chiefly on the east side of the stûpa, characterised by an archaic style of sculpture, and in some instances also with inscriptions in a very early type of alphabet. These must be the oldest sculptures here. They are portions of slabs carved with pilasters and a frieze about 13 inches deep.

Of this class of sculptures two very fine examples of the frieze are given in Plate xlviii, fig. 4. The first is 3′ 10″ long by 13″ high and in very perfect condition. On the lower projecting member it has an inscription preceded by a shield and followed by a symbol resembling in outline the *bhadrâsana* or cane seat,—symbols which occur on the early Bauddha cave inscriptions of Western India and on the Hathi Gumpha inscription at Khandagiri in Orissa. The letters are small but clearly incised, and read—

Sidhaṁ. Kudûranivâsikasa bhayata-Nâgasa atavâsikasa daharabhikhusa Vidhikasa atevâsiniya cha Budharakhitâya natiya cha Chûlabudharakhitâya cha utarâyake paṭo dâna.

"Success! A tablet at the northern gate, the gift of the young monk Vidhika, the pupil of the reverend Nâga, who resides at Kudûra, and of (*his*) pupil Budharakhitâ, and of (*her*) granddaughter, and of the younger Budharakhitâ." [2]

In the recessed face above this are four square holes, the use of which we can only conjecture; and over it is a torus moulding richly ornamented with creepers. On the frieze are three compartments of sculpture, separated by representations of a rail, each consisting of three uprights with three sets of cross-bars, the central one in each case carved with a lion. The sculptures consist of the worship of the Throne with the Dharmachakra behind it; of the Chaitya by two women; and the carrying off by the four Regents of Mâyâ on the night of the conception.

The other slab, though broken, is nearly as long, with a narrower frieze and considerably worn, and the sculptures are not very intelligible.

The next example (Plate liv, fig. 2) shows a pilaster of the type of those found in the

---

[1] From Fergusson's *Tree and Serp. Wors.*, pl. xci, fig. 1, and *Ind. and East. Arch.*, p. 102, also given in *Jour. R. As. Soc.*, N.S., vol. iii, p. 158.

[2] Translated by Dr. E. Hultzsch.

Pitalkhorâ vihâra, with a *chakra* carved on the middle of the shaft, which closely resembles that on the *Śrîpâda* of the Siamese.[1] Above and below this the edges are chamfered off, and the shaft has a half-disc at each end; then a carefully carved capital with a line of beads round it, and another between it and the abacus, the uppermost of the three members of which is minutely carved. On it sit two winged lions, supporting the frieze, the lowest member of which is a quadrantal moulding, on which is the inscription (Pl. lvi, No. 5)—

Sidhaṁ Uvâsikaya Sivalâya saputikaya saduhutukâya deyadhaṁ(ma).

"Success! The meritorious gift of the laic Sivalâ, with her son, with her daughter."

A sunk fascia over this has rectangular holes in it, where the Nâsik friezes have projections to represent the ends of rafters. It may be suggested that these were filled with wooden blocks in which fastenings were inserted, on which to hang garlands. The band above this is carved with small animals, the elephant, boar, bull, winged lions, &c. The zoophorus is divided by two pilasters and their two cross-bars between each pair of compartments. In the two on this stone are the *dâgaba* and the sacred tree, each with two worshippers by the sides of them.

There is one large slab of this series 13 feet 9 inches long by 4 feet 7 inches high and 10 inches thick, on which have been three pilasters—one of which is quite destroyed (Pl. xlix, figs. 5, 6). The base consists of three thin plinths, as in the Nâsik and Junnar caves, supporting a thick lota-shaped body, carved with leaf and bead patterns. Over the lip of this stands a projecting member of about the same height, with three dwarfs carved upon it in one case, and two winged elephants in the other. From this rises the shaft, with a half-disc at each end, and a full one in the middle. Above this is the usual capital, surmounted by winged lions or horses.

A fragment (Pl. xlix, fig. 7) found near this has the base of one of these pilasters, and under it a dado carved with geese, each carrying a flower in its beak, and above and below them a fillet carved with beads.

Another fragment of this kind (Pl. li, fig. 1), more defaced, has had winged elephants on the capital. The boar, buffalo, elephant, and winged horses are carved on the central member; and in the frieze the only compartment left shows the sacred tree again.

On this is the inscription (No. 3) in Maurya characters:—

Sidha Oḍiparivenene vâsikasa dhamakathikasa Budhi. . . . .

"Success! (The gift of) Buddhi . . . . a preacher of the doctrine dwelling in Oḍiparivenena."

The upper portion of this stone, which is 3 feet 8 inches high, is only 5 or 6 inches thick, while below it is double this. Fig. 3 represents another example, but still more injured.

These slabs so closely resemble those round the Jaggayyapetta stûpa, that we cannot mistake in ascribing them to about the same age. They must have belonged to the central building, but whether to an earlier inner rail or to the facing of the central building itself is not clear, though the latter seems the more probable.

That there were additions and alterations executed on the building from time to time is most manifest. Near the last-described slab, and quite close to the east gate, in the line of the outer railing, lie large fragments of at least seven great rail pillars of brownish granite,

[1] Low in *Trans. R. As. Soc.*, vol. iii, pp. 65–124; Alabaster, *Wheel of the Law*, pp. 253–259, 286, 289–310.

which have been hewn or polished exceedingly smooth. The upper portions of all are destroyed, but they have stood much closer together than the marble pillars, and the cross-bars are very much lighter blocks of marble than those belonging to the other portions of the rails, and hewn smooth, with a lenticular section. It is difficult to say to what age these slabs belong. We have no carving or inscription to help us. Was it the first intention to surround the stûpa with such a rail—not unlike that at Sânchi—from which, however, an early departure was made, and the elaborately sculptured rail substituted? Or was it at some subsequent period of decay that these granite pillars and their plain cross-bars were employed to supply a portion of the rail either destroyed or never completed?

On a thin slab, 15 inches by 23, is carved a large chaitya window, in which is a female figure, in rather a poor style of carving, standing under the foliage of a tree, into which she raises her right hand. Another small slab, 16 inches by 24, and more injured, has a similar sculpture, but better carved (Pl. xlix, fig. 8). The female holds open the link or loop attached to her ear with two fingers of her left hand, and has a jewelled ornament in her right hand about to attach it. On the finial of the window in each case is the shield similar to one carved in the Bêḍsâ chaitya.[1]

A portion of another slab (Pl. li, fig. 4), which must be ascribed to the central stûpa, represents the lower parts of three figures—two women and a man clad in very thin garments, and standing on a basement carved with the rail pattern. Their heads are broken off. From inscriptions on other slabs of the same type[2] we infer that they belong to the same age as the large slabs carved with the Bauddha emblems. From the resemblance of this to what we find on the front screen walls at Kaṇheri and Kârlê, we might suppose that they belonged to the base of the stûpa near the gates.

A broken slab 3 feet 10 inches broad and 5 feet 10 inches in height at the left side, brought from Bêjwâḍâ in 1882, is all that is left of a stone 11 feet 1 inch high, which was drawn in October 1816 by Mr. H. Hamilton, one of Colonel Mackenzie's staff.[3] The principal figure is a horse, issuing from a gateway of the Sâñchi type, with bridle, saddlecloth, &c., and followed by a groom carrying an umbrella over it. In front are two runners and overhead two dêvas—one of them with an offering. In Bauddha legend the horse Kaṇṭhaka, styled Aśvarâja ('king of horses'), born on the same day as Gautama, which carried him away from his home when he became an ascetic, and died immediately after, is perhaps the best known, and this might represent him being brought out for the great occasion. But Avalôkiteśvara is also represented under the form of a white horse called Kêśi ('hairy'),[4] 'of most beautiful form, white as the driven snow, his head a rosy tint, his feet swift as the wind, his voice mellow as the softest drum.' Again, one of the seven precious possessions of the Chakravarttin or universal monarch is the purple horse, of a mixed tint of red and blue, which suddenly appears before the king early in the morning. His hair is strung with pearls, which fall off when he is washed or combed, and are instantly reproduced more beautiful and brilliant than before. When he neighs he is heard at the distance of a *yôjana*. He has strength sufficient to fly; and when the king mounts to traverse the world, he sets out in the morning and returns by night without suffering any fatigue. Every grain of dust which his feet touch is converted into gold.[5]

---

[1] *Cave Temples*, p. 231, and pl. vii, fig. 8.
[2] *Tree and Serp. Wor.*, pl. xcv, figs. 1, 3, 4, and pl. xcvi, fig. 1.
[3] *Tree and Serp. Wor.*, pl. xcviii, fig. 2.
[4] Beal's *Rom. Leg.*, pp. 336 ff.
[5] Remusat, *Foe koue-ki*, ch. xvii, n. 12.

The portion now lost of this slab contained the tree with four women to the left, worshipping it, and three dwarfs or goblins—apparently inimical—on the right, with a male seated figure; above are two *dêvatâs* bringing offerings. Over this was a belt carved with birds, and then a panel representing a Dâgaba with two triple-hooded snakes knotted round its dome, and worshipped by a Nâga-râja and his queen on each side, while two men are represented digging in front of it.

Among Colonel Mackenzie's drawings those given on Plate xxxii, fig. 2; Plate xxxviii, fig. 4; Plate xxxix, fig. 4; and Plate l, figs. 1 and 2, in all probability belonged to this class of sculptures. That on Plate xxxii, fig. 2, possibly may be of later date, but the form of the slab and the style seem to indicate that it is of the period of the outer rail, and may have belonged to the central Chaitya. The scenes on it seem to be the court of Suddhodana, the night of the conception, the birth in the Lumbini garden, four Devas in attendance, and a fifth scene in the lower left corner, somehow connected with the birth.

29. Outside Face of a Coping Stone from Bharhut Rail.

CHAPTER XI.

STATUES AND S'RÎPÂDAS.

THREE defaced images of Buddha were found (Pl. lii, figs. 1, 2) which, when complete, must have measured respectively 5 ft. 5 in., 4 ft. (exclusive of a block 9 in. high, on which the second stands), and 3 ft. 2 in. Of the second and third the heads are broken off, the first and third want the feet, and all of them the hands. They are the usual conventional statues of Śâkya Siṁha, with the ample robe thrown over the left shoulder and arm and descending quite to the ankles, and are much superior in sculpture to the later ones at Ajaṇṭâ. The upper part of a fourth standing figure (fig. 3) and the lower portion of one in *alto rilievo* (Pl. lii, fig. 4) were also found, all of the same pattern. The last has an inscription (Pl. lix, No. 43) on the base, much obliterated, but recording that it was the gift of a goldsmith (*heranika*) and his family.

Another image (Pl. liii, fig. 2), of which the head is gone, appears to have been a *śâlikâ* or figure of a worshipper, probably representing some benefactor to the shrine.

Several heads of figures were also found, though in few cases were they those of a Buddha, but probably of chiefs or kings and their wives; as, from the Nânâghâṭ Cave, we know that the Andhra kings had figures of themselves and their families carved, I can hardly doubt that the *alto rilievos* on the inner façades of the Chaityas at Kârlê and Kaṇheri represent families of this dynasty. Four of the pieces found at Amarâvatî are given in Plate lii, figs. 5 and 7.

The footmark or *śrîpâda* of Buddha, like that of Vishṇu among his worshippers, has been an object of veneration among his followers from very early times, and special representations of it, supposed to have been left by the Buddha himself, as that on Adam's Peak in Ceylon, were objects of pilgrimage.[1] And the legends that enumerate the thirty-two marks of personal beauty or superiority ascribed to the Buddha specially mention two beautiful brilliant white wheels (*chakra*) with a thousand rays on the soles of his feet. But though the essential feature in the representation of this footmark, called *charaṇa-nyâsa* or *S'âkya charaṇa*, is the chakra on the middle of the sole, there are almost always others also, and in the eastern peninsula they have been multiplied largely. In Nepâl the *charaṇa* of Śâkya Siṁha is represented with a series of concentric circles on the ball of the great toe or on the posterior part of the sole before the heels, and the eight *maṅgala* or signs in line across the sole; these are the *śaṅkha* or conch, the *chhatra* or parasol, two fishes, two *chauris*, a water-pot, standard, lotus, and *śrîvatsa* figure.[2] In the Siamese *Phrabat* or sacred footprint, the *ashṭamaṅgala* are placed in the first line across the front part of the sole, the rest of the foot being covered by the *chakra* and remainder of the hundred and eight symbols which they reckon. Their eight

---

1. Such a footprint was styled a *padachaitya*, Pâli *padachetyam*.

2. *Asiat. Res.*, vol. xvi, p. 460, n. 8; *Lotus de la Bonne Loi*, p. 647; *J. R. As. Soc.*, vol. xviii, p. 293 and pl. vi. Among the presents sent by Aśoka to King Devanampriya Tishya of Ceylon (*Mahavanso*, p. 70) were apparently most of the eight symbols,—a *chauri* (*vâlavîjanî*), a diadem (*uṇhîsaṁ*), a sword (*khaggo*), a royal parasol (*chhattañcha*), slippers (*pâdukâ*), a head ornament (*molipattaṁ*), a golden vase (*bhiṅkâro*), and yellow sandalwood (*harichandanaṁ*).

maṅgala are the royal spear (or *vajra*), palace, *triśula*, the golden lotus-vase supporting a royal hair-pin, the *mandârava* flower [1] placed on a vase or pedestal, the torch-stand, a book resting on a vase, and the *ankuśa* or elephant-goad on a seat.

Impressions of this kind appear again and again in these sculptures, almost always, if not quite so, under the throne or seat, whether empty or occupied by a relic-casket, and hence we may suppose them emblematic of the Buddha or his authority. They are represented in front of the dâgaba, resting on the folds of the snake which surround them, but more frequently on the upper part of the dâgaba, surmounted by the umbrella of authority. But they also occur on separate slabs, of which the annexed woodcut (No. 30) [2] is an example from those in the British Museum, showing the elaboration of ornament on them, consisting of the thousand-rayed *chakra* in the centre, and the *triśula*, *svastika*, and other emblems more or less common in Bauddha heirogrammy, before and behind. In front of the *chakra* is the *svastika* with another emblem on each side. On the great toe is the *triśula*, and on each of the others a *svastika*, but all in very low relief. On the heel is the *triśula* with the flower or circle behind it, and on each side a *svastika* and two small flowers.

30. Feet of Buddha with emblems.

In the excavations of 1880 and 1881 several examples of *śrîpâdas* were found about the east and west entrances, none at the north or south. One on a small block, 12 inches by 10, merely represents the footprints with a large *chakra* on the sole of each, and some minute and nearly obliterated carving above and below (Pl. lii, fig. 6).

Of a pair which, when entire, must have covered a slab 3 feet wide by nearly the same across, and which has been fixed, perhaps against a wall by iron bolts, we have only a large fragment (Pl. xliii, fig. 14). In the middle of the foot was the *chakra* with the edges formed of small *triśulas*. On the balls of the toes were four symbols,—the *svastika* with curved ends, the flower-pot, the *triśula*-shaped shield, and on the outer sides what appears to have been two double *vajras* with flat oblong objects on each side and between. On each of the toes is the *dharma* symbol or double *triśula* with a small circle or *chakra* between. A sunk border about 5 inches wide, carved with creeper pattern, has surrounded the *śrîpâda*, and outside was a raised ledge with an inscription along the front side, mostly illegible, and only a fragment of it left.

A large pair (Pl. lii, fig. 8), 2 ft. 5 in. long, and 2 ft. 4 in. broad, were found close to the brick building at the west gate, where they appeared to have been venerated till a late date. The central area of the wheel is considerably sunk, and the outer edge of it has been carved with small representations of the *triśula*. On the heel is a *triśula* over a wheel, and at each side of it other symbols [3] too much abraded to be distinguishable, except the *svastika*.

A smaller slab (Pl. liii, fig. 1) broken across, and the front part destroyed, but measuring

---

[1] It resembles the central disc of the Amarâvatî *triśula* (fig. 9, p. 47). It is said to be the *Erythrina fulgens*; Burnouf's *Introd.*, pp. 159, 476; *Lotus*, p. 306.

[2] *Tree and Serpent Worship*, pl. lxxxvii, fig. 3.

[3] See *Arch. Sur. West. Ind.*, vol. ii, pl. xviii, fig. 3, for several of these symbols.

25 inches by about 22, represents the feet 18½ inches in length with the *chakra* on the sole of each, a shield or broadened *triśula* between two *svastikas* on the heel, the shield with some addition on each toe, and the *triśula* on the point of each. On the border or outer edge are two men worshipping on each side.

Among the stones dug up in January 1882, from under the general level of the procession path, was one from the north-east, measuring 4 feet 9 inches by 2 feet 9 inches, but broken across (Pl. li, fig. 2). It will be seen at a glance how different is the style of sculpture from almost anything else, yet with close relations to that on the earliest sculptures. A stout man holds up some pear-shaped object (is it a purse ?) in his left hand, while his right rests on the head of a lad, also holding up what looks like a well-filled bag in his left hand. The turban and heavy ear-ornaments of the man, his broad necklace and *dhôti* or loin-cloth, are carefully treated, and belong to the style represented in the paintings in Cave X at Ajaṇṭâ. Both stand on a low brick wall, very carefully represented, but there is nothing else to suggest what they may have represented. Possibly the man is some bricklayer who made an offering to the stûpa, and had himself and his favourite son carved upon a memorial slab that may have stood outside the enclosure, but fell down and was neglected.

Dug up from behind the outer railing was a fragment of a statue life size (Pl. lii, fig. 9). The head, arms, and lower portion of the legs are destroyed, but what is left is 3 feet 6 inches in height. The bust is bare except a broad necklace of seven strings with a square clasp across it, bearing, perhaps, a triple-hooded cobra. Flowers were held between the hands as if making an offering. The clothing is fixed by a belt round the waist, and is carefully depicted all round. The pattern, too—almost to the threads of the cloth—has been minutely represented. Beside it were found fragments of a rail pillar, a coping stone, and a fragment of an inscription, all thrown in as if to support the outer rail.

In the Madras Government Museum are a number of stone boxes which have enclosed relic caskets of crystal. Of these, five were obtained by Sir Walter Elliot from the Zamindâr of Piṭṭâpur in the Godâvarî district. They had been dug up early in 1848 in a ruined stûpa near the village of Timavaram.[1] Of those represented on Plate liii, figs. 4 to 13, Nos. 8 to 13, most probably belonged to this collection ; that represented in elevation and section with the rock-crystal casket (figs. 4–7) is said to be that obtained by Sir Walter from the successors of the Zamindâr of Chintapalle, as having been found in the Amarâvatî Chaitya. The collection of such objects in the Museum, however, has been so carelessly kept, that there is perhaps some doubts about its identity, or that of the parts of the casket.

[1] *Indian Antiquary*, vol. xii, p. 34.

31. The Death or Nirvâṇa of Buddha, from a Sculpture at Ajaṇṭâ.

CHAPTER XII.

AMARÂVATÎ INSCRIPTIONS.

In the preceding pages, a number of the short donative inscriptions have been noticed, and it only remains to give transliterations and translations so far as they admit of a number of others—many of them only fragments—which occur on slabs of which the sculptures do not call for special description. They have been mostly translated and commented on in German by Dr. E. Hultzsch,[1] from the facsimiles I prepared, and which are photo-lithographed in plates lvi to lxi. Those already translated in the previous pages are of course passed over.

Plate lvi, No. 1.

The most important probably of the series are Nos. 1, 2, and 4 on plate lvi. No. 1 gives the name of Pulumâvi Vasishṭhiputra, of whom we have also inscriptions at Nâsik, Kârlê,[2] and the Sâñchi gateway, whose date we have already assigned with approximate accuracy to about A.D. 135–163. This clearly indicates that in his reign or about the middle of the second century, the Stûpa at Amarâvatî was undergoing additions or embellishments. The slab on which it was found had been broken across, and unfortunately a fragment of the inscription is lost. The first half of the slab I discovered near the west gateway, and the other half had been previously excavated. They had formed parts of a stone about 6 feet 7 inches long and 2 feet broad by 8½ inches thick, with two offsets along one end and one side, the inscription being on the outer edge or most projecting of the three steps, the whole having been used for some coping, possibly the cornice of a pedestal of large size bearing a *Dharmachakra*, or wheel symbol of the Bauddha doctrine. The inscription[3] is in two lines and reads—

(1) [Si]dhaṁ Raño V[âsi]ṭh[i]puta[sa] s[â]m[i]siri-Pulumâvisa savachhara. . . . . Piṁḍasutariyâna[ṁ] Kahûtaragahapatisa Purigahapatisa cha putasa Isilasa sabhâtukasa [sama].[4] . . . .

(2) . . saginikasa[5] bhayâya chasa Nâkânikâya saputaka[sa] . . . . . [to][6] mahâchetiye Chetikiyânaṁ nikâsa[7] parigahe aparadâre dhamachakaṁ dedhaṁ[maṁ[8] ṭh]âpita.

"Hail! (*In*) the year . . . of the king, the son of the queen of the Vasishṭha family, the Lord Śrî-Pulumâvi, at the western gate,—a *Dharmachakra* was established, a meritorious gift to the great Chaitya [*of the Exalted one*] (and) in possession of the school of the Chaitikîyas, by (*two*) Piṁḍasutariyas (*viz.*) by the householder Kahûtara and by Isila (Ṛishila) the son of the householder Puri with his brothers, [*with his mother*] . . . . with his sisters, *and* with *his* wife Nâkânikâ (Nâganikâ), with his sons. . . . . ."

---

[1] In the *Zeitschrift der Deutschen Morgenländischen Gesellschaft*, Bd. xxxvii, Ss. 548–564, and Bd. xl, Ss. 343–346, but without the plates, which are essential for palæographic purposes. Many of them were also translated by the same scholar for my *Notes on the Amarâvatî Stûpa* (Madras, 1882).

[2] *Archæol. Sur. West. India Reports*, vol. iv, pp. 107, 108.

[3] Dr. Bhagwânlâl Indraji gave a translation substantially identical with the following in *Notes on the Amarâvatî Stûpa*, p. 27.

[4] Read *samâtukasa*.

[5] Read *sabhaginikasa*.

[6] Read *Bhagavato*.

[7] Read *nikâyasa*.

[8] Read *deyadhammaṁ*.

The statement that the Stûpa belonged to the Chaitika school, otherwise called the school of the Pûrvaśailas, a subdivision of the Mahâsaṁghikas,[1] has already been referred to (*ante*, p. 24), and as it occurs repeatedly in these inscriptions, it appears sufficient to identify the Amarâvatî Chaitya with the Pûrvaśaila Saṅgharâmâ of Hiuen Thsang.

No. 4.[2]

On a small fragment of stone found in the south-east quadrant, where also the granite pillars and most of the earliest sculptures occurred, was the following fragment of an inscription in letters of the Mauryan type. The characters are thus confirmatory of the early date of the neighbouring sculptures, and prove that, though in the second century vast additions, if not an almost entire reconstruction, was effected, the great Chaitya dates originally from perhaps about 200 B.C. It reads—

. . . Senagopasa Muḍakutalasa thabho . . .

"A pillar of the General Muḍakutala (Muṇḍakuntala ?)"[3]

No. 9.[4]

On a cross-bar of the outer rail,[5] with a disc on each side, is the following fragment,—

. . . . chikâya samanikiya
. . (ya) sabhaginikâya
(dâ)na.

"The gift of the ascetic . . . . . with her sisters."

No. 10.

On the upper left corner of the flange of another cross-bar,[6] bearing a disc, carved with four concentric circles round the centre, the outer one filled with creeper pattern, but much abraded, is the fragment—

[Sama]nikâya
[Si]dhathiyâ
deyadhama.

"The meritorious gift of the ascetic [Si]dhathî (Siddhârthî)."

No. 12.[7]

This is also on the upper right corner flange of a disc of the outer rail,[8] the back of which is pretty entire, but of the face only a fragment remains, showing about a dozen

---

[1] We find the Chaitikas also mentioned in one of the Nâsik inscriptions, and the Mahâsaṅghikas in two of Pulumâyi's reign at Kârlâ. See *Arch. Sur. W. India*, vol. iv, p. 115, No. 6; p. 112, No. 20; p. 113, No. 21.

[2] For No. 2, see p. 61, and for No. 3, p. 94.

[3] *Zeitsch d. Deut. Morg. Gesell.*, Bd. xxxvii, S. 554, No. 18. Dr. Hultzsch points out that a *Mahâsenâpati* of Puḷumâyi is mentioned in the Nâsik inscriptions, and another of Siriyaña Sâtakaṁṇi: *Arch. Sur. W. Ind.*, vol. iv, pp. 111, 114.

[4] For No. 5, see p. 97, for No. 6, p. 53, and for No. 8, p. 37.

[5] No. 185 of the original numbering of the slabs excavated in 1881.

[6] No. 66 of the same.

[7] For No. 11, see p. 48.

[8] This stone and those bearing the inscriptions Nos. 16 and 32, with a fourth, were excavated by me in the south-east quadrant, near Nos. 207 and 208.

heads with peculiarly varied head-dresses. The inscription, however, is in good preservation, and reads—

Chetiavadakasa bha-
yaṁta-Budhino bhâtu-
no Papino â-
nugâmikaṁ
suchi-dânaṁ.

"Of Papi the brother of the reverend Budhi, a Chaityavandaka,[1] the gift accompanying (him after death) of a rail bar (sûchi)."

No. 14.[2]

This fragment is on the upper left corner of a cross-bar, bearing a disc only on the one side, the other side being rounded with the section of the flanges. It is perhaps of older date than the others. It reads,—

(A)ya-Kamâyâ [Sadhugavâ]-
(si)niyâ dâna.

"The gift of the worthy Kamâ, [inhabitant of Sadhuga]."

No. 20 (pl. lvii).[3]

This is from a fragment of a slab which has borne one of the large flower vases. What remains of the inscription reads—

. . . . . bhaya[ṁ]gena sabhaginakena
. . . . . (a)badamala karita satas(i)ch(e).

"An *abadamala*[4] was caused to be made . . . . . . with his sisters."

No. 25.[5]

This inscription is on two fragments of stone, but appears to have belonged to the same block. It reads—

(*a*) . . . . liyanaṁ mahavinayadharasa[6] aya-Budh-
(*b*) isa atevâsikasa pavachi(ta) . . . . . .

"(*The gift of*) the Ascetic . . . . . the pupil of the reverend Budhi, greatly skilled in the Vinaya."

No. 26.

. . . . kasa sadutukasa dânaṁ â . . . . .

"The gift of . . . . with his daughter."

No. 27.

On the upper right-hand corner of a large fragment of an outer rail bar bearing a single disc we have—

Budhilagahapatiputasa heranikasa
Sidhathasa samitanâtibadhavasa suyi
dânaṁ

---

[1] This is equivalent to *Chaityavâda*, evidently the same as *Chaitikîya*, as in No. 1 above. Conf. *Ind. Ant.*, vol. ix, p. 300.
[2] For No. 13, see p. 55.
[3] For No. 15, see p. 62; No. 16, p. 63; No. 17, p. 72; No. 18, p. 84; and No. 19, p. 78.
[4] In a similar fragment we have *abatamâlâ*. *Zeit. d. D. M. Gesell.*, Bd. xl, S. 346.
[5] For Nos. 22 and 23, see p. 85.
[6] See No. 8, p. 37.

"A bar (*sûchi*), the gift of the goldsmith Sidhatha (Siddhârtha), the son of the householder Budhila, with his friends, relatives and connections."

No. 33 (pl. lviii).[1]

. . . . . [ya]sa [sa]matukasa sapitukasa sabhaginikasa sabhâriyasa sap[u]takasa suku . sa d[ânaṁ].

"The gift of . . . . with his mother, father, sisters, wife, sons . . ."

No. 34.

On a broken slab 4′ 11″ high and 1′ 9″ where broadest, which has borne the figure of a flower vase, is the following—

(Si)dhaṁ Mugudasa(ma)putasa marâmu(pama) . . . .
(sadhu)hutukânaṁ sasuṇhikânaṁ sanatu[kânaṁ] . . . .

"Success! (*The gift*) . . . . . of the son of Mugudasa[ma] (Mukundaśarman) . . . . with their daughters, with their daughters-in-law, with their grandsons . . . . ."

No. 37.[2]

This is on a broken fragment in the steps of a well near the village—

. . . . . sa gaha[pati] . . . .
. . . . . sabhâri[yasa] . . . .
. . . . . thaṁbho o[varako] . . .

Perhaps the gift of a pillar and a cell.

No. 38 (pl. lix).

On a piece of a small octagonal pillar which has been cut across at an early date is the following in six lines—

Sidhaṁ Jaḍikiyanaṁ[3] Sidhathagahapa-
tisa bhariyaya Khadaya sadhutukaya
saputikaya samatukaya sabhâtukâsa[4]
(sa)gharasu(nhâ)ya sahajanatihi
Bhagavâto mahachetiyapadamale[5]
apano dhaṁmathâna divakhaṁbho patiṭhavito.

"Success! By Khadâ (Skandâ), the wife of the householder Sidhatha of the Jaḍikiya (*family* or *school*), with her daughters, with her sons, with her mother, with her brothers, with the daughter-in-law in her house, (*and by her*) blood-relations, a pillar for lamps has been placed at the foot of the great Chaitya of the Exalted one as an abode of merit."

No. 39.

In the village, to the east of the large temple, are several small ones built by Vasureddi,

---

[1] For No. 28, see p. 82; Nos. 29–31, p. 85; and No. 32, p. 86.
[2] For Nos. 35 and 36, see p. 91.
[3] The first syllables of this look almost like *Jachi°*.
[4] Read *sabhâtukâya*.
[5] Read *Bhagavato mahâchetiyapâdamûle*.

the Zamindâr, about 1795, and the threshold of one of them, now deserted, is formed of a slab from the stûpa, on which is the following inscription—

[R]âyaselanivâsino vasibhûtasa
(ma)hatherasa ayira-Bhûtarakhitasa (a)-
(te)vâsikasa Chula-ay(i)rasa ara[ha]-
[ta]sa ayira-Budharakhitasa atev(â)-
s(i)niya bhikhuniyâ Nadâya thaṁbho dâ(na).

"A pillar, the gift of the worthy Chula (Kshudra), a disciple of the great *sthavira* of self-controlled mind, the worthy Bhûtarakhita, resident at [R]âyasela (*Râjaśaila*)—and of the nun Nadâ (Nandâ), a disciple of the Arhat the worthy Budharakhita."

No. 40.

On a small fragment, probably of a slab bearing a flower vase, is the following portion of an inscription—

. . . . . Sidhathasa bhariyâya bhagoṁmuya
. . . . . dhuya Bodhiyâ cha dânaṁ ima udhapa(ṭa).

"This *Ûrdhvapaṭṭa* is the gift . . . . . . of the wife of Sidhatha (Siddhârtha) . . . . and of Bodhî."

No. 41.

This is also on one of the tall slabs carved with a flower vase. It reads—

Damila-Kanhasa bhâtuṇaṁ cha Chulakanhasa Nâkhâya cha (dâ)na Mahâche-
tiyapâdamule udhaṁpaṭo.

"An Ûrdhvapaṭṭa at the foot of the great Chaitya, the gift of the Tamiḷ Kanha (Kṛishṇa) and (*his*) brother and sister Chulakanha[1] (Kshullakṛishṇa) and Nâkhâ."

No. 42.

On a portion split off from a pillar[2] near the east gate, and under a carved half disc upon it, is the following in small letters with long stems :—

. . . . . hiralûre Râhulagahapatisa bhâriyâya Bhagîya [bâ]l(i)kâya
. . . . . [Dhaṁ]mâya natukânâṁ [ima ?] khaṁbho.

"[This] pillar (*is the gift*) of the grandsons of [Dhaṁ]mâ (Dharmâ) [*the daughter*] of Bhaṅgî, the wife of the householder Râhula in . . hiralûra."

No. 44 (pl. lx).[3]

On a small fragment of a coping-stone[4] are the following portions of three lines :—

(Si)dhaṁ—Sulasagahapatiputena gaha(pa)[5] . . .
nâgatâya bâlikena ya Sulasena sadhutu[6] . . .
(da)khinapase dâra kârita deyadhama.

"Success ! The house(*holder*) . . . . the son of the householder Sulasa, and Sulasa,

---

[1] That is, "younger" Kṛishṇa. Conf. *Jâtaka* 30, where two brother-oxen named Mahâlohita and Chullalohita appear, and in *Dîpavaṁsa*, ii., Mahodara and Chûḷodara. See Childers' *Dict.* s. v. *Cullo.*

[2] No. 189 of the original numbering.

[3] No. 43 is on the base of a statue mentioned p. 97.

[4] No. 175 of the first enumeration.

[5] Read *gahapatinâ.*

[6] Read *sadhutukena.*

the son of . . . . with his daughters . . . at the southern side (*of the Chaitya*) caused a gate to be made (*as*) a meritorious gift."

No. 46.[1]

On a fragment of an outer rail pillar eight syllables in a later alphabet.

No. 48.

On a fragment of the base of another slab,[2] probably bearing a flower base, are the first halves of two lines,—

Sidhaṁ—Namo Bhagavato Haṁghi(gapa)tiputasa Dusaka(sa)[3] . . . . .
(sa)putakasa saduhutukasa sanati(m)itabaṁdhava(sa) . . . . . .

"Success! Hail to the Exalted one (*Buddha*)! [The gift] of Dusaka (Dûshaka), the son of the householder Haṁghi (Saṁghin) . . . . with his sons, with his daughters, with his relations, friends, and connections. . . . ."

No. 49.

To the west of the south entrance was found a thin pillar[4] 1′ 4½″ by 9¼ inches, and about 4′ 2″ high, with the edges chamfered off, and the usual half rosette above and below on all sides about 11 inches apart. On one side of it is an inscription in ten and a half lines, but much injured. So far as can be made out it reads—

Sidhaṁ namo (Bha)gavato achar(iyâna)
Mahavanasaliyâna Sâripu(tâna a)-
malâna sisihasa[5] (sagharu) . .
gahagûjâkaṁḍasa Dhaṁmilavâni-
yaputasa gadhikasa vâniyasa (Si)-
ri(da)tasa sapitukasa samâtuka(sa sa)-
bha(ri)yakasa sabhatukasa sa . . . .
saputakasa sadhutukasa sa(vadhujana)-
sa sanatuka(sa)[6]
sanatikasa sanatimitabaṁdhava(sa)
saghadeyadhaṁmaṁ padhânama(ḍa)vo
patiṭhav(i)to.

"Success! To Reverence the Exalted one (*Buddha*)! A chief (?) pavilion (*pradhâna-maṇḍapa*) has been established, the meritorious gift to the community (*saṁgha*) of the merchant [Si]ri[da]ta (S′rîdatta) a dealer in perfumery, the son of the merchant Dhaṁmila (Dharmila) . . . (*of the disciple*) of [the pure teacher] Sâripu[ta] living in the hall in Mahâvana, with his father, with his mother, with his wife, with his brothers, with (*his sisters*) with his sons, with his daughters, with [his daughters-in-law], with his grandsons, with his grand-daughters, with his relations, friends, and connections."

---

[1] No. 45 is on p. 87, and No. 47 on p. 86.
[2] Originally numbered 249. *Zeit. d. D. M. G.*, Bd. xxxvii, S. 558.
[3] Read °*gahapati*°.
[4] Numbered 8, see Plate iv.
[5] We should have *sisiyasa* here.
[6] These syllables are inserted between lines 8 and 9.

No. 51 (pl. lxi).[1]

On a large fragment of a pillar, fully 8 feet long and 4′ 4″ in perimeter, with a portion of the rectangular base 13½ by 17½ inches, and an irregular octagonal shaft, is part of a long Sanskrit inscription in early Telugu characters. This probably stood at the eastern entrance. The lines run across three sides of the octagon, but, as Dr. Hultzsch has discovered, they read from the bottom upwards, and consist of eleven complete verses, which contain a dynastic list of Pallava kings, and of a prose passage the end of which is broken off. The verses begin with a series of mythical ancestors and then give the following names—

1. Pallava.
2. Mahendravarman, his son.
3. Siṁhavarman, son.
4. Arkavarman, son.
5. Ugravarman.
6. Srîsimhavishṇu.
7. Nandivarman, son.
8. Siṁhavarman II.

The incomplete prose passage records that Siṁhavarman II. paid honour to the shrine of Buddha at Dhânyaghaṭa or Dhânyaghaṭaka—evidently a vulgar spelling of Dhânyakaṭaka. In another early Pallavaâ inscription,[2] we also find mention of a Siṁhavishṇu and a Mahendravarman, then Narasiṁhavarman, Mahendravarman II., Parameśvaravarman, Narasiṁhavarman II., Parameśvaravarman II., Nandivarman, and Pallavamalla-Nandivarman.

On the other side is the Pâli inscription (No. 51) in two lines—

Gahapatino Vâ[su]mitasa putasa Himalasa sabhâriya[sa]
Saputakasa sabhâgineyasa saduhutukasa thabhâ dâna.

"Pillars the gift of Himala, son of the householder Vâsumita, with his wife, with his sons, with his sister's sons, with his daughters."

No. 54.[3]

Sidhaṁ Kaṭakasolakasa upâsakasa Utarasa samat[ṇka]-
sa sabhaginikasa saputakasa sadhutukasa [dânaṁ].

"Success! [*The gift*] of the layman Utara, (Uttara) a native of Kaṭakasola, with his mother, sisters, sons, and daughters."

---

[1] For No. 50, see p. 93.

[2] *Ind. Antiquary*, vol. viii, pp. 273 f.; and conf. *ib.* p. 167.

[3] For No. 52, see p. 67; for No. 53, p. 90; and No. 56, p. 38. Other inscriptions are given on pp. 58, 67, 85, &c.

CHAPTER XIII.

THE JAGGAYYAPEṬA STÛPA.

THIRTY miles north-west from Amarâvatî, on the Pâler River, a tributary of the Kṛishṇâ, and about four miles north of their junction, is the flourishing town of Bêtavôlu, rebuilt by the same Vâsu-reddi who destroyed so much of the Amarâvatî stûpa, and renamed by him Jaggayyapeṭa. About a mile to the east of the town is a hill of no great height, known as Dhana Bôḍu or "Hill of Wealth," on which is one of the stations of the great Trigonometrical Survey. The people of the village had been in the habit of digging for many years past into brick mounds that covered a portion of the south-west of this hill, and in 1881 they excavated some carved slabs. The local native officer, a more than usually intelligent man, hearing of this, took possession of the slabs and promptly reported the matter to Madras.[1] In February 1882 I visited the place, and found that there had at one time been on the hill a group of stûpas, mostly small, together with some other buildings of a very early date. But they had been so long dug over for bricks and slabs, that of one only was there any very distinct remains left. It was to the south-west of the other traces, and had long ago lost the whole of the dome and rail, and had been rifled of its relic-casket. No doubt Vâsu-reddi Venkaṭâdri Nayaḍu had largely utilised the materials of this as well as of the others in the buildings of the neighbouring town; indeed, in the roof of a small temple, built about a century ago at the foot of the hill, I found, among other slabs of the same sort, a portion of one of the five tall pillars which had adorned the east face of the stûpa, bearing a copy of the same inscription as I found engraved on other two of them.

On excavating round the mound, it was found to be 31½ feet in diameter, and had been faced with slabs of the same stone as those used at Amarâvatî. They had been quarried on the bank of the Kṛishṇâ immediately to the south; and there can be little doubt that the Amarâvatî slabs were all brought from the same place. The slabs surrounding the base of the stûpa, of which many were *in situ*, stood about 3′ 9″ above the level of a procession path, 10½ feet wide, which surrounded the whole. But the rail around this had entirely disappeared: not a fragment of it could be found. It had been carried off apparently while the stûpa itself was tolerably entire. The stûpa had next been attacked, and, if it had a casing of carved stone, as is quite probable, it also had been carried away, and then the material of the dome, on being thrown down, covered the procession path and the slabs round the basement, and conduced to their preservation. On some portions of the outer edge of the procession path were found portions of the brick and lime base that had been made to support the pillars of the outer rail.

To the south-east of the stûpa, over an area of about 170 feet by 120, were found the lower portions of pillars, scarcely rising above the surface of the ground, but which must have been arranged at regular intervals about 11 feet apart. From the south-west corner of this area extends a low fence of large stones laid together along part of the two adjacent sides. This area and the lines of the pillars does not face the stûpa, but, as it were, looks

[1] This report came to the hands of Mr. R. Sewell, who was at the time collecting information for the *Lists of Antiquarian Remains*, and he naturally conjectured that this mound might represent an old stûpa.

past the east side of it. The first impression regarding these pillars is that they had formed one of those groups, perhaps supporting a roof, and forming a large hall, of which we have several examples in Ceylon.[1] That they did form a large maṇḍapa of some sort, there can be little doubt: a place of assembly for visitors to the Stûpa.

Inside the outer casing of slabs the stûpa was formed of earth in layers about two feet thick, over each of which was laid a close flooring of very large bricks closely fitted together. In this way little or no water could percolate into the centre and so swell the earth as to injure the outer casing. The relic must have been deposited not lower than the base of the dome, for in the loose disturbed earth on the top a small fragment of the outer stone casket was found, and the flooring of brick over the first layer of earth below this was intact.

The slabs surrounding the base of the stûpa are about 3′ 6″ to 3′ 9″ wide, and very few of them have any carving except a small pilaster up the edge. Over a carefully carved base of very early type is a *makara*, sea-horse, or other monster, and on it stands a male or female figure whose head reaches to the top of the shaft. These figures are probably Yakshas, and the counterparts of those found on the Bharhut pillars. The capital is heavy, and of the pattern already noticed in what are believed to be the earliest of the Amarâvatî sculptures and in the Pitalkhorâ vihâra. On it sit two winged animals. These reach to a flat projecting member, much injured all round. These pilasters are carved on one edge of each slab, and the back of the outer side of each is hewn away, so as to allow the plain edge of the next slab to be inserted with a hold of a few inches behind it, so concealing the joint and strengthening the whole casing. But the base of the stûpa could hardly have stopped here: a frieze almost certainly surmounted this, but was all carried off.

These pilasters are so interesting for comparison with those at Bharhut, the earliest Western caves, and the oldest sculptures at Amarâvatî, that a pretty full illustration from the few that remain has been given in Plates liii, figs. 14–17, liv, figs. 3, 4, 6, and lv, figs. 1 and 4. These render any detailed description unnecessary.

The stone of which these slabs consists burns into excellent lime, and no fragments being noticeable in the town of Jaggayyapeṭa is perhaps accounted for in this way, that the slabs were all thrown into the limekiln and converted into mortar.

On the upper facia of some of the slabs were a few letters of inscriptions, in no case sufficient to yield a name or complete word, but in characters of the Maurya type, and which may belong to as early a date as the beginning of the second century B.C.

A longer inscription on the pillars that had ornamented the eastern gate is in a much later character and will be given below; and a still later one was discovered on a relief of Buddha on the pavement west of the stûpa.

The few carvings on the slabs of the basement are in very low relief and of archaic type.

One slab (pl. lv, fig. 2), much broken, has upon it a drawing of a shrine or *Puṇyaśâlâ*. The front is supported by four pillars standing on a basement to which the ascent is by steps. Inside is seen the *śrîpâda* under a rudely drawn seat or altar, over which is a *chhatra* or umbrella with two garlands hanging from it. From the lintel also depend what seem intended for ornamental hangings or garlands, and on the floor are several round objects, but whether intended to represent blossoms offered or not is uncertain. In each side division of the front is a female, that on the left much defaced, but the other bearing a vessel probably of flowers as an offering. The proportions of this and of a male figure outside to the right

---

[1] Fergusson, *Indian and East. Architecture*, pp. 196 f.

are very poor, but her head-dress, &c., are so exact a copy of some of those in Cave X. at Ajaṇṭâ, that there can be no doubt they represent the same caste or race, and that the Ajaṇṭâ frescoes are only a later representation of Andhra worshippers. The Ajaṇṭâ Chaitya, Cave No. X., may be almost as old as this stûpa, and it is only from the style of its paintings that we can conjecturally fix its age: they are by far the oldest at Ajaṇṭâ or even in India, and can hardly be placed later than the Christian era, if not before it. The paintings in that cave, the sculptures in the Pitalkhorâ vihâra and in the small vihâra at Beḍsâ, and these fragments with the earlier sculptures found at Amarâvatî, are among the most important discoveries made in the peninsula for the elucidation of the earliest Bauddha art. Nor should the Bharhut sculptures be overlooked in any comparison of these early remains. If more boldly executed than these of Jaggayyapeṭa, it will be found that there are underlying characteristics common to both and pointing to the same age.

The upper part of the building represented on this slab seems intended to represent a second storey with an arched or chaitya window on each side of a large latticed centre compartment, and over this an arched roof with a large chaitya window in front, the apex of which rises over the ridge of the roof, and on the latter are four ornamental finials—reminding one of those on the monolithic Raths at Mahâvellipuram. To the right of the building is a man standing on a cushion, with a scarf passed across his breast, worshipping towards the shrine. To the left is a date palm-tree rising to the height of the building. Parts of two other similar buildings were found on two fragments of broken slabs.

On another slab (Pl. lv, fig. 3) is a tall male figure, standing on a cushion with a high turban, broad necklace, armlets and bracelets, and his clothing gathered principally round his waist. An umbrella is over his head, in front is the *chakra* on a short pillar, and behind his head is an object like a drum, also on a short supporting pillar. Above are clusters of objects which may be compared to the lower ends of bags, and from five different points among them stream down square objects, which, it may be, represent pieces of money. There seem to be rude devices on them similar to what are represented on the pieces of money in the Bharhut scene of the purchase of the Jetavana by Anâthapiṇḍika.[1] Before or to the right of the man stands a woman, also on a cushion, with heavy anklets and bunches of balls attached, as is sometimes worn to the present day. She has very large ear-rings, and her head-dress is of the peculiar style only found in these very early representations. Below her is a horse saddled and with a plume, but the figure is altogether below proportion even to the woman, who is about half the height of the man. Behind the central figure are two young men paying reverence to him, each with a scarf across the chest and with heavy ear-rings and large turbans; they, like all the figures, stand on cushions—possibly a conventionalism. Below them is an elephant about half their height, saddled, and with his trunk raised towards the tall man. Who this represents we know not: some great person, the owner of horse and elephant, with wife and sons, and symbols of authority.

On two pieces of another slab was found part of the representation of a Dâgaba having a very simple capital or relic-box without the usual abacus, but supporting five *chhatris* of various sizes, each having two garlands depending from it. A garland is carried round the dome, hung apparently from projecting horn-shaped supports.

Another broken slab (Pl. liii, fig. 17) represents the base of another Dâgaba, with a

---

[1] Cunningham's *Bharhut Stûpa*, pp. 84, f. pl. xxviii, fig. 3, and pl. lvii.

man and woman offering flowers before it. The basement of a shrine appears on another fragment (Pl. liv, fig. 7); and what seems to have been part of the front of a throne in fig. 5. The low relief of all these carvings, as compared with those of the great rail at Amarâvatî, cannot fail to strike one.

The portions of the drum or base of the stûpa facing each of the gates or cardinal points projected between 2 and 2½ feet from the rest for a length of from 12 to 15 feet. This was distinctly marked at the south and west sides, as also at the north,—though most of the stones had been carried off from the last. At the east front the only stones left had been disturbed, but there can be little doubt the same arrangement existed at it as on the other sides. It was only at these fronts that any slabs were found bearing sculptures other than the pilasters on the edge of each.

At three of the sides large pillars or stelæ were found lying, and at the east side one bearing an inscription lay where it had fallen. It was about 17 feet long, but the upper portion of it had been broken off; and how long it may have been originally is unknown. For the lower 7½ feet it was square, and above this octagonal. There had been five such stelæ on each face, and on the lower portion of the octagonal shaft of this one was an inscription in characters that belong to about the third or fourth century A.D., but possibly earlier. Two other copies of it were also found on fragments of similar pillars,—one on a portion carried off by the villagers and broken, but secured by the local native officer; and another in the roof of a small ruined temple at the base of the hill. Reduced copies of these inscriptions are given on Plate lxii, Nos. 1 and 2, and the third on Plate lxiii, No. 1. They read thus :—

No. 1.

. dhaṁ Raño Mâḍhariputasa Ikhâ
. . . r(i)vira-Purisa(da)tasa saṁ-
vachhar(a) 20 vâsâpakhaṁ 8 divasaṁ
10 (1) . . ka . ṭhe Ṇaḍatûre
vathavasa avesaṇisa Nâkachaṁdasa
put(o) gâme Mahâkâṁḍurûre vathavo
(2) avesaṇi Sidhatho apaṇo mâtaraṁ
Nâgilaniṁ purato katûnaṁ gharaniṁ
cha Samudaniṁ bâlaka . cha Mûla-
siri bâ-(3)l(i)kaṁ cha. akabudhanikaṁ
bhâtukaṁ cha Budhinakaṁ tasa
gharaniṁ cha Kanikaṁ bâlakâ
cha Nâgasiri - Chaṁdasiri bâlikaṁ
(cha) (4) Sidhathanikaṁ evam nâti-
mitasaṁ . . ívagena sahâ gâ.
Velagiriyaṁ Bhagavato Budhasa
puvadâre aya - (5) ka - khaṁ-
bhe 5 save niyute apano deya-
. . satânaṁ hi . sukhâya
paṭiṭhapita ti || (6)

No. 2.

. . . . riputasa Ikhâ-
kuṇâm sirivíra - Purisadatasa saṁ-
v . . r . . . . (1) divasaṁ
10 Kaṁmâkarathe gâme Ṇaḍatûre
vathavasa âvesaṇisa Nâkachaṁdasa
puto gâme Mahâka . u . (2)rûre vathavo
âvesani Sidhatho apaṇo mataraṁ
Nâgilaniṁ purato kâtûnaṁ gharaniṁ
cha Samudani (3) bâlakaṁ cha Mula-
siriṁ bâlai . . . .
. . . .
. raniṁ cha Kaṁnikaṁ bâlakâ
cha (4) Nagasiri-Chaṁdasiri bâlika
cha Sidhathanikaṁ evaṁ nâti-
mitasaṁbaṁdhivagena sahâ game
Ve(la) . iri . (5) Bhagavato Budhasa
Mahâchetiyapuvadâre âyaka-khaṁ-
bhe paṁcha 5 savaniyute âpaṇo deya-
dhaṁmaṁ. (6)savasatâṇam hitasûkhâ-
ya paṭith(a)pita ti (7)

No. 3.

Sidham Raño Mâḍhariputasa Ikhâ-
khuṇaṁ Sirivira-Purisadatasa saṁ-
vachhara 20 vâsâpakhaṁ 8 divasaṁ(1)
10 Ka(ṁ)mâkaraṭhe Ṇaḍatûre
âvenisa Nâkachaṁdasa
pûto gâme Mahâkâṁḍurûre
âvesani (2) Sidhatho âpaṇo mâtaraṁ
Nâgilaniṁ purato katûnaṁ gharaniṁ
cha Samudaniṁ bâlakaṁ cha Mûla-
siriṁ (3) bâlikaṁ cha Nâkabudhani-
kaṁ bhatuka(ṁ) cha Budhinakaṁ tasa
gharaniṁ cha Kanikaṁ bâlakâ
cha Nâgasiri-Chaṁda-(4) siri bâlikaṁ
ya S(i)dhathanika(ṁ) eva(ṁ) nâti-
mitasaṁbadhivagena sahâ gâme
Velagiriyaṁ Bhagavato (5) Budhasa
Mahachetiyapuvâdare âyaka-khaṁ-
bhe 5 savaniyute apaṇo deya-
dhaṁmaṁ savasatânaṁ hi(6)tasukhâ-
ya paṭithapita ti || (7).

Translation.

"Success! On the 10th day of the 8th fortnight of the rainy season, in the 20th year of the king Purisadata (Purushadatta), the glorious hero (*śrîvîra*) of the Ikhâkus

(Ikshvâkus) *and* son of the Mâḍhara (*mother*),—the artisan (*âvesaṁi*) Sidatha (Siddhârtha) resident in the village of Mahâkâmḍurûra, the son of the artisan Nâkachaṁda (Nâgachandra) resident in the village of Naḍatûra in the province (*rathe*) of Kaṁmâka, having associated (*with him*) his mother Nâgilani, and his wife Samudani (Samudrâṇî) and his son Mûlasiri (Mûlaśrî) and his daughter Nâkabudhanika (Nâgabuddhanikâ) and his brother Budhanika, and the wife of the same Kanika (Kanyakâ, Kṛishṇâ, *or* Karṇikâ) and (*their*) two sons Nâgasiri (Nâgaśrî) and Chaṁdasiri (Chandraśrî) and daughter Sidhathanika (Siddhârthanikâ), erected thus, together with the multitude of his blood-relations, friends and connexions, in the village of Velagiri, near the eastern gate of the Great Chaitya of divine Buddha, five (5) Âyaka-pillars,[1] which were dedicated by all (*the above persons*), as his own meritorious gift for the good and the welfare of all living beings."[2]

Who this king Purushadatta was we do not know, but further discoveries may yet reveal something more of his dynasty. Ikshvâku is famous in Indian legends as the mythical founder of the Solar race,[3] and of an early dynasty, the Aikshvâkas, which, according to the *Vâyu* and *Matsya Purâṇas*, lasted through twenty-four descents.[4] The Buddhists and Jainas also trace the descent of their sacred personages from the same hero. The Ikshvâkus are sometimes mentioned as a warlike tribe or race.[5] The claim of Purushadatta to be of this race, however, is most probably an idle boast. He may have belonged to some local dynasty which succeeded the Andhras on the Lower Kṛishṇâ. But the character of the alphabet in which these documents are engraved probably belongs to a later period than the original construction of the stûpa. A few letters found on the capitals of the pilasters surrounding the base of the stûpa are of a very much earlier form; indeed they so closely resemble the Maurya alphabet, that there can be little doubt that the original structure belongs to a date considerably before the Christian era.

A much later sculpture was found lying on its face on the procession path north-west side. This was a standing figure of Buddha in high relief in a panel with an inscription underneath in five lines of different lengths, and in an alphabet of about 600 A.D. (see Plate lv, fig. 5).

The stone measures about 3′ 11″ by 2′ 1″, and the image is in a sunk recess 2′ 7″ by 14″, with the robe disposed as usual, and the right hand raised as if in blessing: the face is very short and the figure ill proportioned. On the border of the panel above the head is a crude conventional representation of the sacred tree, and down each side are (1) a *Vidyâdhara* or other superhuman being with a conical cap, among what may represent clouds; (2) a dâgaba, very rudely represented, with the five-hooded snake carved on the drum or base; and (3) a standing figure with a conical cap. The Buddha stands on a lotus which is spread

---

1 *Âyaka* perhaps means "entrance" or gate pillars; there were five on each of the four fronts of the Chaityas, as shown in many of the Amarâvatî sculptures.

2 This translation was given by Dr. G. Bühler, C.I.E. (by whom it now has been revised), in the *Ind. Antiq.*, vol. xi, p. 258, and scarcely differs from that of Pandit Bhagvanlal Indraji, Ph.D., in the *Notes on the Amarâvatî Stûpa*, p. 58.

3 *Râmâyaṇa*, i, 5, 3; 23, 6; 47, 12; 70, 11, 20, 21; ii, 110, 6 ff.; iii, 74, 4; iv, 17, 9; v, 7, 10; *Mahâbhârata*, i, 3140; xiii, 88; xiv, 66; *Harivaṁśa*, 443, 614, 667, &c.

4 Wilson's *Vishṇu Pur.* (Hall's ed.), vol. ii, pp. 171, 181, 184; *Mahâbhârata*, i, 3719; xii, 1023; xiii, 189; *Harivaṁśa*, 1996; *Râmâyaṇa*, i, 26, 12; ii, 36, 1; *Śatapatha Brahm.*, xiii, 5, 4, 9.

5 Pâṇini, iv, 1, 168 sch.—*Ikshvâkurâjñaḥ subalasya;* In Draupadîramâtha, ii, 9,—*kshuvatastu manorjajña Ikshvâkurghrâṇataḥ sutaḥ; Bhâg. Pur.*, ix, 6, 4, in Wilson's *Vish. Pur.* (Hall's ed.), vol. iii, p. 259.

over part of the base and interferes with the Sanskrit inscription (Pl. lxiii, No. 4). This reads :—

> Svasti Bhadanta Nâgârju- nâchâryyasya
> śishya[shyo] Jayaprabhâchâryya[ḥ] Tach-chhishyeṇa Cha(ndra)-
> prabheṇa kârâpitâṁ satu[tya ?] - Sugata - gata - prasâda - viśesha - viśishṭa-saṁsâre dêvamanu(ja)
> vibhûtipûrvvakaṁ Buddhattva-prâpti-nimittaṁ Buddha-pratimâṁ pratisthâ[shṭhâ]pitâṁ anumôdanâ
> (pakshe ?) kurvvantu sarvvê Saugaty-âgryâ(?)nyo pi

"Hail ! The disciple of the reverend Nâgârjunâchârya (*was*) Jayaprabhâchârya. May everybody—even one who is different from the best of Saugatas—approve of the image of Buddha caused to be made by his (*Jayaprabha's*) disciple Chandraprabha, and established for the purpose of the attainment of the condition of a Buddha after [*the enjoyment of*] greatness in the world of gods and men in the course of existences characterised by the great favours of the real Buddha (*of whom this is an image*)." [1]

As Mr. J. Fergusson has handled so exhaustively the sculptures of the Mackenzie and Elliot collections from Amarâvatî, and the contents of this volume are simply supplementary to his work, much need not be said by way of conclusion. With the additional information we have accumulated since Mr. Fergusson's *Tree and Serpent Worship* was prepared, his main conclusions have not been shaken but rather confirmed. That buildings did exist on the site of the Amarâvatî stûpa before the Christian era is amply confirmed by the style of the earlier sculptures and the inscriptions upon them, which point to a period about a century or more before that epoch ; and they evidently belonged to a stûpa,—possibly the same that continued all through the later history of the place. Next the inscription of Pulumâyi and others, which, on palæographic grounds, must belong to about the same age or within the next half century, afford evidence that the repair and embellishment of the stûpa and the erection of the outer rail were begun in the second century, and perhaps completed before the end of it, or at latest during the earlier part of the third. The sculptures of the inner rail would seem to be of a somewhat later date, and may not have been completed much before the end of the third century.

All that has of late been discovered bearing on the history of Indian art is perfectly in accordance with this. The farther the palæographical indications carry us back from about the beginning of the second century, the less elegant and perfect the style of the sculptures is. About that point of time it seems to have culminated in refinement, and after a short period of elaborate richness of detail conventionalism began to set in.

The remains of the Jaggayyapeṭa stûpa throw light upon this history. What fragments of sculpture remain are so closely allied to what had previously been considered the oldest of those at Amarâvatî and to the sculptures in the oldest of the Western caves, that they strongly support the accuracy of our previous determinations, while they show that most of the slabs of this early age found at Amarâvatî may most probably have belonged to the facing of the base of the first stûpa of the Pûrvaśaila school at this place.

Few as they are, they indicate that the Amarâvatî stûpa was first raised as early as perhaps the second century B.C. and decorated with sculptured marbles ; at a later date possibly, it was greatly enlarged and covered with new sculptures ; and it was in the height of its

---

[1] Translated by Prof. R. G. Bhandârkâr, M.A., Ph.D., Poona. The doubtful readings in the inscription are marked with a query.

popularity when the great rail was erected, shortly before A.D. 200. That very large reconstructions have taken place is abundantly evidenced by the numerous fragments of carved slabs that are found propping the pillars of the rail and buried beneath the procession path. Further excavations in the vast accumulations of earth and bricks round its site, if only carried out under skilled supervision, may yet disclose other remains of interest.

32. The Buddhist Chaitya Cave at Elura.

TRANSCRIPTS AND TRANSLATIONS

OF THE DHAULI AND JAUGADA VERSIONS OF AS'OKA'S EDICTS,

By Dr. G. Bühler, C.I.E.

The subjoined transcript of the truncated Dhauli and Jaugada versions of Aśoka's fourteen edicts has been prepared directly from Dr. J. Burgess's excellent paper impressions, from which also the accompanying plates (lxiv–lxix) are photo-lithographed. The impressions, for which a double layer of Indian country paper has been used, are by far the best productions of this kind which I have seen, and furnish, for the greater portion of the inscriptions, a perfectly trustworthy and easily intelligible text. Even in places where the stone has suffered considerably, an examination of the *reverse* of the impression frequently permits one to distinguish the original strokes of the mason from the numerous accidental rents and scratches. It is only in one passage of the fourth edict (Dhauli iv. 19) and at the end of the fourteenth edict that the real reading remains doubtful.

The chief results deducible from the new text are the following. First, it is now evident that the Dhauli version, which hitherto was considered to be one of the worst and most carelessly executed, is in reality quite as well engraved as the others. The general maxim that the Aśoka inscriptions offer no inexplicable words and forms, and that Aśoka's masons were both skilled and careful, is confirmed here quite as much as by the previous publication of trustworthy texts of the Girnâr, Khâlsî, Jaugada, Dehli, and Allahabad edicts.

The lesson which this discovery again inculcates is, that the interpreter of these documents is not entitled to make many and great conjectural changes in the text. When his readings become inexplicable, it will be necessary for him to carefully consider whether his copy is really to be depended upon, and whether he himself has read correctly, before he ventures on a conjectural emendation. Commonplace as these remarks may seem, they are yet very necessary. For, until quite lately, all Orientalists held most erroneous views regarding the condition of Aśoka's inscriptions, as they were misled by the imperfect reproductions published by Prinsep, H. H. Wilson, and others.

Secondly, the new text shows that the Dhauli and Jaugada versions of the fourteen edicts are copies made from one and the same MS. Their agreement is nearly complete. The apparent differences are *savata* (Dh. ii. 7) against *savatu* (J. ii. 8); *seto* at the end of Dh. vi., omitted in J.; *hîlaṁna°* (Dh. viii. 5) against *hilaṁna°* (J. viii. 12); [*pa*]*jopaddâye* (Dh. ix. 6) against (*pa*)*jupaddâye* (J. ix. 14), and possibly *vasevû tî* (Dh. vii. 1) against *vasev*[*u t*]*i* (J. vii. 7). The notes show, however, that the first case is also doubtful. It will further be clear from the explanation[1] of the word *seto*, that the latter does not belong to

[1] See below, note 32 on the text of Dh.

the edict after which it stands, and that it would have been out of place in the Jaugada version. Thus the real difference is the quantity of one vowel and the character of another.

Thirdly, a supposition which I have long held, that the alphabet of the Aśoka inscriptions was not the only one known and used in his times, receives a strong support from some peculiarities of the Dhauli alphabet. Twice, in the word *u.pânâni* (ii. 8) and in *hilamnapaṭividhâne* (viii. 1), we meet, it seems to me, with unmistakable instances of the use of the *serif.** Moreover, if the word *seto* has been incised by the same mason who engraved the body of the inscription, it is evident that he knew an alphabet closely resembling that of the Guptas and the *Brâhma aksharas* of the ancient palm-leaves from Japan. It may be objected that the form *seto* for *śvetaḥ* is itself a late one, and that the usage of the Dhauli dialect would require *svete.* Yet it is difficult to imagine how, in later times, anybody could have an interest in making such an addition. A full discussion of this subject would here lead too far, and I reserve it for my remarks on the palæography of Aśoka's inscriptions, which will shortly appear in the *Zeitsch. der Deutsch. Morg. Gesellschaft.*

As regards the Separate Edicts, my text differs from M. Senart's in minor details only. M. Senart has also used Dr. Burgess's impressions, and, as might be expected, succeeded in settling nearly all the essential difficulties. Every case where I have thought it necessary to differ from him has been pointed out in the notes, and the reasons why I differ have been given, where it was possible to do so. It is well known that the Dhauli and Jaugada versions of the Separate Edicts do not entirely agree, but show such differences as might be expected in two separate letters addressed to officials residing in two different towns. I may add, however, that the characters of the two inscriptions likewise differ not inconsiderably. Those of the Dhauli version resemble throughout the alphabet used for the ten Rock-edicts of Dhauli and of Jaugada. Those of the Jaugada version are in a few cases, *e.g.*, in the form of *kha*, similar to the Khâlsî letters. Some characters, especially *ha* and *la*, show forms which I have not seen in any other inscription of Aśoka, but which are common enough on the documents of the Andhras and in later times. *La* especially has frequently a very modern appearance. This circumstance, too, is an important argument in favour of my belief that in Aśoka's times more than one form of the Southern or Lâṭ alphabet existed.

THE DHAULI AND JAUGADA VERSIONS OF AŚOKA'S ROCK EDICTS.†

EDICT I.

Dhauli, middle face.	*Jaugada.*
(Iyaṁ). . . . . .si [1] (pa)vatasi (d)evâ-naṁ pi(ye) . . . . jin[â] (likhâ)	Iyaṁ dhaṁmalipî Khapiṁgalasi [1] pavatasi devâ-naṁ piyena Piyadasinâ lâjinâ likhâpitâ[.] Hida no

* See notes 5 and 34 on the text.

† The sign ( ) indicates that the letter or letters are slightly damaged; the sign [ ], that they are so badly damaged as to be *almost* effaced. See Plates lxiv to lxix.

Dhauli Version.

[1] The inscription seems to have suffered considerably since the time when the first facsimiles were taken. The latter give a large portion of the beginning of the first edict and some other letters which are not now recognisable.

Jaugada Version.

[1] A dot is inscribed in the angle of the vowel of *pi.* Though it stands rather high, its regular form and depth show that it cannot be accidental, and must be taken for the *anusvâra*, which in the Jaugada and Dhauli versions is regularly placed in the vowel *i*, not after the *akshara* which bears the latter.

Dhauli.

. .i .îvaṁ âlabhitu pajoh. . . . [1] (no) [pi]. cha samâ . . . . .i . . . (tiyâ) [sa](m)â[jâ] (sâ)dhumatâ devâ . . . . [2] [Piya]-(dasi)ne [lâ](ji)[ne] . . . mah . . . . . . (naṁ) . . . Piya . . . . . . .n . . . . i (pânasa-tasa) . . . [â](la)bhiyis(u) sûpaṭhây(e)[. 3] Se [aja] adâ (i)[ya]ṁ dhaṁ(ma)lipî likhitâ tiṁn[i] . . . . . . [la]bhi(ya) . . . . tiṁni pânâni pachhâ (no â)l(a)bhiyisaṁt[i][. 4]

Jaugada.

kichhi jîvaṁ âlabhi(tu) [2] pajohitav(i)ye[, 1] (no) [3] pi cha samâje kaṭaviye[.] Bahukaṁ hi dosaṁ samâjasi [4] d(a)khati devânaṁ piye Piyadasî lâjâ[.] Athi pi chu ekatiyâ samâjâ sâdhumatâ devânaṁ piyasa [2] Piyadasine lâjine[.] Puluvaṁ mahâ(nasa)si [5] devânaṁ piyasa Piyadasine lâjine anudivasaṁ bah(û)ni pânasatasah(a)sâni [6] âlabhiyisu sûpa(ṭh)âye[. 3] Se aja adâ iyaṁ dhaṁmalipî likhitâ tiṁni yeva pânâni (â)labhiyaṁti[,] duve majûlâ[,] eke mige[.] Se pi chu mige no dhuvaṁ[.] Etâni pi ch(u) [7] tiṁni pânâni [4] pachhâ no âlabhiyisaṁti[. 5]

EDICT II.

(Sa)vata (v)i(ji)tasi [2] (d)e(v)ânaṁ piyasa Piyadasi(ne) l). . . . . [Aṁ]tiyoke nâma (Y)o(na)lâjâ[, 5] [e] vâ .i .sa Aṁtiyo[ka]sa sâmaṁtâ lâjâne s(a)vat(a) (devâ) . ṁ (pi)y(e)n(a) P(i)ya(d)asin[â] [3] . . . . . ch . . . . sâ cha pa . .i .isâ (cha)[.] . . dhâni [6] ân(i m)un(i)[so](pagâ)ni pasuopagân(i) cha atata nathi[,] sa-[va]t(a) (h)âlâpit(â) cha (lopâpi)tâ [4] cha (mûlâ) . . . . (va)ta (hâ)lâpitâ cha [7] lo(p)âpitâ cha [.] Ma(g)e[su] u [5] . pânâni khânâpitâni l(u)khâni cha lopâ(p)itâni paṭibhogâye . . . . . naṁ[.8]

Sa(v)ata vijitasi devânaṁ piya(sa) Pi(ya)dasine lâjine[,] e vâ pi aṁtâ[,] athâ Choḍâ Paṁḍiyâ Satiyapu[t]e . . . . .î [8] Aṁtiyoke nâma [6] Yonalâjâ[,] e vâ pi tasa Aṁtiyokasa sâmaṁtâ lâjâne[,] savata devânaṁ piyena Piyadasinâ lâji . . . . (ch)ikisâ (cha) [7] pasuchikisâ cha[.] Osadhâni âni munisopagâni pasuopagâni cha atata nathi[,] sava[ta] [9] . . . . cha atata nathi[,] savat(u) [10] hâlâ(pi)tâ [11] cha lopâpitâ cha [.] Magesu udupânâni khânâpitâni lukhâni cha . . . . [9]

EDICT III.

Devânaṁ piye Piyadas(î) lâjâ hevaṁ âhâ[:] (D)u(v)âdasavasâbhisitena me iy(a)ṁ ân(apa) .i . . . . (ta vi)jitasi me yut(â) [6] la [j]uke [cha] . . . i[ke] . [9]

Devânaṁ piye Piyadasî lâjâ hevaṁ âhâ[:] Duvadasavasâbhisitena me .i(ya)ṁ (â) [12] . . . . cha pâ(de)sike cha [10]

---

[2] There is a mark after *ta* which might have been an *anusvâra*, but its shape is so irregular that I believe it to be accidental, especially as indisputable cases in which the form *ṃsi* is used for the locative are not to be found.

[3] Though these words are a little damaged, the instrumental terminations are perfectly plain.

[4] The correctness of the reading *lopâpitâ* becomes perfectly certain, if one looks at the reverse of the impression.

[5] A very short stroke is attached to the left of the top of *u*. Hence it might be thought that we ought to read *odupânâni*. But this is impossible, as the sign for *o* in *pasuopagâni* (l. 7) differs very much, being a reversed *u* with an *â*-stroke attached to the right of the top. For the explanation see below, Note 34.

[6] The *â* of *yutâ* is not quite certain.

Jaugada Version.

[2] The left half of the letter *ta* is gone, but its right side and the vowel *u* are distinct.

[3] *No* is much damaged, but the *o*, at least, very probable.

[4] The vowel of the final *si* is very faint, but clearly traceable on the reverse of the impression. The *akshara* is damaged by a long slanting scratch, which goes from the middle of the left upstroke of the *sa* upwards.

[5] The *aksharas nasa* are much damaged, and the latter has lost its left-hand curve almost entirely.

[6] The reading *°sahâsâni* is possible, though in my opinion not probable.

[7] It may be *chû*, but the upper *u*-stroke is faint, and probably an accidental scratch. There is no certain case where *chû* appears instead of *chu*.

[8] No more than ten letters seem to have been lost. The final *î* of last lost word [*Taṁbapaṁn*]*î* is very plain.

[9] Only the straight upper stroke of *ta* is visible.

[10] The impression seems to decide for the reading *savatu*, though an apparent *e*-stroke is visible on the left of the *ta*. It is, however, not improbable that the apparent *u*-stroke is also accidental, since its shape is irregular.

[11] *Hâlâpitâ* is, according to the impression, more probable than *hâlâpetâ*.

[12] Only the upper left-hand part of this letter is visible.

Dhauli.

paṁchasu paṁchasu vasesu anusayânaṁ [7] nikhamâvû athâ aṁnâye (pi k)aṁ(ma)ne hevaṁ imâye (dh)aṁ(m)ânu . thiy(e)[:] (s)âdhu mâtâpit(i)su [8] (s)u(s)ûs[â] [9] . . . . [10] nâtisu cha[,] baṁbhanasamanehi sâdhu dâne[,] jîvesu anâlambhe sâdhu[,] apaviyati (a)pabh(a)ṁḍatâ sâdhu[.] Palisâ pi cha . . na[s]i [10] (yu)[tâ](n)i ânapayi(sati) [11] . tut(e) cha viyaṁ(ja) . . . [11]

Jaugada.

paṁchas(u) [13] paṁchasu vasesu anusayânaṁ nikhamâvû athâ aṁnâye pi kaṁmane . . . . .
. . . .
. . sâ mitasaṁthutes.[14] [11] nâtisu cha[,] baṁbhanasamanehi sâdhu dâne[,] jîvesu anâlaṁbhe sâdhu
. . . .
. . . . [12] hetute cha viyaṁjanate cha[.13]

EDICT IV.

Dhauli.

Atikaṁ(ta)ṁ aṁtalaṁ bahûni vasasatâni[,] vaḍhiteva pânâ(la)ṁbhe vihisâ cha bhûtânaṁ nâtisu asaṁp(a)ṭipati sa(ma)nabâbha(ne)su a(sa)ṁpaṭipa[ti][12] [12.] Se aja devânaṁ piyasa (P)i(y)adasi(n)e l(â)ji(n)e (dha)ṁmachalanena bheligho(sa)ṁ a(ho) dhaṁma(gho)saṁ vimânadasanaṁ ha(thî)ni (a)gi(k)aṁdhâni aṁnâni cha (d)ivi(y)âni [13] lûpân[i] da(s)ayitu munisânaṁ[.] Âd(i)se (b)ahûhi va(s)a(s)a(t)ehi no hûtapuluve[,] tâdise aja vaḍhi . (de)vânaṁ pi(ya)sa Pi(yad)asine lâjine dhaṁ(m)ânusathiyâ [14] (anâ)(la)ṁbhe pânânaṁ avihisâ bhûtânaṁ nâtisu saṁpaṭi pat(i) . manaba(ṁ)bh(a)nesu [13] saṁpaṭipati mâtipitususûsâ vu[ḍha]susûsâ[.] Esa aṁne cha ba(hu)vidhe [15] (dh)aṁmachalane vaḍhite[,] vaḍhayis(a)ti chev(a) (de)vânaṁ piye Piya(da)sî lâj(â) dhaṁmachalanaṁ imaṁ[.] Putâ pi (cha)[13b] natipana[t]i. [14] cha devânaṁ piyasa Piyadasine lâ(j)ine [16] pavaḍhayisaṁti yeva dhaṁmachalanaṁ (i)maṁ âk(apa)ṁ dhaṁma[s]i (s)îlasi cha [ch]i[ṭh]itu [15] dh[aṁ](ma)ṁ (a)nu(sâ)sisaṁ(ti)[.] Esa h(i) se[ṭhe] (ka)ṁme yâ dhaṁmânusâsanâ[.] Dhaṁmachalane pi chu [17] no hoti asilasa[.] Se imasa a(ṭha)sa vu(ḍh)î ahîni cha sâdhu[.] Et(â)[y]e . . . (i)yaṁ likhite[,] imasa aṭhasa vaḍhî yujaṁtû hîni cha mâ alochayis(u)[.18] Duvâdasa vasâni abhi-

Jaugada.

A(t)ikaṁtaṁ aṁtalaṁ bahûni vasasatâni[,] vaḍhiteva pânâlaṁbhe . . . .
. . . . [14.]
Se aja devânaṁ piyasa Piyadasine lâjine dhaṁmachalanena bhel . . . .
. . . .
. . . . [15] diviyâni lûpâni dasayitu munisânaṁ[.] Âdise bahûhi vasasate . .
. . . .
. . . . [16] dhaṁmâ(nu)sathiyâ anâlaṁbhe pânânaṁ avihisâ bhûtânaṁ nâtisu (saṁpa)[15] .
. . . .
. . . . [17] Esa aṁne cha bahuvidhe dhaṁmachalane vaḍhite[,] va(ḍhayi) . . . .
. . . .
. . . .
. . . [18] Piyadasine lâjine pava(ḍhayisaṁti) [y]e(va) dhaṁmacha . . . .
. . . .
. . . .
. . [19] Dhaṁmachalane pi chu no ho(ti) . . . .
. . . .
. . . . [.20]
h[î]ni [16] cha mâ alocha(y)i . . . .

---

[7] There is a dot standing in the proper position after *sa*; but as it is smaller and not quite so deep as the other *anusvâras*, I take it to be accidental.

[8] The tops of the letters *pa*, *ta*, and *sa*, are much damaged, and the reading °*pitâsu* is not quite impossible.

[9] The lower portions only of the three consonants are visible, and the *û* under the second is not quite certain.

[10] Only the *na* and the *i* are certain, but the reading was doubtlessly [*gana*]*na*[*s*]*i*, as in the Khâlsî version.

[11] The tops of the letters *sa* and *ta* are much damaged, and a really certain reading impossible.

[12] It would seem that two more letters followed this word, but it is impossible to make out any word.

[13] The reading °*baṁbhanesu* is more probable than *bâ*°, as the back of the impression shows a deep circle detached from *ba*.

[13b] Possibly *chu*.

[14] One more letter, *kâ*, seems to have stood after *pana*[*t*]*i*, and the reading has probably been *panatikâ*, similar to that of Khâlsî.

[15] This may also have been *chithitu*. The middle sign is too much defaced to allow a certain reading.

Jaugada Version.

[13] The impression shows clearly that the apparent second *u*-stroke in the first *paṁchasu* is merely an accidental scratch.

[14] The left half of the final *sa* of *mitasaṁthutes*[*u*] is distinct; the right and the vowel are lost. It is, however, perfectly clear what the reading has been. It is also possible that a *cha* stood at the end of the line.

[15] *Saṁpa* is on the impression less distinct than on the photograph.

[16] The shape of the vowel-mark above *ha* makes it probable that it was *î*, not *i*. The omission of the following *cha* in my first transcript, given in the *Zeitsch. D. Morg. Ges.*, is due to a clerical mistake.

Dhauli.

sitasa devâ(n)aṁ (p)i(ya)sa Piyadasine lâjine (ya)ṁ . .[16]
likhite[.19]

Jaugada.

. . . .
. . . [21]

EDICT V.

. . â(na)ṁ piye Piyadasî lâ(j)â h(eva)ṁ âhâ[:] Kayâne dukale[.] E . . . . kayân(a)sa[,] se dukalaṁ kal(e)ti[.] Se me b(ahu)ke kayâ(n)e kaṭe[.] Taṁ ye me (put)[â] va [20] n(a)t[i] (va) . . ṁ cha t(e)n(a) (ye) apati(y)e me âva kapaṁ tathâ anuvatisaṁt(i)[,] se(suka)ṭaṁ kachh(a)ṁti[.] E (he)ta desaṁ pi hâpayisat(i)[,] se (d)ukaṭaṁ kachh(a)ti[.] Pâ(pe) hi[nâma] [21] sup(a)dâlaye[.][17] S[e] at(ika)ṁtaṁ aṁtalaṁ[,] no hûtapuluvâ dhaṁmamahâmâtâ nâma[.] Se ted(a)sava(sâ)bhisitena me dhaṁmamahâmâtâ nâ(m)a kaṭâ[.] Te sa(v)apâsaṁḍes[u] [22] v(i)y(âpaṭâ) dhaṁmâdhithân(â)ye[18] dhaṁmavaḍhiye hitasukhâye cha dhaṁ(mayu)tas(a) Yona-Kaṁbocha-Gaṁdhâlesu Laṭhika-Pi(te)nikesu e vâ pi aṁne âp(alaṁ)ta[.] Bhaṭi[mayes]u[19] [23] bâbha(n)ibhi[ye](s)u[20] anâthesu ma[hâ](la)kesu cha h(i)tasukhâye dhaṁmayutâye a(pa)libodh(â)ye[21] viyâpaṭâ se[.] Baṁdha(naba)dhasa p(a)ṭivi[dhâ](nâ)ye apali(bodhâ)ye mokhâye cha [24] iyaṁ anubaṁdh(a)[22] (pa)[ja] ti va [ka]ṭâbhîkâ[le] ti va mahâlake ti v(a) viyâpaṭâ se[.] Hida cha (b)âhilesu cha nagalesu savesu s(a)v(e)su ol(o)dhane(su) (m)[e] e vâ pi bhât(i)naṁ[23] me bhaginînaṁ va [25] aṁnesu (v)â nâ(t)i[su][24] (savata viyâpa)ṭâ[.] E iyaṁ dhaṁ(man)isite ti va[25] dhaṁmâdhithâne ti v(a) dânasayute va savapu(ṭha)viyaṁ[26] dhaṁmayutasi viyâpaṭâ ime dhaṁmamahâ(mât)â[.] (Im)âye aṭhâye [26] iyaṁ dhaṁmalip(i)[27] likhi(tâ)[,] chilaṭhi(tî)kâ[28] [ho](t)u [tathâ][29] (cha) me pa[jâ] (anu)vatatu[.27]

Devâ(naṁ) piye Piyada . . . . . .
. . . .
. . . .
. . . . [22] (na)t(i) va palaṁ cha te .
. . . .
. . . .
. . . . [23]
s(u)padâla(ye)[.] Se a . . . .
. . . .
. . . .
. . . . [24] . . . .
. ṁ(mâ)dhi(ṭhâ)nâ . . . .
. . . .
. . . .
. . . . [25] . bhanibhi . . . .
. . . .
. . . .
. . . . [26] mokhâye . . .
. . . .
. . . .
. . . . [27] . . e vâ
. . . .
. . . .
. . . .
. . . . [28] . . . . .
. . . .
. . . .
. . . . [29][16a]

EDICT VI.

Dhauli: Middle face.

Devâ(naṁ p)iye Pi(yada)sî lâjâ (h)evaṁ âhâ[:] A(t)ikaṁ(taṁ) (a)ṁ(t)alaṁ[,] no (h)û(ta)puluve savaṁ kâlaṁ

Jaugada: Second side.

. . ânaṁ piye Piyadasî lâjâ hevaṁ âhâ[:] Ati (k)aṁtaṁ aṁtalaṁ[,] no hûtapuluve savaṁ kalaṁ

---

[16] I am unable to say what the two signs after *yaṁ* may have been. The remnants of the second point rather to a *dha* than to a *pa*, which other facsimiles give. The sense requires the reading *iyaṁ*, as the other versions read, or some similar phrase.

[17] There is a small vertical stroke under *pa*, but a look at the reverse of the impression shows that it is accidental.

[18] The vowel of *nâ* is slightly damaged, but recognisable on the reverse.

[19] The lower portions only of the letters *mayes* are visible.

[20] Two large slanting fissures or scratches deface the lower left and the top of *ye* on the right. Nevertheless the *e*-stroke is plainly visible.

[21] *Dhâ* is plain on the reverse of the impression.

[22] Though the top of *dha* is defaced (as well as that of the following *pa*), it is not probable that a vowel sign or an *anusvâra* was attached.

[23] This may have been *bhâtînaṁ*. It is only possible to recognise that the vowel was an *i*, but not its quantity.

[24] The reverse of the impression shows *nâti* with tolerable distinctness. The final *su* is much defaced, and the reading *taṁ* not impossible.

[25] There is a dot after *va*, the shape of which, however, shows clearly that it is not an *anusvâra*.

[26] Possibly *savaputhaviyaṁ* with a dental *tha* is to be read.

[27] Possibly °*lipi* is to be read.

[28] *Tî* is pretty clear on the reverse of the impression.

[29] *Ho* and *tathâ* are visible on the reverse of the impression.

Jaugada Version.

[16a] Though there are only remnants of twenty-eight lines on this face of the Jaugada inscription, the total must have been twenty-nine; for, as the first four show, each line contained from fifty to fifty-five *aksharas* only.

Dhauli.

aṭha(kaṁ)me va (p)aṭiveda(n)â va[.] Se mamayâ kaṭe[,] savaṁ [kâlaṁ] . . [mî]nasa me [28] aṁte olodh(a)-na(s)i gabh(âgâla)si v[achas]i [v]inîtasi (u)yân[asi cha] savata paṭivedakâ janasa aṭhaṁ paṭived(a)yaṁtu me (t)i[.] Sa(vata) cha janasa a(ṭh)aṁ kal(â)ṁi [30] ha-[ka]ṁ[.29] Aṁ pi cha ki[ṁ](chh)i mukh(a)te (ânapa)-yâm(i) dâpakaṁ v[â] (sâ)v(a)kaṁ vâ[,] e vâ mahâm[â-teh]i [31] atiyâyike âlopite hoti[,] tasi aṭhasi v(iv)âde (va) nijhatî vâ saṁtaṁ palisây(a) [30] ânaṁtaliyaṁ paṭ(ive)detav(iye) me ti sava(ta) savaṁ kâ(la)ṁ he(va)ṁ me anusathe[.] Nath(i) [hi m]e [to](s)e u[ṭhâna]s-aṭh(a)saṁtîl(a)nâya cha[.] Kaṭaviya(mate) hi me sa valokahite[.31] T(asa) cha pan(a) iyaṁ mûle (u)ṭhân(e cha aṭha)saṁtîl(an)â cha[.] Nathi hi kaṁmata. (sava)-lo[ka](hitena)[.] (Aṁ cha) . chh[i] palakamâm(i h)a kaṁ[,] kiṁti[?] bhûtânaṁ â[na]niyaṁ yehaṁ ti [32] (hida) (cha kâni su)khayâmi pal(a)t(a) cha sva(ga)[ṁ] [â]lâdhayaṁtû ti[.] (Etâye) . . . . yaṁ dhaṁmalipî likhitâ[,] ch(ilaṭhi)tîkâ hotu t(ath)â cha putâ papotâ me palakamaṁt(u) [33] [sava] . (ka-hitâ)ye[.] Dukale chu iyaṁ aṁna(ta agena pa)-lakamena[.] (Se)to.[32]

Jaugada.

aṭhakaṁme paṭivedanâ va[.] Se mamayâ kaṭe[,] savaṁ kâlaṁ [1] . . . . (sa) me aṁte olodha-nasi gabhâgâlasi vachasi vinîtasi uyânasi cha savata paṭivedakâ janasa aṭhaṁ paṭivedayaṁtu me ti[.] Savata cha janasa [2] . . . . (ka)ṁ[.][17] Aṁ pi cha kiṁchhi mukhate ânapa-yâmi dâpakaṁ vâ sâvakaṁ vâ[,] e vâ mahâmâ-tehi a(t)i(yâ)yike (â)lopite hoti[,] (ta)si aṭhasi vivâde va [3] . . . . lisâ(ya) (â)naṁ(ta)liyaṁ paṭivedetaviye me ti savata savaṁ kâlaṁ hevaṁ me anusathe[.][18] Nathi hi me tose uṭhânasi aṭhasaṁtîlanâya cha[.47] . . . . me sa-valokahite[.] Tasa cha pana iyaṁ mûle uṭhâne cha aṭhasaṁtîlanâ cha[.] Nathi hi kaṁmatalâ[19] sava-lokahitena[.] Aṁ cha kichhi [20] p(a)lakamâmi ha-kaṁ[, 5] . . . . . . (na)niyaṁ yehaṁ ti[,] hida cha kâni sukhayâmi palata cha svagaṁ âlâdhayaṁtû ti[.] · Etâye (a)ṭhâye i(ya)ṁ dhaṁmalipî likhitâ[,] chilaṭhitîka hotû [6] . . . . . . (po)tâ me palakamaṁtu saval(o)ka-hitâye[.] Dukale chu iyaṁ aṁnata agena pa-lakamena[.]

EDICT VII.—*On Right face.*

Devânaṁ (p)iye Piyadasî lâjâ savata ichhat(i) [sava](p)âsaṁ[ḍâ] vasevû t(i)[.][33] Save h(i) t[e] (s)ayamaṁ (bh)âv(a)sudhî cha ichhaṁti[.] Mun(i)sâ cha[1] [u]ch[â]v[u]chachhaṁdâ uchâvuchalâgâ[.] T(e) s(a)vaṁ vâ ek(ade)s(aṁ) v[a] (kachhaṁti)[.] V(i-p)u(l)e pi ch(a) dâne as(a) n(a)th[i][,] (s)a(y)ame (bh)â-vasudhî cha nîche bâḍhaṁ[.2]

. . . . . . yada(sî) lâjâ savata ichhati savap(â)saṁḍâ vasev. . i[.] (Sav)e hi te sa(y)amaṁ bhâvasudhî cha ichhaṁti[.] Munisâ cha uchavuchachhaṁdâ uchâvuchalâgâ[.8] . . . (v)[â] ekadesaṁ va kachhaṁti[.] (V)i-(pu)le pi cha (d)â . e . . . . [dh]i cha nîche (b)âḍhaṁ[.9]

EDICT VIII.

. . (kaṁtaṁ) aṁ(talaṁ) lâ(jâ)ne (vi)h(â)layâtaṁ nâm(a) . i(kha)m(i)su[.] . t[a] m[i](ga)viy[â] (a)ṁnâni cha edisâni (abh)i(l)â(m)âni huvaṁti (n)aṁ[.] Se dev(â)naṁ piye [3] P(iyada)sî lâjâ d(a)s(avas)âbhi-si(t)e (n)ikhami saṁbodh(î)[.] . e[n]atâ dha- . . . [.] (Ta)[t]esa (ho)ti[,] samanabâbhanânaṁ d(a)-s(a)n(e) ch(a) d(ân)e cha v(u)ḍhânaṁ dasane cha [4]

. (t) . kaṁtaṁ aṁtalaṁ lâjâ . . . . iyâ (a)ṁnâni cha e . . . . . . (m)âni huvaṁti naṁ[.] Se devânaṁ piye [10] Piyadasî (l)âjâ dasa . . . . [.] (Ta)te(sa ho)ti[,] (sa) . . . . cha dâne cha vuḍhânaṁ dasane cha [11]

---

[30] Read *kalemi.* Horizontal strokes are apparently attached on both sides of the top of *la*, one of which must be accidental, because *o* is never marked in the Dhauli version by two horizontals placed at the same height. The *â*-stroke looks more regular and distinct than that on the left.

[31] Among the four letters placed between brackets *â* alone is recognisable, though with difficulty. The remainder has disappeared, but the very distinct final *i* makes the restoration certain.

[32] The word *seto* follows *palakamena* at a distance of about two inches, and cannot therefore belong to the preceding edict. The upper part of the first *akshara* is damaged, but it seems to me certain that it represents a *sa* similar in shape to that of the Gupta alphabet with a superscribed *mâtrâ.* After *to* follows a long slanting fissure or scratch, which, as far as I can see, does not conceal a third letter.

[33] Possibly *vasevû tî* is to be read.

Jaugada Version.

[17] The right side of the cross-bar and a part of the vertical of *ka* are visible.

[18] The dental *tha* of *anusathe* is perfectly distinct.

[19] A piece of the rock between the top of *ka* and the *anusvâra* has peeled off and produces a semblance of *kâ.* But the *anusvâra* is nevertheless undoubtedly the correct reading.

[20] The impression shows no *anusvâra.*

Dhauli.

hilaṁnapaṭivi(dhân)e [34] cha (j)â(n)apada(sa) (j)anasa d(a)s(a)ne cha dhaṁmânu(sa)thî ch(a) . (ma) . (l)i(p)u-chhâ cha[.] (Tado)pa(yâ esa bhûy)e abhilâme hoti devânaṁ piyasa Piyada(s)in(e) (l)âjine bhâge [aṁ](n)e[.5]

Jaugada.

hilaṁnapaṭiv(idhâ)ne (cha) . . . .
. . . . ṁmapâli(p) .
. . . . ilâme hoti
devânaṁ piyasa [12] Piyadasine lâjine bhâge (a) . . [.13]

Edict IX.

Devânaṁ piye Piyadasî lâjâ hevaṁ âhâ[:] (Athi) [ja](n)e uchâvuchaṁ maṁga(l)aṁ kal(e)ti (âbâ)dh(e) . . . . . .îvâ . . . [j]opadâye pavâsasi[. 6] Etâye aṁnâye cha hed(i)sâye j(a)ne bahukaṁ maṁgalaṁ ka[let]i[.] [Eta] (tu) ithî b(ah)u(ka)ṁ ch(a) (bah)u[v]i(dhaṁ) ch(a)(khuda)[kaṁ](cha) (nilaṭhiya)ṁ cha maṁgalaṁ kaleti[.7] Se kaṭ(a)viye (ch)e(va) (kho) (m)aṁ(ga)le[.] (Ap)aphale chu kho esa hedise maṁ(ga)[le][.] . [ya]ṁ [cha kho] (mahâ)ph(a)le e [dha]ṁmamaṁ(ga)le[.] (Ta)tesa [dâsabhaṭakas]i saṁ-m(y)âpaṭipati [35] [8] gulûnaṁ apa(chi) . . . . . . [me] (sama)nabâbha(n)ânaṁ dâ(n)e[.] Es(a) aṁne ch(a) . . . (dha)[ṁma]maṁga(le) [nâ](ma)[.] [Ta] vata . . (p)it(i)nâ . p[ute]na pi bhâtinâ pi [9] suvâmike(na) [pi][:]
. . . .
(le) âva tasa aṭhasa niphatiy(â)[.] (Athi p)[i] . [v]aṁ v[u]te[:] [36] dâne s[â]dh[û] ti[.] Se (nathi) . . . . . anugahe vâ[, 10] [âd]i[s]e (dh)aṁmadâne dhaṁma-(nugahe) . . . . [m]i . . . . .i(k)e(n)a sahâye(na)[p]i viyovadit(avi). . . i [ta]si pakalanasi [11]
. . . . [l]âdhayitave[,
. . . . ṭav . . . . . . (svagasa) âl(adh)î[.12] [37]]

Devân(aṁ) [21] piye Pi(y)adasî l(âjâ) . . . . . .
. . . .
. . . . (pa)jupadâye pavâsasi[.]
Etâye aṁnâye cha [14] hedisâye jane (bah)u(ka)ṁ .
. . . .
. . . .
. (ma)ṁga(laṁ) kaleti[.] Se kaṭaviye cheva kho maṁ(ga)le[.16] Apa(pha)le chu (kho) e(sa hedise ma) . . . .
. . . . (bhaṭa)kasi saṁ-myâpaṭipati [22] gulûnaṁ apachi(ti) pâne(su) sa(ya)me [16] sama(na)bâbhanâ [23] . . . e[.] Esa aṁne) .
. . . .
pi)tinâ pi putena pi bhâtinâ pi suvâmikena pi[:] i(yaṁ (sâdhu)[,] iyaṁ kaṭavi(y)e [17] . . . .
. . . .
. . . . (se) dâne (a)nugahe vâ[,] âdi[s]e [24] dh(aṁ)madâne dhaṁmâ-(nu)ga(h)e cha[.] Se chu kho miten(a) [18] . . . . .
. . . .
. yaṁ (sâ)dhû[,] imena sakiye svage âlâdh(a)yitave[,] kiṁ hi imena kaṭaviyatalâ [19] . . . . [20]

Edict X.

. v[â]naṁ piye Piyadas[î] (lâjâ) (yaso vâ k)iṭi vâ n(a) . . (ṭhâ) . (haṁ) maṁn[a]t(e) . . . . . i (yaso vâ ki)ṭî vâ ichh(a)ti tadatvâye (a) . . . . [:](ja)ne[13] . . . . (saṁ) s[u] . (satu me) (dha)ṁma . . . .

. . . .
. . . . (ya)so [25] vâ ki(ṭ)î vâ ichhati tadatvâye â(ya)tiye cha [:] (ja)ne dhaṁmasu(sû)saṁ susûsatu (me) [21] . . . . . .

---

[34] I write *paṭividhâne* instead of *peṭi°*. Though a horizontal stroke is attached to the top of the left-hand vertical of *pa*, its shortness shows that it is not an *e*-stroke. A similar peculiarity has been noticed above in the initial *u* of *u[du]pânâni* (ii. 8), where, as has been pointed out, the reading *odupânâni* is impossible. In the latter case the horizontal stroke can only serve to define the end of the vertical stroke. In other words, it must be a *serif*. I think that in this second instance it has to be taken in the same manner. Exactly similar forms of the serif are common on the Andhra inscriptions.

[35] Read *samyâsaṁpaṭipati*. The subscribed *ya* is perfectly distinct on the reverse of the impression.

[36] There are two copies of this passage on the impression. On the reverse of one *vaṁ* is distinctly visible, and on the obverse of the other *vute*, not *vate*, is the probable reading. It is not in the least doubtful that this misunderstood passage has to be read "*Athi pi hevaṁ vute.*"

[37] Possibly *âlâdhi*.

Jaugada Version.

[21] *Naṁ* looks nearly like *nâ*. But the position of the apparent *â*-stroke and its form on the impression show that it is an *anusvâra* which has been joined with the *na* through the peeling of a piece of the rock.

[22] Read *samyâ°* instead of *saṁmyâ*.

[23] *Samabâbhanâ*, in my former transcript in the *Zeitsch. D. Morg. Ges.*, is a misprint.

[24] *Âdise* looks even on the impression like *âdive*. But the position of the circle under the vertical stroke and its enormous size, as well as a large flaw on the spot where the right-hand curve of *sa* ought to stand, show that the letter has been a *sa*, not a *va*.

[25] Only a small piece of the right side of *ya* is visible.

Dhauli.

. . . . . (me)[.] Etakâye ya . . . . î (vâ) . . . . . .
. i (p)ala . kama(t)i devânaṁ piye (p)â(la)[t]i[k]â[y]e . [,
14] kiṁti[?] (sa)ka(le apa)pal(i)save h[u]v[eyâ] (t)i[.]
Palisa . . . . [D]ukal[e] . . . . . . (ta age) . . . . . (na)
savaṁ cha pa[l]itiji[tu][15] khudak(e)na v(â) usa(ṭe)na
vâ[.] U(saṭena) chu (dukala)ta[le].16][38]

Jaugada.

. . . .
. . . . . . (t)i devânaṁ piye pâl(a)ti(kâ)yevâ[,]
(k)i(ṁ)ti[?][26] sakale apapalisave huv(ey)â ti[.22] . . .
. . . .
. . . . [i]itij(i)t(u) khu(da)kena vâ u(sa)ṭe(na)
v(â)[.] Usaṭ(e)na chu dukalatale[.23]

EDICT XIV.

Dhauli.

Iyaṁ dhaṁmalipî devânaṁ piyena Piyada . inâ
lâj . . [likh] . . . . athi
majhi(m)ena . . . .[No[39] h]i save sav(a)ta
ghaṭite[.17] Mahaṁte hi vijaye ba(h)u(k)e cha
likhite likhiyisâ . [ch]e[va] . . [.] Athi (cha) [he] .
. . . . ây[e] [18]
(k)iṁti cha[?] jane tathâ paṭipajeyâ t(i)[.] E pi chu
heta (asa)mati likhite (sa)ṁ . . . . saṁ .
(lochayitu) . . . . kala . . . . . ti [19][40]

Jaugada.

. . . .
. . . .
. jhim(ena athi) vith(a)ṭena[.] (No) hi save savata
ghaṭite[.] Mahaṁte hi vijaye [24] . . . .
. . . .
. . . . (sa) mâdhuliyâye[,]
kiṁt(i) cha[?] jane tathâ paṭipajeyâ ti[.] E pi chu
heta [25] . . . . , ...
. . . . [26]

TRANSLATION.[1]

EDICT I.

This religious edict has been incised by order of King Piyadasi, beloved of the gods, on Mount Khapiṁgala:—No animal may be slaughtered and offered here as a burnt-sacrifice; nor shall any festive assembly be held. For King Piyadasi, beloved of the gods, sees much evil in festive assemblies. There are, however, also some *kinds of*[2] festive assemblies considered meritorious by King Piyadasi, beloved of the gods.

Formerly many hundred thousand animals were slaughtered daily in the kitchen of King Piyadasi, beloved of the gods, in order to *prepare* curries. Now, when this religious edict is incised, only three animals are slaughtered *daily*, two peacocks *and* one deer; the deer, however, not even regularly. But in future even these three animals will no *longer* be slaughtered.

---

38 The *ta* of *dukatale* is clearly distinguishable; *le* is very faint.

39 Only the *ó*-stroke of the *o* in *no* is distinct; *hi* is more probable than *pi* when seen on the reverse. A vertical stroke is visible after *hi*, but it must be an accidental scratch, as there is no room for a letter between *hi* and *sa*.

40 The reading of the Dhauli version seems to have differed from that of the other three recensions (G., Kh. and Sh.), but I am unable to guess its precise tenor from the remains.

Jaugada Version.

26 It is certain that *kiṁti* is the correct reading. The *anusvâra* stands as usual in the angle of the *i*. The remark on my transcript in the *Zeitsch. D. Morg. Ges.* has to be corrected.

1 With respect to the translations appended, I must note that they are based on my German rendering, published in the *Zeitsch. der Deutsch. Morg. Gesellsch.*, Bd. xxxvii, (1883–84), pp. 87–108, 253–281, 422–434, 572–593, and Bd. xl, pp. 127–143. The notes given there show the reasons why I differ from my predecessors. Full explanations of the Separate Edicts will be published in one of the next numbers of the same journal. I have also to state that Dr. E. Hultzsch and Dr. M. Winternitz have assisted me in the preparation and collation of the transcripts.

2 The italics indicate that the words have been added for clearness' sake, and the sign [ ] that the passage has been destroyed in the text, and restored according to the other versions.

Edict II.

Everywhere in the empire of King Piyadasi, beloved of the gods, as well as *among those nations and princes* that are *his* neighbours, such as the Choḍas, the Paṇḍiyas, the Satiya[puta, the Kelalaputa, Taṁbapaṁn]î, the Yona-king, called Aṁtiyoka,[1] as well as *among those* who are the vassal-kings of that Aṁtiyoka,—everywhere King Piyadasi, beloved of the gods, has founded two *kinds of* hospitals, both hospitals [for men] and hospitals for animals. Everywhere where herbs wholesome for men and wholesome for animals are not found, they have been imported and planted by *the king's* order. [Moreover, everywhere where *medicinal* roots and fruits] are not found, they have been imported and planted by *the king's* order. On the roads wells have been dug and trees been planted by his order for the enjoyment [of men and beasts].

Edict III.

King Piyadasi, beloved of the gods, speaks thus :—*When I had been* anointed twelve years this *following* order was given by me :—"[Everywhere] in my empire both *my* loyal writers and vassals shall go forth on a tour every five years, as for other business, even so for the sake of preaching the sacred law in this wise: Meritorious is the obedience towards mother and father, towards *venerable* friends and acquaintances, and towards *venerable* relatives; meritorious is the liberality towards Brahmans and ascetics, meritorious is the abstention from killing living creatures, meritorious is the abstention from reviling heterodox *men*. Moreover, *the teachers and ascetics of all* schools will inculcate *what is* befitting at divine service, both according to the letter and according to the spirit."

Edict IV.

A long period, many hundreds of years, have passed, *during which* the slaughter of animals, the cruel treatment of created beings, the unbecoming behaviour towards relatives *and* the unbecoming behaviour towards ascetics and Brahmans have only increased. But now, in consequence of the fulfilment of the sacred law by King Piyadasi, beloved of the gods, the sound of drums, or rather the sound of the law, *has been heard*, while the sight of cars of the gods, elephants, and other heavenly spectacles were exhibited to the people. As has not happened formerly in many centuries, even so have grown through the god-beloved King Piyadasi's preaching of the law the non-destruction of animals, the good treatment of living creatures, the decorous behaviour towards relatives, the decorous behaviour towards ascetics and Brahmans, the obedience towards parents, the obedience towards the aged. Thus and in many other ways the fulfilment of the sacred law has grown, and King Piyadasi, beloved of the gods, will make this fulfilment of the sacred law grow *still more*. Moreover, the sons, grandsons, and great-grandsons of King Piyadasi, beloved of the gods, will make this fulfilment of the sacred law grow until the end of time, *and* will preach the sacred law, abiding by the sacred law and by virtuous conduct. For that is the best work, *viz.*, the preaching of the sacred law; but the fulfilment of the sacred law is not *possible* for a man destitute of virtuous conduct. The growth of this very matter and its non-diminution are meritorious. For this [purpose], *viz.*, *that* they may cause the growth of this matter

---

[1] The Choḍas are the Cholas of Kâñchî, the Paṁḍiyas the Pâṇḍyas of the extreme south, the Satiyaputa is probably the king of the Satvats, the Kelalaputa the king of Kerala or Malabâr, Taṁbapaṁnî, Tâmraparṇî, or Ceylon, the Yonas are the Yavanas or Greeks, and Antiyoka is Antiokhos.

and may not permit its diminution, this *edict* has been incised. This *edict* has been incised when King Piyadasi, beloved of the gods, had been anointed twelve years.

Edict V.

King Piyadasi, beloved of the gods, speaks thus :—Good *works* are difficult of performance. [He who is fully occupied] with good *works* does something difficult of performance. Now much good has been done by me. *If* then my sons and my grandsons, and those *among* my descendants who *may come* after them until the end of time, will thus follow *my example*, they will do *what is* meritorious. But he who will give up even a portion of these *virtuous acts* will commit sin. For sin easily develops.

Now a long period has passed, *and* the *officials* called the Overseers of the sacred law have formerly not existed. Now when I had been anointed thirteen years, I appointed Overseers of the sacred law. They are busy among all sects with watching over the sacred law, with the growth of the sacred law, and with the welfare and happiness of *my* loyal *subjects, as also* among the Yonas, Kaṁbochas, Gaṁdhâlas, Laṭhikas, Pitenikas,[1] and *all* other *nations* which are my neighbours. Among *my* hired servants,[2] among Brahmans and Vaiśyas, among the unprotected and among the aged, they are busy with the welfare and happiness, with the removal of obstacles connected with the sacred law. With the prevention of *unjust* imprisonment and of *unjust* corporal punishment, with the removal of obstacles and with loosening bonds, for these purposes they are busy, *considering* that *there is* a *numerous* progeny, or, ... , or, that *the person concerned is* aged. Here[3] and in all the outlying towns they are everywhere busy in all my harems, as well as *in those* of my brothers and sister and among my other relatives. These Overseers of the sacred law are busy with what concerns the sacred law, with watching over the sacred law and with what is connected with *pious* gifts, on the whole earth, among *all my* loyal *subjects*. This religious edict has been incised for the following purpose, *viz*., that it may endure for a long time, and that my subjects may act accordingly.

Edict VI.

King Piyadasi, beloved of the gods, speaks thus :—A long period has elapsed, *during which* formerly the despatch of business and the hearing of the informers have not regularly taken place. Now I have made *the following arrangement, that* the informers may report to me the concerns of the people at any time, [while I dine,] in *my* harem, in *my* private rooms, in the latrine, in *my* carriages, and in *my* pleasure garden, and everywhere I despatch the business of the people. Moreover, if, with respect to anything which I order by *word of* mouth to be given or to be obeyed as a command, or which as a pressing *matter* is entrusted to my officials, a dispute or a fraud happens in the committee *of any caste or sect*, I have given orders that it shall be brought forthwith to my cognisance in any place and at any time. For I am never satisfied with *my* exertions and with the despatch of business. For I consider the welfare of all people as something for which I must work. But the root of that is exertion and the despatch of business. There is no more important

---

[1] *i.e.*, Yavanas or Greeks, Kambojas or Kâbulîs, Gândhâras or the north-western Pañjâbîs, Ṛishṭikas, and Pitenikas, two southern people.

[2] The new reading, *bhaṭimaya*, makes it necessary to render the word by *bhṛitimaya*, and to explain it by "hired servants."

[3] *i.e.*, in Pâṭaliputra, the capital of Aśoka.

work than *to secure* the welfare of all. And what is the purpose of every effort which I make? It is that I may discharge the debt *which I owe* to the creatures, that I may make them happy in this world, and that they may gain heaven in the next. This religious edict has been incised for the following purpose, that it may endure for a long time, and that my sons and grandsons may thus exert themselves for the welfare of all men. But that is difficult *to carry out* without the utmost exertion. The white one.[1]

EDICT VII.

King Piyadasi, beloved of the gods, desires that sectarians of all kinds may dwell everywhere. For they all seek after self-control and purity of mind. But men *possess* various desires and various likings. They will put in practice either the whole or a part only *of what they profess*. But self-control and purity of mind are laudable in a lowly man, to whom even great liberality is impossible.

EDICT VIII.

A long period has elapsed, *during which* the kings used to go forth on so-called pleasure-tours. On such *occasions* the chase and other similar amusements used to be *pursued*. Now when King Piyadasi, beloved of the gods, had been anointed ten years, he went forth *in search* after true knowledge. Owing to this *event*, religious tours *have become a regular institution* here *in my empire*. On that *occasion* the following happens, *viz.*, the reception of and almsgiving to Brahmans and ascetics, the reception of the aged, the distribution of gold, the reception of the people of the provinces, the preaching of the sacred law and inquiries concerning the sacred law. *It is thus that*, in exchange *for past pleasures*, King Piyadasi, beloved of the gods, since then enjoys the pleasures *which* these *virtuous actions procure*.

EDICT IX.

King Piyadasi, beloved of the gods, speaks thus:—The people performs various auspicious rites in misfortunes, [at marriages of sons and daughters], on the birth of sons, at *the time of* starting on a journey. On these and similar occasions the people performs many auspicious rites. But at such *times* the women perform many and various despicable and useless rites. Now auspicious rites ought indeed to be performed. But rites of this description produce no results. But the following, the auspicious rite, *which consists in the fulfilment of* the sacred law, produces, forsooth, great results. That includes kindness towards slaves and servants, reverence towards venerable persons, self-control with respect to living creatures, liberality towards ascetics and Brahmans. These and other similar *virtuous actions are* called the auspicious rites of the sacred law. Now a father, or a son, or a brother, or a master, ought to speak *as follows*:—"This is meritorious; this [auspicious rite] must be practised until the *desired* aim is attained." Now it has also been said, "Alms-

[1] This word is of course separate, and has no connection with the edict. In all probability it refers to the elephant, sculptured in relievo, just above the middle part of the inscription which ends with this edict. In like manner, we have the subscription *gajatame*, "the best elephant," under the Khâlsî relievo, and a mutilated sentence, *va sveto hasti sarvalokasukhâharo nâma*, "the white elephant that brings happiness to the whole world," which, according to M. Senart's very plausible conjecture, also originally illustrated a relievo. Professor Kern has pointed out that the elephant may be a symbol of S'âkyamuni Gautama, who became incarnate in the shape of a white elephant. It ought, however, to be noted that the same myth is told regarding the founder of the Jaina sect, Jñâtiputra Mahâvîra.

giving is meritorious." But there is no such alms and no such charity as the almsgiving of the sacred law and the charitable gift of the sacred law. Therefore a friend, or a master, or a companion, ought to give advice on this or that subject, *saying*, "[This ought to be done]; this is meritorious; through this heaven can be gained." For what is more important than gaining heaven?

Edict X.

King Piyadasi, beloved of the gods, does not think that glory and fame [bring much profit, except that] he desires glory and fame *with the view* that at present and in the future the people may practise obedience to the sacred law, and that they observe [the duties] of the sacred law. For this *purpose* [he desires] glory and fame. But all the efforts of King Piyadasi, beloved of the gods, are made with reference to the *results* for a future life. How so? *It is his wish* that all may be free from danger. [Now the danger is sin.] But assuredly the thing is difficult to accomplish, whether for the low or for the great, [except by the greatest exertion] and by renouncing everything. But it is most difficult for the great.

Edict XIV.

These religious edicts[1] have been incised by order of King Piyadasi, beloved of the gods, *under a form*, [whether abridged,] whether of moderate length or expanded. For not everything is suitable in every place. For my empire is large, and much has been incised, and I shall incise *still more*. Certain *sentences* [have been repeated over and over again] because of the sweetness of their import. And for what purpose *has that been done?* *It is with the intention* that the people may act thus. [But it may be that] something has been engraved here incompletely, [be it on account of the space, be it on account of some reason to be *specially* determined, or through a mistake of the writer.][2]

The Separate Edicts of Dhauli and Jaugada.

Separate Edict I.

Dhauli.

[Dev]ânaṁ (pi)y(a)[sa va](chane)na Tosa(l)iyaṁ mah[â]mâta (naga)lavi(yohâla)k[â][1] [1] . . vataviya[2][:] (a)ṁ [ki](chhi da)[kh]â(mi) hakaṁ taṁ ichhâmi[;] kiṁ[t]i[?] [kaṁma]na (pa)ṭi[ve]d(ay)e[2a] haṁ [2] duvâ(la)te cha âlabhe haṁ[.] Es(a) cha me mokhyamata duva[l . e . s] . (aṭha)si[3] aṁ tuphe[su 3] anusathi[.]

Jaugada.

Devânaṁ piye hevaṁ âhâ[:] Samâpâyaṁ mahâmâtâ n(a)galaviyohâlaka he . ṁ vatav(i)yâ[:] aṁ kichh(i)[1] dakhâmi ha(k)aṁ taṁ ichhâmi[;] kiṁti[?] . [kaṁ]man(a)[2] [p]aṭ(i)pâtaye[3] haṁ [1] duvâlate cha âla(bhe) haṁ[.] E(s)a cha me mokhiyamat[a] duvâlaṁ[4] a(ṁ) tuphesu anus(a)thi[.]

---

[1] The text has the singular *lipî*, which is used in a collective sense, like *sûtram*, *kârikâ*, *smṛitiḥ*, &c.

[2] The restoration has been made according to my reading of the Khâlsî version.

Dhauli Version.

[1] *Kâ* is probable from the reverse.

[2] The loss of two letters [*hevaṁ*] is probable. M. Senart's reading *vataviyaṁ* is not quite impossible.

[2a] Read *paṭipâdaye*. The third *akshara* is so much defaced, that it may have been originally *pâ*, not *ve*, which latter it now most resembles.

[3] Possibly *athasi*.

Jaugada Version.

[1] The final vowel of *kichhi* may have been long.

[2] Between *kiṁti* and *kaṁmana* a letter, probably *hâ* or *hi*, has been erased.

[3] *Paṭi°* looks like *saṭi°*. The additional curve is probably accidental.

[4] This may have been *mokhiyamate*, or *°mataṁ duvâla*. The *anusvâra* is doubtful, because the dot, though it is very regular, stands above *la*.

Dhauli.

Tuphe hi ba(h)ûsu pânasahasesu â[yatâ,] p(a)na . (gachhema) sumunisâ(na)ṁ[.] Save [4] munise pajâ mamâ[.] Athâ[4] pa(jâ)ye ichhâmi haka[ṁ;](ki).[t.?] (savena hi)tasukhena hidalo(k)i[k.- 5] pâlalokik[ây]e yû[jev]û[5] (t)i[.] (Tathâ) . . (muni)sesu pi (i)chhâmi hakaṁ[.] (No) cha (p)â(p)u(nâtha) âvâga- [6] (mak)e iyaṁ a(ṭhe)[.][6] (K)e(chha)v[a]ekapuli(s)e . nâti et(aṁ)[,] (se) pi desaṁ n(o) savaṁ[.] Dekhat[a] (hi t)uphe etaṁ[,7] suvi(hi)tâ pi (niti)[.] (I)yaṁ ekapulise pi [athi] ye baṁdhanaṁ vâ (pa)likilesaṁ vâ pâpu(n)âti[.] Tata hot(i)[7] [8] a(kasmâ) t(e)na ba(ṁ)dhan(aṁ)tik[a,] aṁne cha . . [ba]hujane da-(v)iye dukhîyati[.] Tata ichhitaviye [9] tupheh(i)[;] kiṁti [?] majhaṁ paṭipâdayemâ ti[.] Ime(hi) chu [j.](tehi) no saṁpaṭipajati[,] isâya âsulopena [10] (nithû)liyena tûlanây[a] anâvûtiya âlasiyena k . lama-(the)na[.][8] Se ichhitaviye[;] kiti[?][9] ete [11] j(âtâ) n(o) huvevu (mam)â ti[.] Et(as)a cha sava(sa) mûle anâsu(lo)pe a[t .](la)nâ cha niti(yaṁ)[.] E kilaṁte siyâ [12] . (t)e uga(chh.)[.]
Saṁchalitavi(ye t)u va . ita[v]iy(e) etaviye vâ[.] Hevaṁmeva e da(khi)ye tuphâka[.] Tena vata-

Jaugada.

Phe h(i) bahû(su)[5] pânasahasesu [â](yata)[,] p(a)nayaṁ gachhema (su)m(u)[ni]sânaṁ[.] S(a)vam(u)ni(s)e [2] pa(jâ)[.] (Ath)a ·pa(jâ)ye ichhâm(i)[;] ki(ṁti)[?] me sav(e)na hita(su)khena y(û)jeyû .[6] ti hida(log)ik(a)-pâlalokikena[.][7] (He)meva m(e ichha) savamuni-[se]su[.] No cha [tuphe etaṁ] pâpunâtha âv(â)ga-make[8] [3] iyaṁ aṭhe[.][9] Kechâ ekapu(l)ise p(i) [ma]nâti[,] (s)e pi desaṁ no savaṁ[.] D(a)khata hi [tuphe,] (hi)suvitâ[10] p(i) bahuka[.][10a] A(th)i y(e) eti[11] e(kamunise) baṁdhanaṁ (pa)lik(i)lesaṁ hi[12] pâpunâ(t)i[.] Tata [ho]t(i aka)- [4] smâ tena ba(ṁ)dhan(aṁ)t(i)k(a) . .[13] cha vage bahuke veda-(ya)ti[.][14] Tata tuphehi [i](chi)taye[;][15] kimti[?] majhaṁ (paṭi)pâtayema[.] Imehi jâtehî[16] no (saṁṭipa)[ja]ti[,][17] is(â)[ye][18] âsulopena niṭhu-liyena [5] tulâye (a)nâ(vu)tiye[19] âlas(yena)[20] (k)ilama-then(a)[.] Hevaṁ ichhit(a)viye[;][21] kiṁti[?] me etâni jâtâni no heyû ti[.] (S)avasa cha[22] iyaṁ mûle anâsulope at(ulan)â[23] cha niti . [.] E yaṁ[24] [kilaṁte si] . . .[25] [6] saṁchalit(u) uth(â)[ye.][26] (Saṁcha)litavye[27] tu vajitaviya[28] pi etaviye pi[.] Nîtiyaṁ e ve de(khe)yi[29]

---

[4] The long vowel of *thâ* is visible on the reverse.

[5] The form *yûjevû* corresponds to Sanskrit *yujyeran.*

[6] *ṭhe* seems plain on the reverse.

[7] *Ti* is not quite plain, but probable.

[8] The vowel after *k* is not distinguishable. But it must have been *i.*

[9] There is an *anusvâra* above *ki*; a large hole above *ti* is clearly accidental.

Jaugada Version.

[5] The vowel of *hi* may be long. The last vowel of *bahûsu* looks like *û*, probably owing to an accidental scratch.

[6] *Yûjeyû* is the correct reading, just as in the Dhauli version.

[7] *Pâlalokikena,* not °*kikâye*, as M. Senart writes, is plain on the impression. The reading of the facsimile °*kikoye* is due to a correction.

[8] M. Senart's reading *tuphe etaṁ pâpunâtha* seems to be correct, though the first four *aksharas* are nearly effaced. The final vowel of *âvâ* is not distinct.

[9] The *e*-stroke of *aṭhe*, for which M. Senart reads *aṭha*, is distinct on the impression.

[10] *Hisuvitâ* seems plain, but is, as M. Senart says, a mistake for *suvihitâ.*

[10a] *Bahuka* must be a clerical mistake. The sense requires *niti*, the reading of the Dhauli version.

[11] Read *eta.*

[12] Read *pi*, which M. Senart gives in his transcript.

[13] The last two *aksharas* of *baṁdhanaṁtika* are recognisable. It is impossible for me to say if the following two signs may be read *aṁne*, as M. Senart thinks.

[14] *Vedayati* seems more probable than M. Senart's *vedayaṁti.*

[15] Read *ichhitaviye.*

[16] Possibly *jatehî.*

[17] There are only four half-effaced *aksharas* and the reading may either be that given above, or *paṭipajati.* M. Senart's correction *saṁpaṭipajati* is, however, necessary.

[18] *Isâye* seems more probable than M. Senart's *isâya.* But the last syllable is half effaced.

[19] Read *tulanâye. Anâvutiye,* instead of M. Senart's *anâvûtiye*, is plain.

[20] *Âlasyena* is on the impression much more distinct than on the facsimile. M. Senart's *âlasiyena* is probably a clerical mistake.

[21] *Ichhitaviye* looks like *ichhitâviye,* owing to a probably accidental scratch.

[22] Possibly *savasa chu.*

[23] The quantity of the second vowel of *atulanâ* is uncertain.

[24] After *niti* a letter has been erased. Then follows *e yaṁ*, not *iyaṁ*, as M. Senart reads. These syllables have been transposed by mistake. The correct reading is *nitiyaṁ e*, just as in the Dhauli version.

[25] I am unable to recognise on the impression M. Senart's *yâ na*, but agree that *siyâ na se* must have been the original reading.

[26] I read *uthâye* instead of M. Senart's *uthi[he]*, but must admit that the last vowel is very uncertain and that *uthâya* is possible. *Uthâye* or *uthâya* might be the 3d pers. sing. of the optative of *uthâti*, Pali *uṭṭhâti.*

[27] *Saṁchalitavye* is perfectly distinct. M. Senart's *saṁchalitaviye* seems to be a clerical mistake.

[28] *Vajitaviya,* instead of M. Senart's *vajitaviye* is perfectly distinct.

[29] Read *dekkhiye,* as M. Senart proposes.

Dhauli.

viye[: 13] (aṁ)naṁ ne dekhata[.] [10] Hevaṁ cha hevaṁ cha [d]evânaṁ piyasa anusathi[.] Se mahâ . (le) etasa (saṁpa)tipâda [11] [14] (mahâ) apâye asaṁpaṭipati[.] Vipaṭipâdayamînehi etaṁ nathi svaga(s)a âladhi no lâjâladhi[. 15] Duâhale hi i(ma)sa kaṁ(masa) m(e) kute man(e) atileke[.] [11a] (Saṁ)paṭipajamî(n)e chu [12] (e)t[aṁ] svagaṁ [16] âlâ(dhayisatha) [ta]. . . . [â]naniyaṁ ehatha[.]

Iyaṁ cha lip(î) [13] t(i)sanakhatena s[ota]viya [17] aṁtalâ pi cha [tis]e (kha)nasi kha[na]si [14] ekena pi so(ta)viya[.] Hevaṁ cha kalaṁtaṁ (t)uphe [18] (cha)gha(tha) saṁ(pa)[ṭi]pâdayitave[.] (Etâye athâye i)yaṁ li(pi) likhit(a) hida ena [19] nagalavi(y)o[hâ]lakâ sa(sva)taṁ samayaṁ y[uje]vû [ti nagalaja]nasa akasmâ (pa)libodhe [15] va [20] akasmâ palik(i)[les]e va no siyâ ti[.] Etâye cha a(ṭh)âye hakaṁ [dhaṁ]mate paṁchasu paṁchasu vase[- 21] su [n]i[khâ]may(i)sâmi e akhakhase a[cham]ḍ . sakhinâlaṁbhe [16] hosati[.] Etaṁ (a)ṭhaṁ jânitu [ta]thâ [22] kalaṁti [17] atha mama anusathî ti[.] Uje(ni)te pi chu [18] kumâle etâyeva aṭhâye (ni)khâma(yisa) . [23] hedis(aṁ)meva vagaṁ no cha atikâmayisati tiṁn(i) [19] vasâni[.] Hemeva T(a)kha(si)lâte pi[.] Adâ a . . . [24] te mahâmâtâ nikhamisaṁti anusayânaṁ tadâ ahâpayit(u) [20] atane kaṁmaṁ etaṁ pi jânisaṁti [25] taṁ pi tathâ kalaṁti a(tha) lâjine anusathî ti [. 26]

Jaugada.

aṁn(a) n(e ni)jhapetaviye[. He]vaṁ [30] (h)evaṁ cha devânaṁ pi(ya)sa anusathi[.] . . . . [31] [7] taṁ mahâphale h(o)ti asaṁpaṭipati ma(hâ)pâye hot(i)[.] Vipaṭip(â)tayaṁtaṁ no svag(a) âladh(i) no lâjâdhi[.] [32] Du(â)hale etasa [kaṁ]mas(a) sa me kute [ma]ne a . . . . [33] [8] cha ânan(e)yaṁ esatha svagaṁ cha âlâdhayisathâ[.] Iyaṁ cha lipî (a)nutisaṁ sotaviyâ . alâ [34] pi (kha) . na [35] s. taviyâ ek . . pi . . va . . . . mane cha . . . . [36] [9] tave[.] Etâ(ye) cha aṭhâye iyaṁ . khitâ lipî [37] e(n)a mahâmâtâ nagalaka sasvataṁ samayaṁ (yu . yu ti) [38] . . . . ne hi . . . . [39] [10] paṁchasu paṁchasu vase(su) anusaṁyânaṁ nikhâmayisâmi [40] ma(hâ)mâtaṁ achaṁ(ḍa)ṁ [a]phalahata . vachanele [41] . . . .

. . . i . mâlevâ . . . .

. . . .

. . [42] [11] . . . . âjavachanika[.]

Adâ anusaṁyânaṁ nikhamisaṁti

atane kaṁmaṁ e . ṁ

pi . n . . . .

. . . . . [12].

Edict II.

Dev(ânaṁ) piy(a)s(a) v(a)ch(a)nena Tosaliyaṁ (k)umâle mahâmâtâ cha vataviy(a)[:] Aṁ kichhi dakhâm(i ha)[kaṁ] . . . .

Devânaṁ piye hevaṁ âha[:] Samâpâyaṁ mahamatâ lajavachanika [43] vataviyâ[:] Aṁ kichhi dakhâmi hakaṁ taṁ ichhâmi hakaṁ[,] kiṁti[?] kaṁkamana [1] [44]

---

[10] *Dekhata* is probably the correct reading.

[11] The apparent *e*-stroke after *da* is not deep enough to be real. *Saṁpaṭipâda* stands, as the *varia lectio* of Jaugada [*saṁpaṭipâ*]*taṁ* shows, for °*pâdaṁ* and is a neuter.

[11a] *Mane* is more probable than *mana*.

[12] The *u*-stroke goes downwards, but is distinct; compare above, line 10, and below, line 23.

[13] *Pî* is not quite certain.

[14] *Na* is visible on the reverse.

[15] Possibly *pâlibodhe*.

[16] Apparently *sekhinâ*°. But the stroke before *sa* is accidental. The corresponding Sanskrit word is *ślakshṇârambhaḥ*.

[17] The *anusvâra* of *kalaṁti* is plain.

[18] The *u*-stroke is again slanting downwards.

[19] The *anusvâra* of *tiṁ* is probable.

[20] The *u*-stroke is a little damaged, but perfectly certain.

Jaugada Version.

[30] The first syllable looks, owing to sundry accidental rents, like *che*.

[31] Probably eight *aksharas* lost.

[32] Read *lâjâladhi*.

[33] *Dele* the second *sa* after *kaṁmasa*. *Mane a* after *kute* seems certain. Both versions seem to have read *mane atileke* instead of *mana atileke*. Probably eleven or twelve *aksharas* lost.

[34] Read *aṁtalâ*.

[35] After the somewhat indistinct *kha* a consonant has been lost, which bore an *i* at the top. The reading may have been *khasina*, a mistake for *khanasi*.

[36] Probably twenty-two *aksharas* lost.

[37] The long *î* of *lipî* is distinct.

[38] Possibly a letter may have stood between *samayaṁ* and *yu*[*je*]*yu*.

[39] Probably twenty-six *aksharas* lost.

[40] The final long *î* of *nikhâmayisâmî* is plain.

[41] I consider M. Senart's emendation *aphalusa* to be correct. But the impression shows apparently *aphalahata* and *vachanele* or *vavanele*, the last vowels of which are uncertain. The whole passage seems to be corrupt.

[42] Probably eleven *aksharas* lost.

[43] Read *mahâmâtâ lâjavachanika*.

[44] M. Senart reads *kaṁkaṁmana*. The reverse of the impression shows the reading given above with perfect plainness. It is, however, a mistake for *kaṁmana*, *i.e.*, *karmaṇâ*.

Dhauli.

. . . . . . [1] du(vâla)te cha (â)labhe haṁ[.] Es(a) cha me mokhyam(ata duvâ)lâ etasi (a)ṭhasi aṁ tuph(e)[su] . . . . (mama) [2.] Atha pajây(e) ichhâm(i) hakaṁ[,] k[iṁ]ti (sa)vena hi[tasukhe](na)

hid(a)lo[kika](pâla)lokikâye yujevû ti h(e)v . . . . (uni . . u) [3] siyâ[.] Aṁtânaṁ avijit(ânaṁ) kichh(aṁ)d. su lâj. . [phe]s . . . . . mav(e) [21] i(chha ma)ma aṁt(e)su . . (p)â(p)unevu te iti[,] devânaṁ p[i[y . . . . . . a . (vi)g. n(a) ma(m)â(ye)[4] huvevû ti asvasevu cha sukhaṁmeva lahevu mama (te) no dukha(ṁ)[.] [22] Hevaṁ . . n[e]vû [i]ti[,] khamisati [23] ne devânaṁ p(i)y(e) (aphâ)ka(ṁ) [24] ti e ch(a)kiye khamitave[;] mama (ni)mit[aṁ] cha dhaṁmaṁ chalev(û)[, 5] hidaloka palaloka(ṁ) cha (â)lâdhayevû[.] (E)tasi aṭhasi hak(aṁ) anusâsâmi tuphe[.] Anane) eta(k)ena hakaṁ[,] anusâsitu chhaṁdaṁ) cha veditu â (hi) [25] (dhi)ti, paṭiṁnâ cha mam(â) [6] (aja)l(â)[.] S(e) hevaṁ kaṭu kaṁme chal(i)t(a)vi(y)e[,] asv(â) . . . .i (cha tâni)[,] ena pâpunevû iti atha pitâ tatha [26] devânaṁ piy(e) aphâka[,] [27] athâ cha atânaṁ [28] hevaṁ devânaṁ pi(y)e [a]nu(kaṁpati) aphe[, 7] athâ cha paja h(e)vaṁ may[e] devânaṁ piyasa[.] Se hakaṁ anusâsitu chhaṁdaṁ cha v . . . . . phâka

de(sâv)utike hosâmi etâye (a)thâye[.] [29] Paṭibalâ hi tuph(e) asvâsanâye (h)itasu(khâ)ye cha [te](sa)[8] [30] hidalokikapâla(lokikâ)ye[.] Hevaṁ cha kalaṁtaṁ tuphe svagaṁ (â)lâ(dha)yisatha mama cha ânaniyaṁ ehatha[.] (Etâ)y(e) cha aṭhâye iyaṁ lipi (l)ikhitâ hida

Jaugada.

paṭipâtaye haṁ duvâ(la)te cha âlabhe haṁ[.] Esa cha me mokhiyamataṁ [45] duvâl(a) etas(a) athasa aṁ tuphesu anusa[thi][.] [46] Savamuni [2] sâ me pajâ[.] Atha pajâye ichhâmi[,] kiṁti[?] me savenâ [47] hitasu(khe)na yu[je]yû atha pajâye ichhâmi[,] kiṁti[?] m[e] savena hitasu-[3] khena yujeyû ti hidalogikapâlalokikena[.] Hevaṁmeva me ichha [48] savamunisesu siyâ[.] Aṁtânaṁ avijitâ [4] naṁ kiṁchhaṁde su lâjâ aphesû ti[,] etâ kâ v(â) [49] me ichha aṁtesu[,] pâpuneyu[,] lâjâ hevaṁ ichhati anuvigi(n)a heyu [5] mamiyâye asvaseyu cha me sukhaṁmeva cha laheyû [50] mama te no khaṁ[.] [51] Hevaṁ cha pâpuneyu[,] khamisati ne lâjâ [6] e chakiye khamitave[;] mamaṁ nimitaṁ cha dhaṁma chaley(û) ti h(i)dalogaṁ cha palalo(ga)ṁ cha âlâdhayeyu[.] Etâye [7] cha aṭhây(e) h(a)kaṁ tupheni anusâsâmi[.] Anan[e] [52] etakena hakaṁ[,] tupheni anusâsit[u] chhaṁdaṁ cha vedi[8]t[u] â mama dhiti paṭiṁnâ cha achala[.] Sa [52a] hevaṁ (kaṭu) kaṁme chalitaviye asvâsaniyâ cha te[,] ena te [53] pâpune [9] yu athâ pita hevaṁ ne lâjâ ti[,] atha atânaṁ anukaṁpati hevaṁ apheni anu(k)aṁpati[,] athâ pajâ he[10]vaṁ maye lâjine[.] Tupheni hakaṁ anusâsit[u] [54] chhaṁdaṁ cha vedit[u] [55] . mama dhiti paṭiṁnâ [56] châ achal[a] . . . [11] desâ [57] âyutike (hos)âmî [58] etasi athasi[.] Alaṁ hi tuphe asvâsasanâye h(i)tasukhâye (cha t)esaṁ hida- [12] logikapâlal(o)kikâye[.] Hevaṁ cha kalaṁtaṁ svagaṁ [cha] âlâdhayisatha [59] mama cha ânaneyaṁ esatha[.] E [60][13]tâye cha athâye i[yaṁ] lipî likhitâ [61] . da

---

[21] *Mave* is tolerably plain on the reverse, but remains inexplicable.

[22] The *anusvâra* of *dukhaṁ* is quite plain on the reverse.

[23] The *sa* of *khamisati* stands above the line.

[24] *Aphâkaṁ* is superfluous, as *ne* occurs in the same sentence. The letters are defaced, perhaps intentionally.

[25] *Hi* is plain on the reverse, and farther on *mamâ* instead of *mama*.

[26] *Tatha*, not *tathâ*, as M. Senart reads, is as plain as possible.

[27] There is no trace of an *anusvâra*.

[28] *Naṁ* stands above the line.

[29] The character of *tha* in *athâye* is uncertain. It may be *ṭha*.

[30] The reverse shows clearly that *sa*, not *se*, is the correct reading. The *e*-stroke before *ta* is much defaced.

Jaugada Version.

[45] The reverse of the impression favours this reading rather than M. Senart's °*mate*.

[46] *thi* stands somewhat lower than the other letters, and the *i* is much defaced.

[47] *Savenâ* is as plain as possible. The phrase *atha—yujeyu* has been written twice over by mistake.

[48] M. Senart's *ichhâ* seems not possible.

[49] The long *â* in *vâ* is tolerably plain.

[50] The long *û* of *laheyû* seems distinct.

[51] Read *dukhaṁ*. Perhaps *du* was written above *khaṁ*.

[52] The *ne* of *anane* is indistinctly visible on the reverse of the impression. M. Senart's *anena* is impossible, as the second *akshara* is very plain.

[52a] Read *se hevaṁ*.

[53] *Te* has been omitted by mistake in M. Senart's transcript.

[54] The vowel after the *t* of *anusâsit* is no longer recognisable; but I believe it to have been *u*, not *a*, as M. Senart reads.

[55] *Vedit* is plain enough, but the final vowel very doubtful. It must have been *u*.

[56] *Dhiti paṭiṁnâ* is plain enough, but the whole phrase may be a mistaken repetition from line 10, where *paṭiṁnâ* is also most distinct.

[57] *Desâ âyu*° is plain.

[58] The *î* of *hosâmî* is perfectly distinct.

[59] There is a dot after *tha*, which, on account of its shape, cannot be taken as an *anusvâra*.

[60] The *e* of *etâye* stands not in the beginning of line 14, but at the end of line 13.

[61] *Lipî* is perfectly plain.

Dhauli.	*Jaugada.*
ena (m)ahâmâtâ sva(sataṁ) [sa]ma [31] [9] yujisaṁti (a)-(sv)â(sa)nâye dhaṁmachalan(â)ye (cha t)e(sa) [32] aṁtâ-naṁ[.] Iyaṁ cha li(pi anuch)â(t)uṁmâsaṁ tisena nakhatena sotaviyâ kâmaṁ cha khaṇas(i) [33] khanasi aṁtalâ pi tisenae(k)ena (pi)[10](so)taviya[.] [34] He(va)ṁ kalaṁ(taṁ tu)phe chaghatha saṁpaṭipâdayitave[.11]	e(n)a mahâmâtâ sasvataṁ s(a)maṁ yujeyû [62] a-svâsanâye cha [14] dhaṁmachalanâye (cha a)ṁtâ-naṁ[.] Iyaṁ cha *lipî* [63] a(nu)châtuṁmâsaṁ [64] sotaviyâ tisena aṁtalâ pi cha sotaviyâ[.15] Khane saṁtaṁ (e)kena pi sotaviyâ[.] Hevaṁ cha kalaṁtaṁ chaghatha sampaṭipâtayitave[.16]

TRANSLATION.

EDICT I.

By order of the beloved of the gods, the officials at Tosalî, the administrators of the town, should be addressed *as follows* :[1] " Whatever I understand *to be right*, with respect to that I conceive a desire. How so ? I desire to practise it in *my* deeds and to carry it out by *efficacious* means. But I consider this to be the chief means for *my* present purpose, *viz.*, *to give* you instructions. For you dwell *as rulers* among many thousands of creatures, *desiring*, 'May we gain the affection of *all* good men.' All men are my children. *For them*, as for *my* children, I desire—what ? that they may enjoy complete happiness and welfare in this world and in the next. Even this I desire for *all* men. But you do not understand *all* that the sense *of these words* implies. Some single *private* individual understands it, at least a portion, if not the whole. Look then to this *meaning of my words ;* the maxims of *good* government, too, are well determined *and teach the same lesson.* It happens that such a single *private* individual undergoes either imprisonment or *other* serious trouble. Then that *trouble*, which ends with imprisonment, falls upon him without any cause, and the other multitude is deeply sorry *for him.* In such *a case* you ought to desire —what ? 'May we act justly.' But that is impossible with the following dispositions, *viz.*, envy, want of perseverance, harshness, hastiness, neglect of repeated efforts, sloth, want of energy. Hence, *each of you* ought to desire—what ? 'May these dispositions not be found in me.' But the root of all this [2] *is* perseverance and the avoidance of hastiness in *the application of* the maxims of government. He who is destitute of energy is unable to rouse himself ; but it is necessary to move, to walk, and to advance. Even thus *it is with*

---

31 Read *sasvataṁ*. There is no trace of an *anusvâra* after *sama*.

32 M. Senart's reading, *tesu*, seems at first sight possible. But on a closer examination of the reverse, it becomes evident that the apparent *u* is due to a large rent in the rock, which passes diagonally under *tesa*, and through the lower part of the following *a*.

33 M. Senart's reading, *khano*°, is impossible, because in the Dhauli version the two horizontal strokes forming the *o* are never attached at the same height. The right-hand stroke is usually attached to the top of the *akshara*, and the left-hand one lower down. But the contrary arrangement occurs also. The lingual *ṇa* occurs also once in the Jaugada version. The final syllable *si* stands above the line.

34 *Taviya*, not *taviyâ*, as M. Senart reads, seems plain enough. I am not able to confirm M. Senart's assertion that the facsimile B. appears to read *taviyaṁ*. The dot above *ya* cannot be an *anusvâra*, because in Aśoka's edicts the *anusvâra* hardly ever stands at the top of the *akshara* to which it belongs, except if the latter is followed by the vowel *i*.

Jaugada Version.

62 M. Senart's *yujevû* must be a clerical mistake, as °*yû* is perfectly plain.

63 *Lipî* is again very plain.

64 *Nu* is faintly visible on the reverse of the impression.

---

1 The text of Jaugada says : " The beloved of the gods speaks thus. The officials at Samâpâ, the administrators of the town, should be informed of the *following* order of the king.

2 Of all this, *i.e.*, of the due discharge of one's duties.

respect to the affairs which you have to decide. Hence it is necessary *for me* to tell *you*: 'Pay attention to my orders.' Such, even such, *are* the instructions of the beloved of the gods.

"Now, the due fulfilment of this *my intention* secures great rewards, the neglect of *its* due fulfilment causes great evils. For those who do not fully carry out this *my intention*, there is neither *the possibility of* gaining heaven nor *of* gaining the favour of the king. For I have made *true* zeal in this cause bear a twofold *reward*. If *you* fully carry out this *my intention*, you will gain heaven and pay the debt *which you owe to* me.

"But this edict shall be read *publicly* under the constellation Tishya,[1] and *in the intervals*, too, between the Tishya-*days* it may be read on every fit occasion, even before one *man*. And acting thus, you will strive to fully carry out *my intentions*.

"This edict has been incised here for the following purpose, *viz.*, that the administrators of the town may ever fulfil their covenant saying: 'The citizens shall neither without cause suffer imprisonment, nor without cause *any other* serious trouble.' And for this purpose I shall send forth[2] in accordance with the law *an official* who is neither harsh nor passionate, *but* gentle in his doings.[3] Understanding this purpose, they will act[4] according to my instructions. And from Ujjain, too, the royal prince[5] will send forth *men of* the same class, and he will not let pass more than three years.

"In like manner *officials will be deputed* from Takshaśilâ.[6] When . . . these officials go forth on tour, they will, without neglecting their own business,[7] pay attention to this *order of mine*, and will act in accordance with the instructions of the king."

Edict II.

The beloved of the gods speaks thus:—The officials in Samâpâ must be informed of the *following* order of the king:[8]—"Whatever I understand *to be right*, with respect to that I conceive a desire. How so? I desire to practise it in *my* deeds, and to carry it out by *efficacious* means. But I consider this to be the chief means for *my* present purpose, *viz.*, *to*

---

[1] The text of Jaugada says: "But this edict shall be read *publicly* on every *Tishya* day." Aśoka follows here the practice of the old Brahminical Sûtras, according to which each lunar day is named after the *nakshatra* or constellation with which the moon is supposed to be in conjunction. The number of the public readings prescribed here is, of course, twelve.

[2] The text of Jaugada adds: "On tour an official."

[3] The verb of this sentence, *kalaṁti*, stands in the plural, though in the preceding one only one man is spoken of. Probably the first sentence is inaccurately worded, and in reality several officials were sent out. The extent of Central India is so great, that one man could not have effected much.

[4] With Aśoka's promise to send officials on tour in order to superintend the administration of justice by the subordinate local authorities, compare his utterance in Rock-edict iii, and the rule given by Manu vii, 120–123, which inculcates the necessity of the king's appointing superintendents over the subordinate officials, "the lords of one, ten, or a hundred villages," and of his having their doings examined by the superintendents and their spies. Aśoka's proceeding agrees with the Brahmanical law, and this agreement is probably indicated by the word *dhaṁmate*, "in accordance with the law."

[5] A royal prince seems to have been viceroy at Ujjain, one of the most important towns in the western portion of Aśoka's dominions. According to the Buddhist tradition, Aśoka himself was viceroy of Ujjain at the time when his father died.

[6] In the legend of Kuṇâla, this town is mentioned as the seat of a viceroy who was a royal prince.

[7] "Their own business" probably means "appeals in revenue and judicial matters, the collection of taxes from recusant vassals, and so forth."

[8] The text of Dhauli says: "The *following* order of the beloved of the gods should be addressed to the prince and the officials at Tosalî."

give you instructions. All men are my children. *For them* as for my children I desire—what? that they may enjoy through me complete happiness and welfare, both in this world and in the next. My desire is that it may be even thus with all men. *If you ask* what is the order of the king for us with respect to *his* unconquered neighbours, or what my desire here is with respect to the neighbours, *viz.*, *what I wish* them to understand, *the answer is*, the king desires that they should not be afraid of me, that they should trust me, and that they should receive from me happiness, not misery. Moreover they should understand 'The king will bear with us when forbearance is possible,'[1] that they should follow the law for my sake, and that *thus* they should gain this world and the next. And *it is* for this end *that* I give to you my instructions. I discharge my debt *to them* thereby that I instruct you and make known to you *my* will, *i.e.*, my unshakable resolution and proposal. Now you must discharge your functions, acting accordingly, and must make them trust me, in order that they may understand 'The king is to us even as a father; he loves us even as he loves himself; we are to the king even as *his* children.'

"Instructing you *thus*, and making known to you *my* will, *i.e.*, my unshakable resolution and proposal, I shall have superintendents in *all* countries as far as this matter *is concerned*. For you have power to make them trust me, and to *ensure* their welfare and happiness in what concerns this world and the next. Moreover, acting thus you will gain heaven, and you will pay the debt *which you owe* to me. And for this purpose this edict has been incised here, in order that the officials here *in my empire* may always exert themselves, both in order to make *my* neighbours trust me and in order to make them follow the law. And this edict shall be read *publicly* at the commencement of every season on a Tishya-day. It may also be read in the interval. When there is a fit occasion, it may also be read before one *man*.[2] And acting thus you will strive to fully carry out *my intentions*."

---

[1] *Chakiye* is the future passive participle of a Prakrit root, *chak*, which is equivalent to, and possibly allied to, the Sanskrit root *śak*. The Mahârâshṭrî form *chay* is mentioned in the *Pâiyalachchhî*, vs. 202, and by Hemachandra, *Prakrit Grammar*, iv. 86.

[2] This passage differs somewhat in the Dhauli version, where we read, "And this edict shall be read *publicly* at the commencement of every season under the constellation Tishya; and optionally it may be read on every fit occasion, in the interval also on a Tishya-day before one *man*." But the general sense of both versions is the same. The edict *must* be read at the commencement of each season (literally, period of four months), on a day when the moon is in conjunction with the Nakshatra Tishya. It *may* be read on intermediate Tishya-days, and on other fit occasions. For *châturmâsya*, "the commencement of a season," see Böhtlingk's smaller Sanskrit Dict. *sub voce*. The passage proves that in Aśoka's time the year was officially divided into three seasons, not into six. The same division occurs in all the official documents of the Andhra kings.

THE END.

1

2

SCALE 1-10TH OF THE ORIGINALS

1

2

SCALE 1/10TH OF THE ORIGINALS.

1

2

SCALE 1/10TH OF THE ORIGINALS.

1

2

SCALE 1-10TH OF THE ORIGINALS.

1

2

SCALE 1-10TH OF THE ORIGINALS.

AMARÂVATÎ: PILLARS OF OUTER RAIL.

1

2

3

SCALE 1-10TH OF ORIGINALS.

AMARÂVATÎ : OUTER RAIL PILLARS

PLATE XI

SCALE : [illegible]TH OF THE ORIGINALS

SCALE 1/10TH OF ORIGINALS.

1

2

3

4

SCALE 1-10TH OF THE ORIGINALS

2

1

6

3

5

SCALE 1-10TH OF ORIGINALS.

AMARÂVATÎ: PILLARS FROM THE OUTER RAIL.

AMARÂVATÎ RAIL SCULPTURES. PLATE XVI

1

2

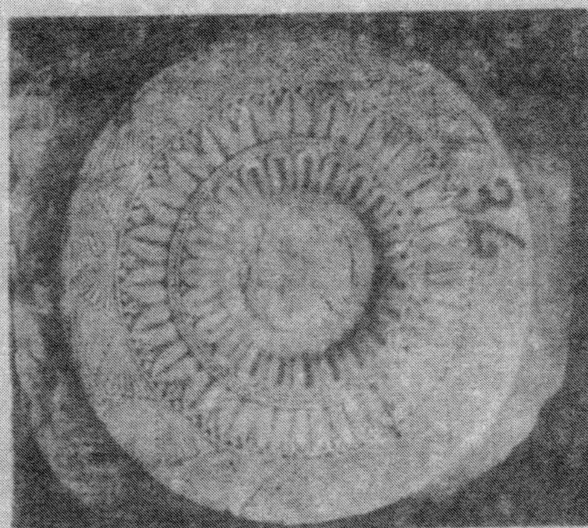

3

4

SCALE 1-10TH OF THE ORIGINALS.

1

2

3

4

SCALE 1/10TH OF ORIGINALS.

1

2

3

4

SCALE 1-10TH OF ORIGINALS.

PLATE XX

AMARÂVATÎ OUTER RAIL.

1

2

SCALE 1-10TH OF THE ORIGINALS.

1

2

SCALE 1/10TH OF ORIGINALS.

AMARÂVATÎ OUTER RAIL.

SCALE 1/10TH OF THE ORIGINALS.

AMARÁVATÍ :—FRAGMENTS OF THE OUTER RAIL.

Fig. 1

Fig. 2

Fig. 3

Fig. 4

Plate XIX.

LONDON. TRÜBNER & C°.

Scale 1-fifth of originals

FRISCH. BERLIN.

PLATE XXIV.

SCALE 1/10TH OF THE ORIGINALS.

AMARÂVATÎ OUTER RAIL.

SCALE 1-10TH OF THE ORIGINALS.

PLATE XXV.

AMARÂVATÎ OUTER RAIL.

1

3

2

4

6

5

SCALE 1/10TH OF THE ORIGINALS.

1

2

3

4

5

6

SCALE 1-10TH OF THE ORIGINALS.

1

2

3

4

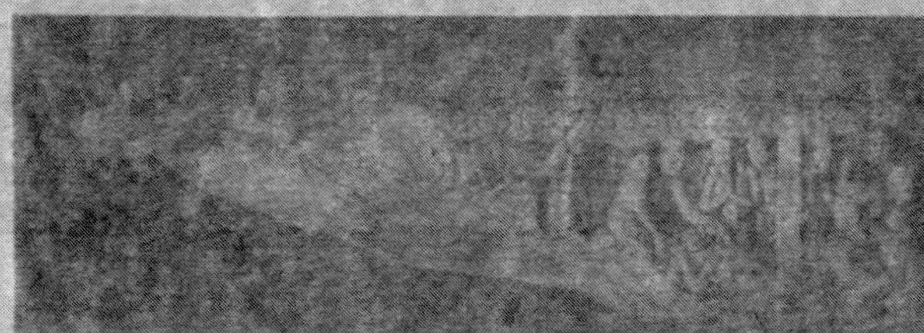

5

6

SCALE 1-10TH OF THE ORIGINALS

1

2

3

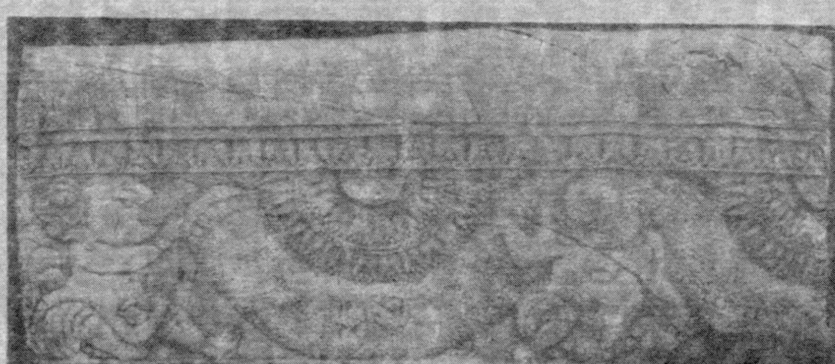

SCALE 1-10TH OF THE ORIGINALS.

1

2

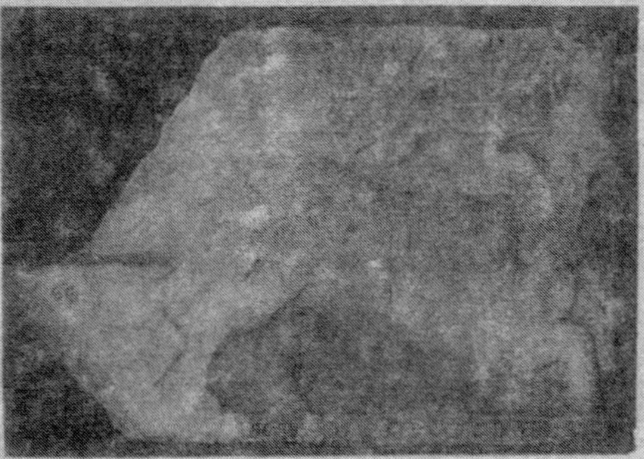

3

4

5

SCALE 1-10TH OF THE ORIGINALS.

1

2

3

4

5

6

7

SCALE 1/10TH OF THE ORIGINALS.

PLATE XXXII

AMARÂVATÎ.—CHAITYA AND PILLAR SLABS FROM THE INNER RAIL.

AMARÂVATÎ CHAITYA SLABS.

PLATE XXXIV

AMARÂVATÎ CHAITYA SLABS.

PLATE XXXV

AMARÂVATÎ CHAITYA SLABS.

PLATE XXXVI

AMARÂVATÎ CHAITYA SLABS.

1

2

1.

2.

4.

3.

1

2

4

3

SCALE 1-10TH OF ORIGINALS.

1

2

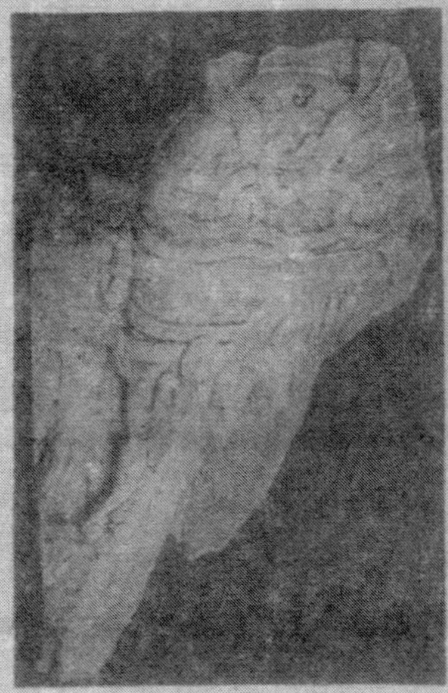

3

4

5

6

SCALE 1-10TH OF THE ORIGINALS.

SCALE 1/10TH OF THE ORIGINALS.

AMARĀVATĪ INNER RAIL. PLATE XLIII.

SCALE 1-10TH OF THE ORIGINALS.

SCALE 1/10th OF ORIGINALS

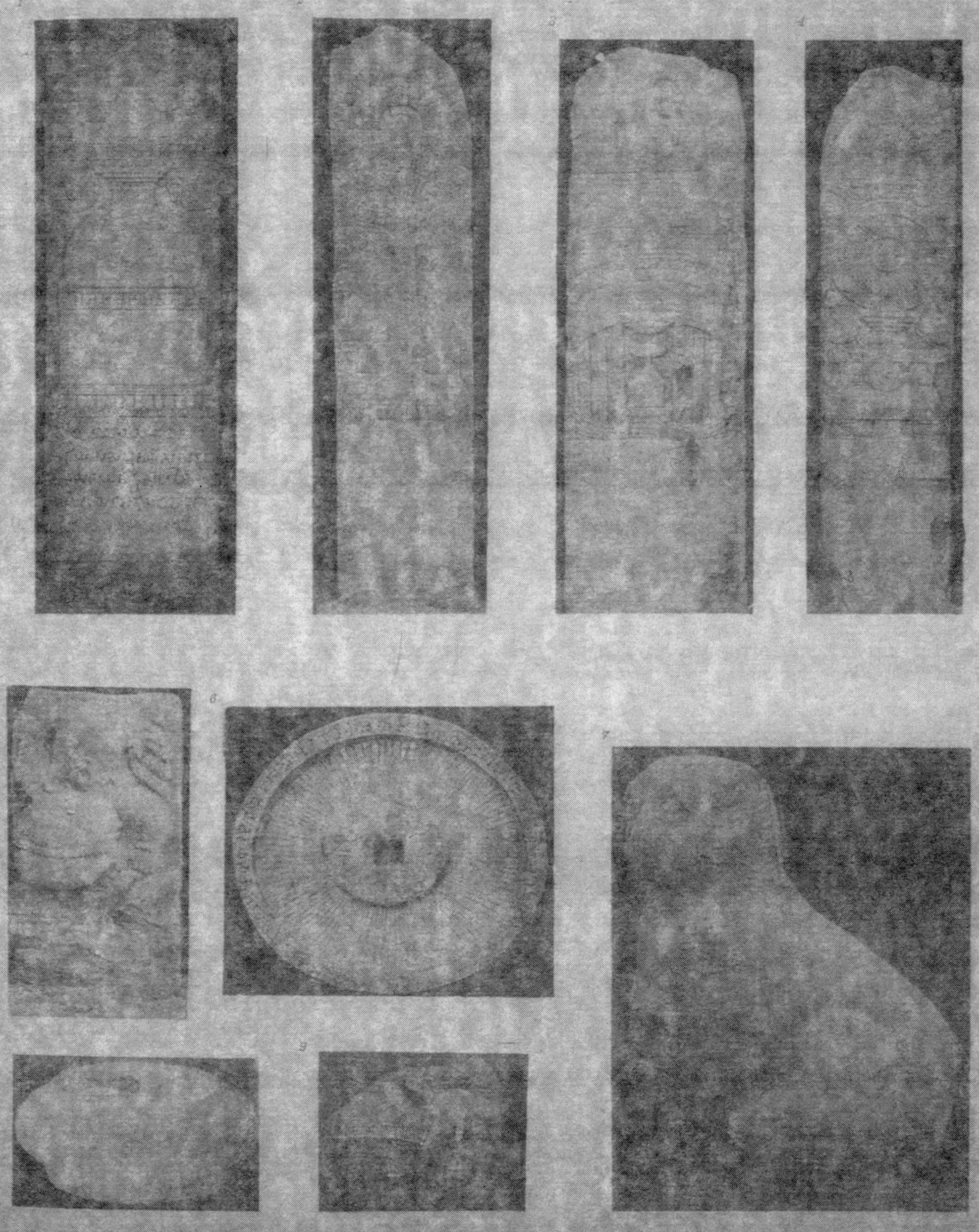

SCALE 1/40TH OF ORIGINALS.

1

2

3

4

SCALE 1/10TH OF THE ORIGINALS.

1

2

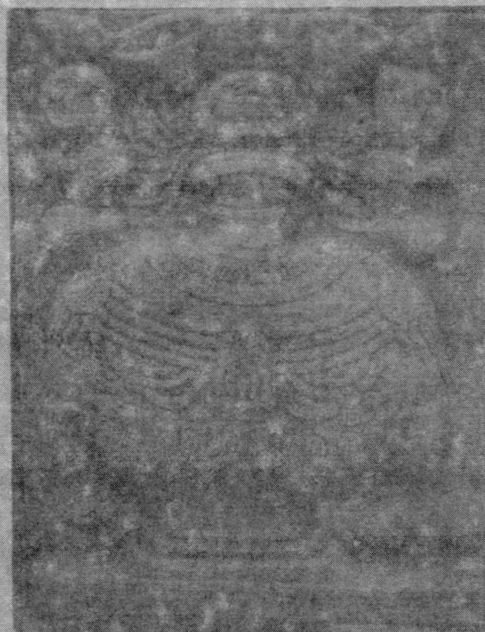

3

4

SCALE 1-10TH OF ORIGINALS.

1

2

3

4

SCALE 1/10TH OF THE ORIGINALS.

J. Burgess, fecit.

AMARÂVATÎ: SLABS FROM THE STÛPA.

PLATE L.

1

2

3

4

SCALE 1-10TH OF THE ORIGINALS.

SCALE 1-10TH OF THE ORIGINALS.

AMARÂVATÎ & JAGGAYYAPETA SCULPTURES.

PLATE LIII

SCALE 1-10TH OF THE ORIGINALS.

SCALE 1-10TH OF ORIGINALS.

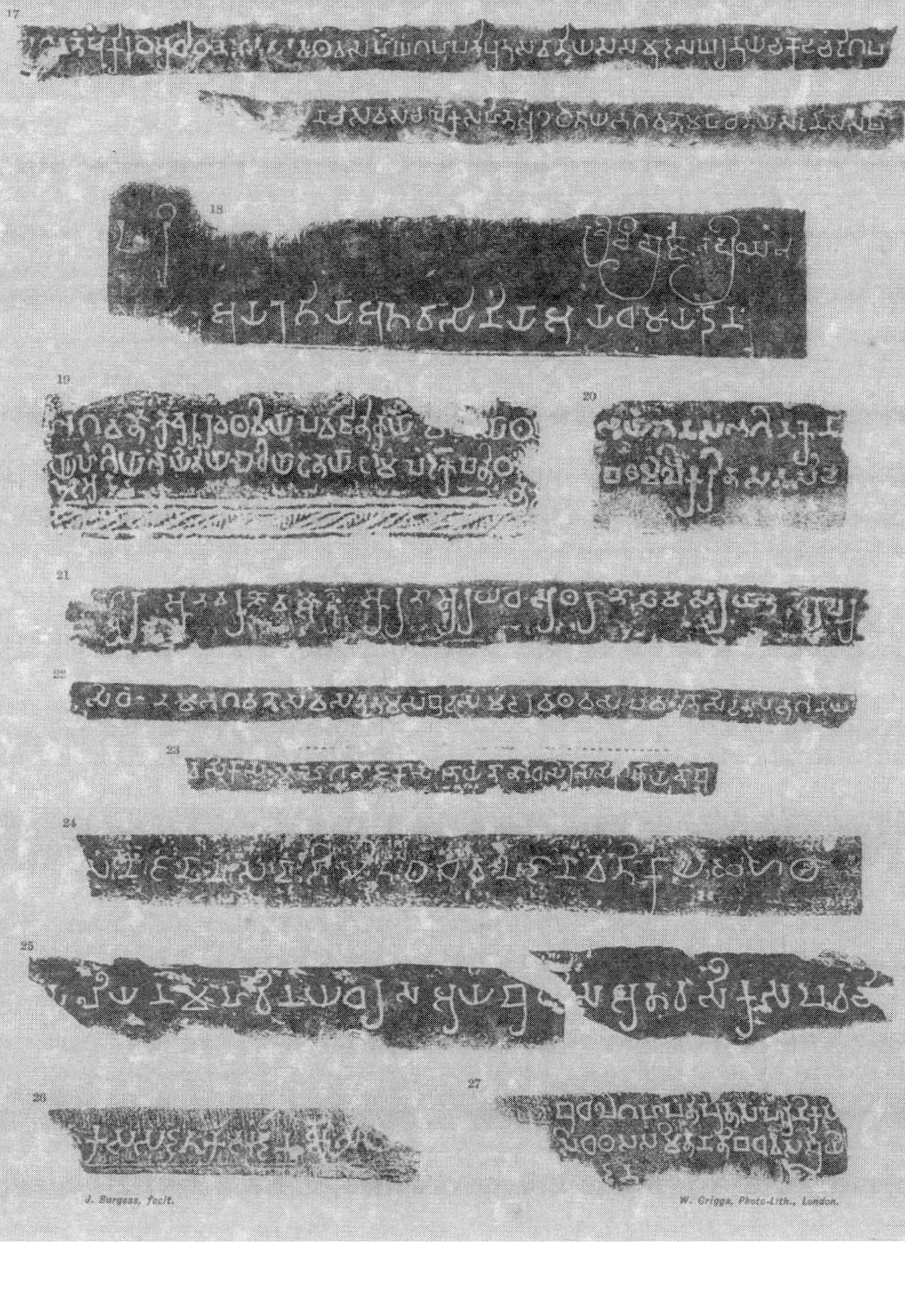

J. Burgess, fecit. *W. Griggs, Photo-Lith., London.*

28

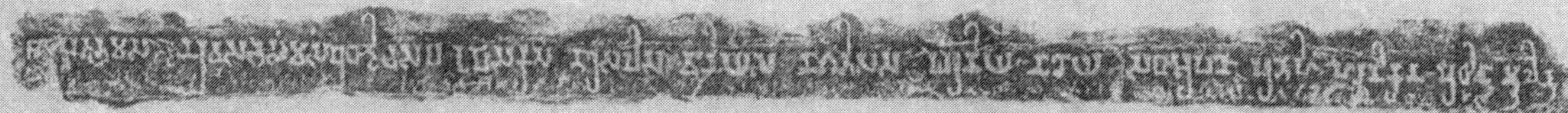

29

30

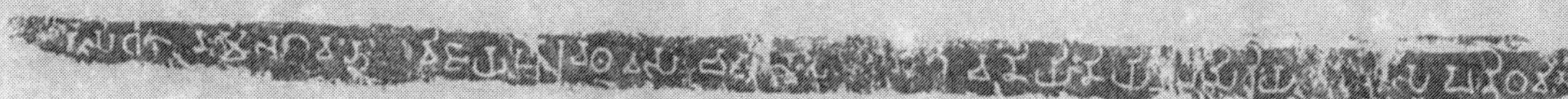

31

32

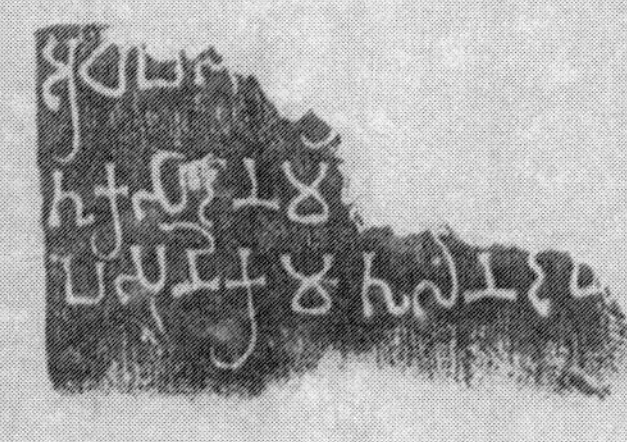

33

34

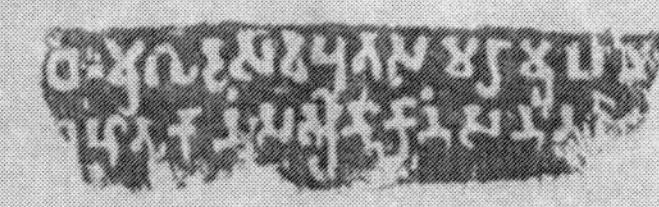

35

36

37

J. Burgess, fecit.

W. Griggs, Photo-Lith., London.

38

39

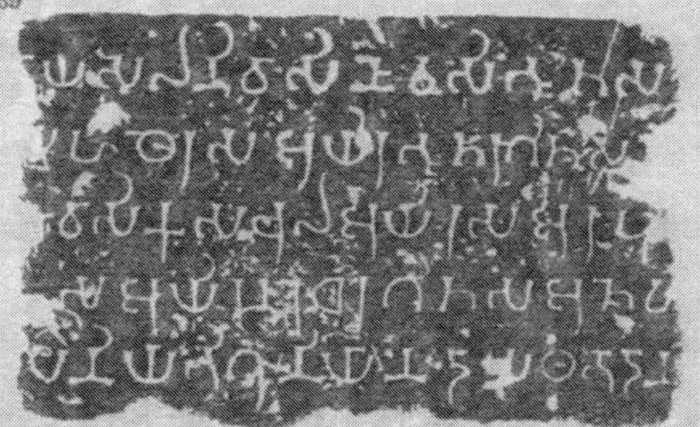

40

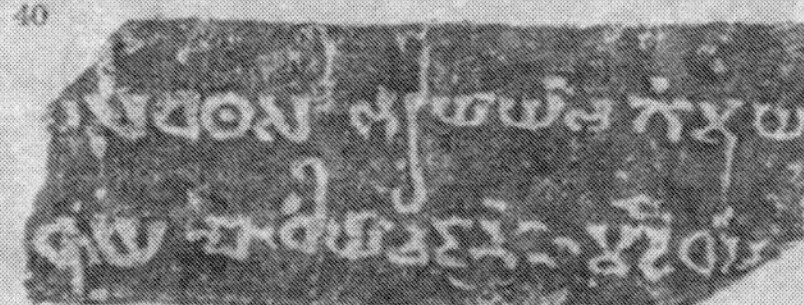

41

42

43

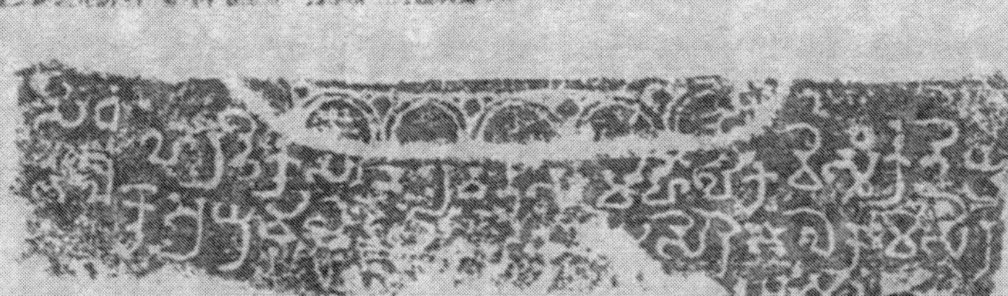

J. Burgess, fecit.

J. Burgess, fecit.

W. Griggs, Photo-Lith., London.

51

52

53

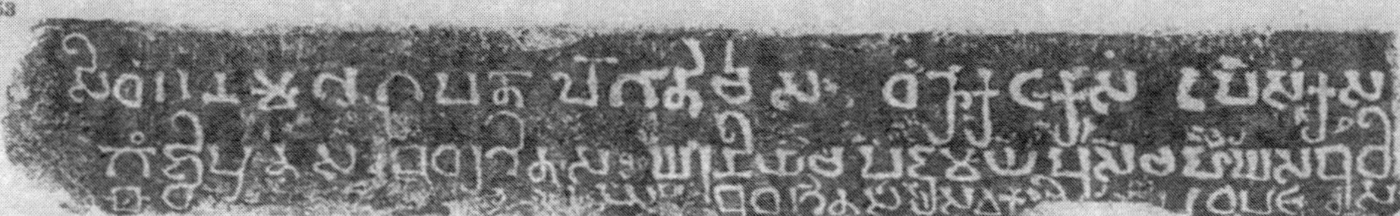

54

55

56

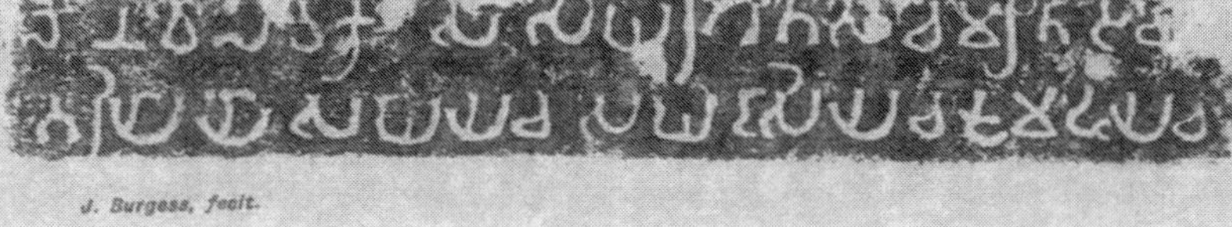

J. Burgess, fecit.

1

2

J. Burgess, fecit.

3

4

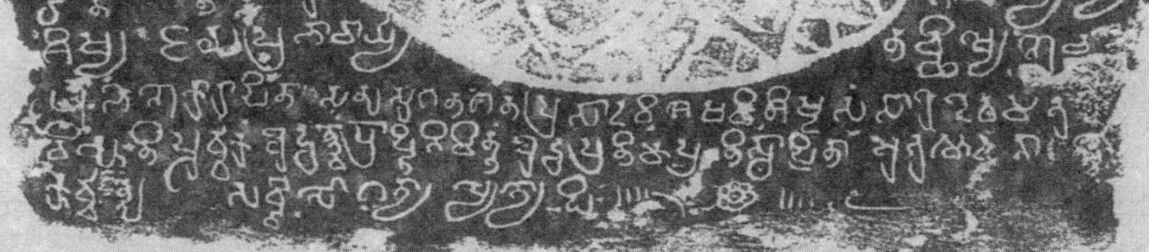

5

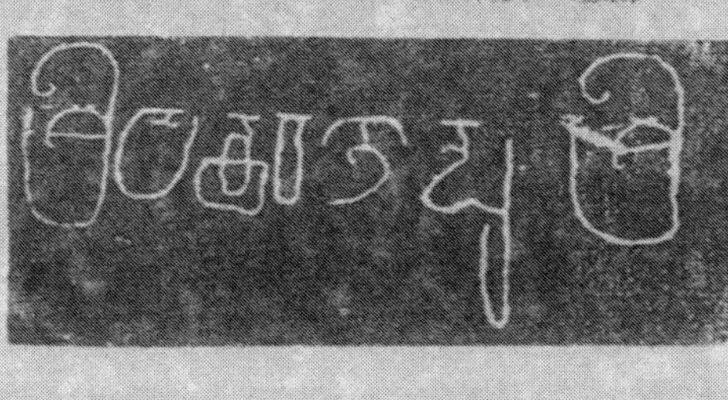

J. Burgess, fecit.

AŚOKA INSCRIPTIONS AT DHAULI.

I. Edicts I-VI.

Middle Column on the Rock.

J. Burgess, fecit. W. Griggs, Photo-Lith.

SCALE 0·12.

ASOKA INSCRIPTIONS AT DHAULI.

II. Edicts VII to X, XIV and 2nd Separate Edict.

Right hand Column on the Rock.

J. Burgess, fecit.

W. Griggs, Photo-Lith.

SCALE 0·12.

III. FIRST SEPARATE EDICT.

LEFT COLUMN ON THE ROCK.

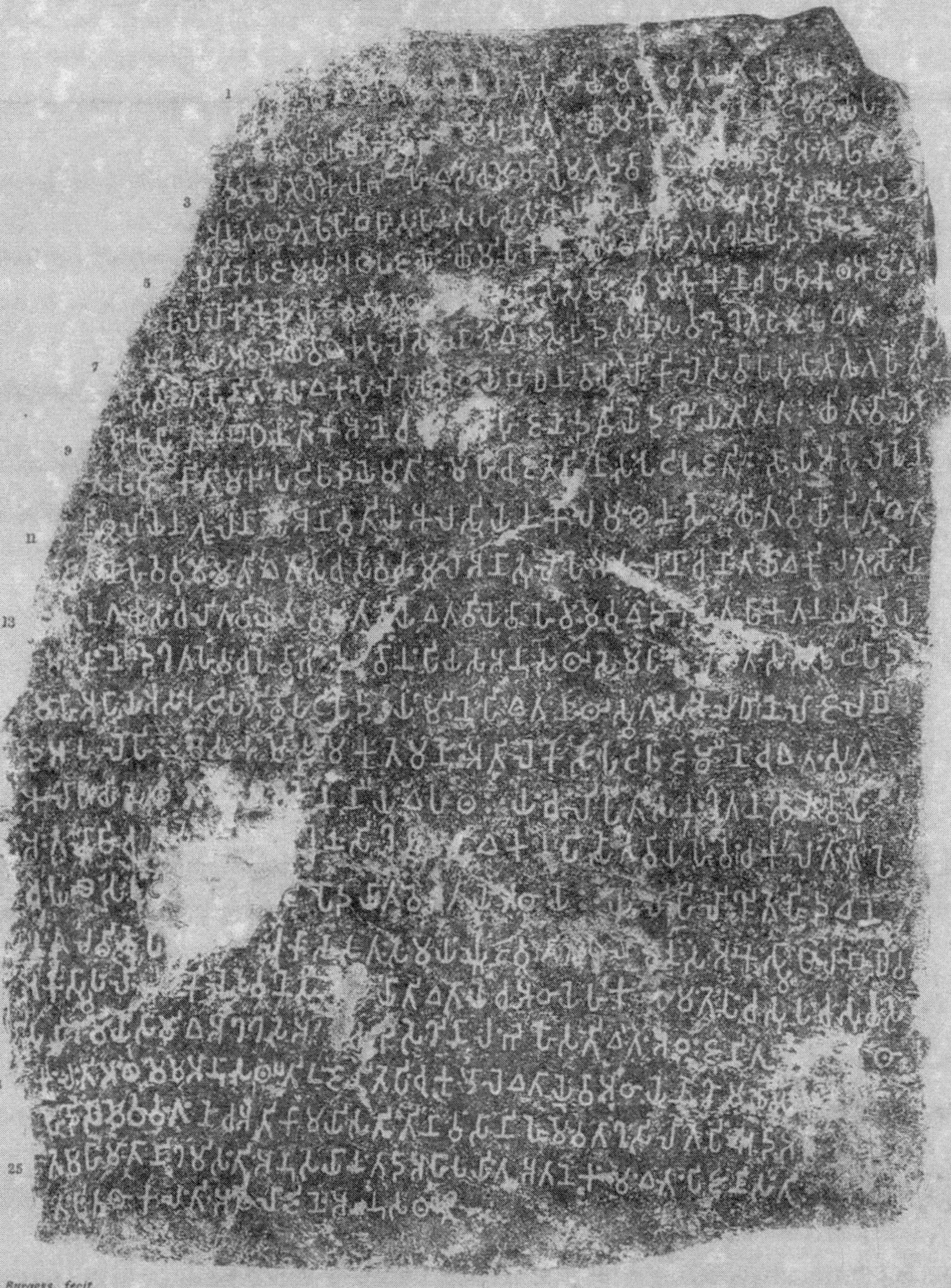

J. Burgess, fecit.

Scale 0.12.

Edict I. Edict II. Edict III. Edict IV. Edict V.

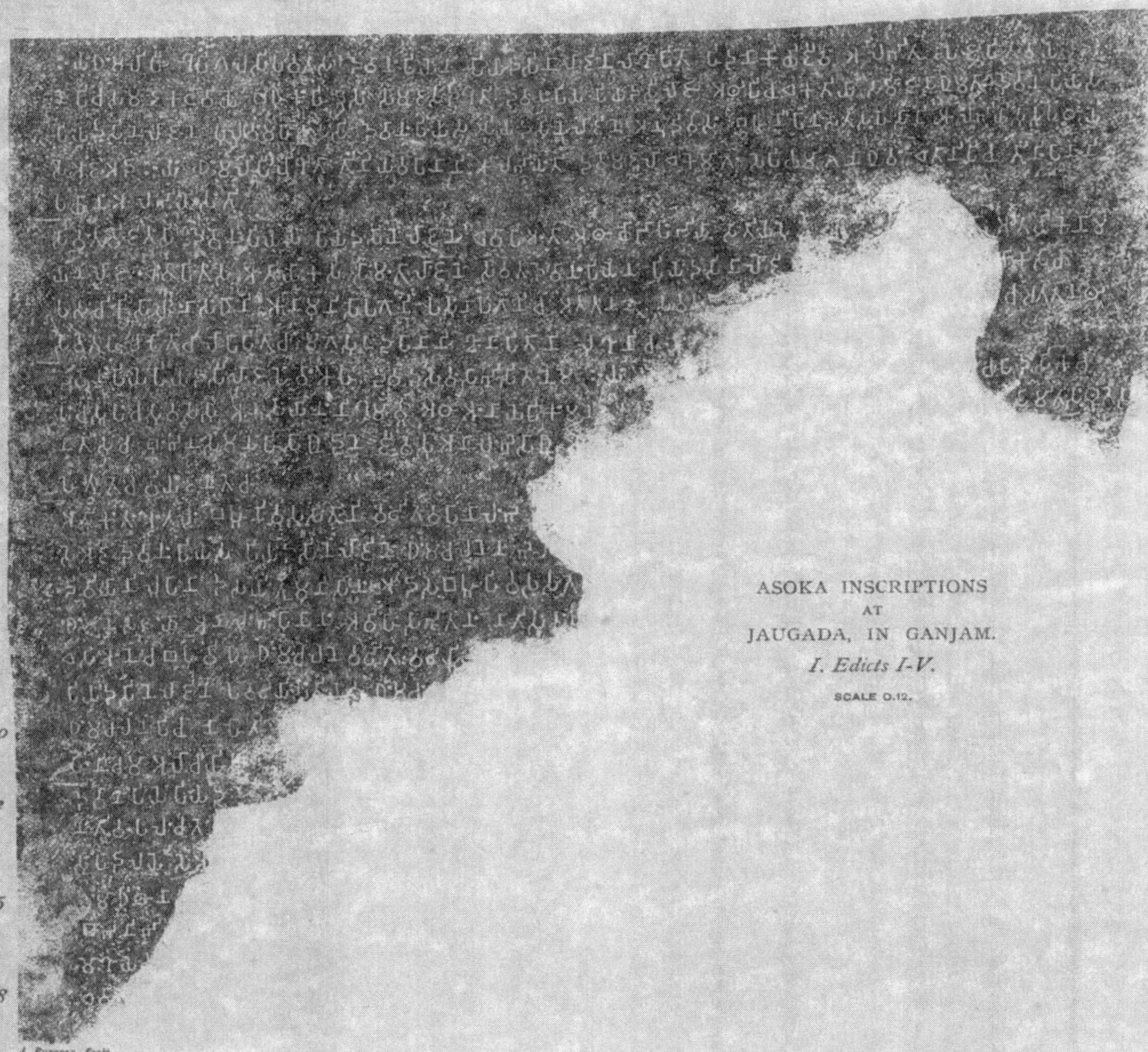

ASOKA INSCRIPTIONS
AT
JAUGADA, IN GANJAM.
I. Edicts I-V.
SCALE 0.12.

J. Burgess, fecit

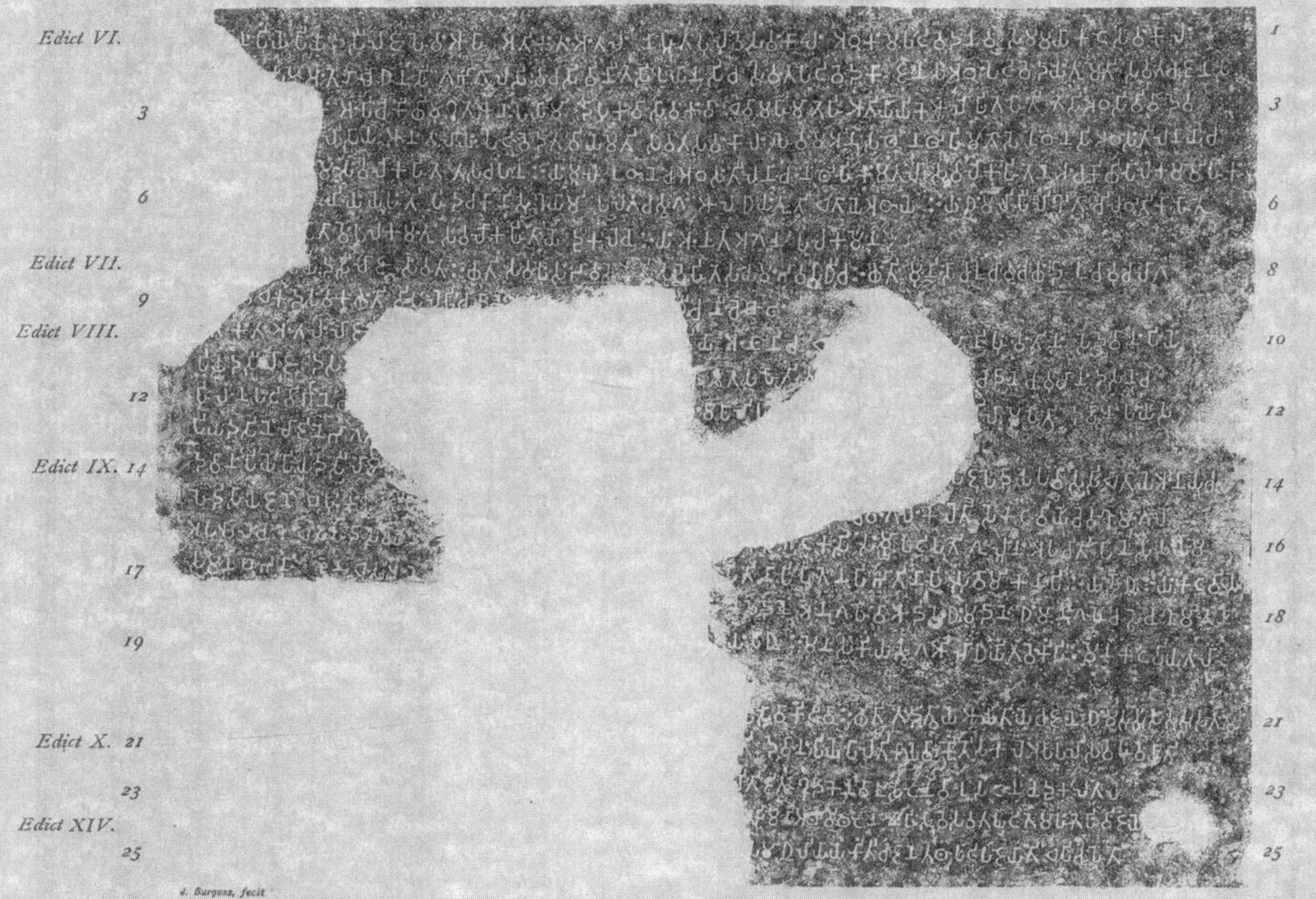
Edict VI.
Edict VII.
Edict VIII.
Edict IX.
Edict X.
Edict XIV.
J. Burgess, fecit

ASOKA INSCRIPTIONS
AT
JAUGADA, IN GANJAM.
III. Separate Edicts.
SCALE 0.12 OF ORIGINAL.

Edict II.

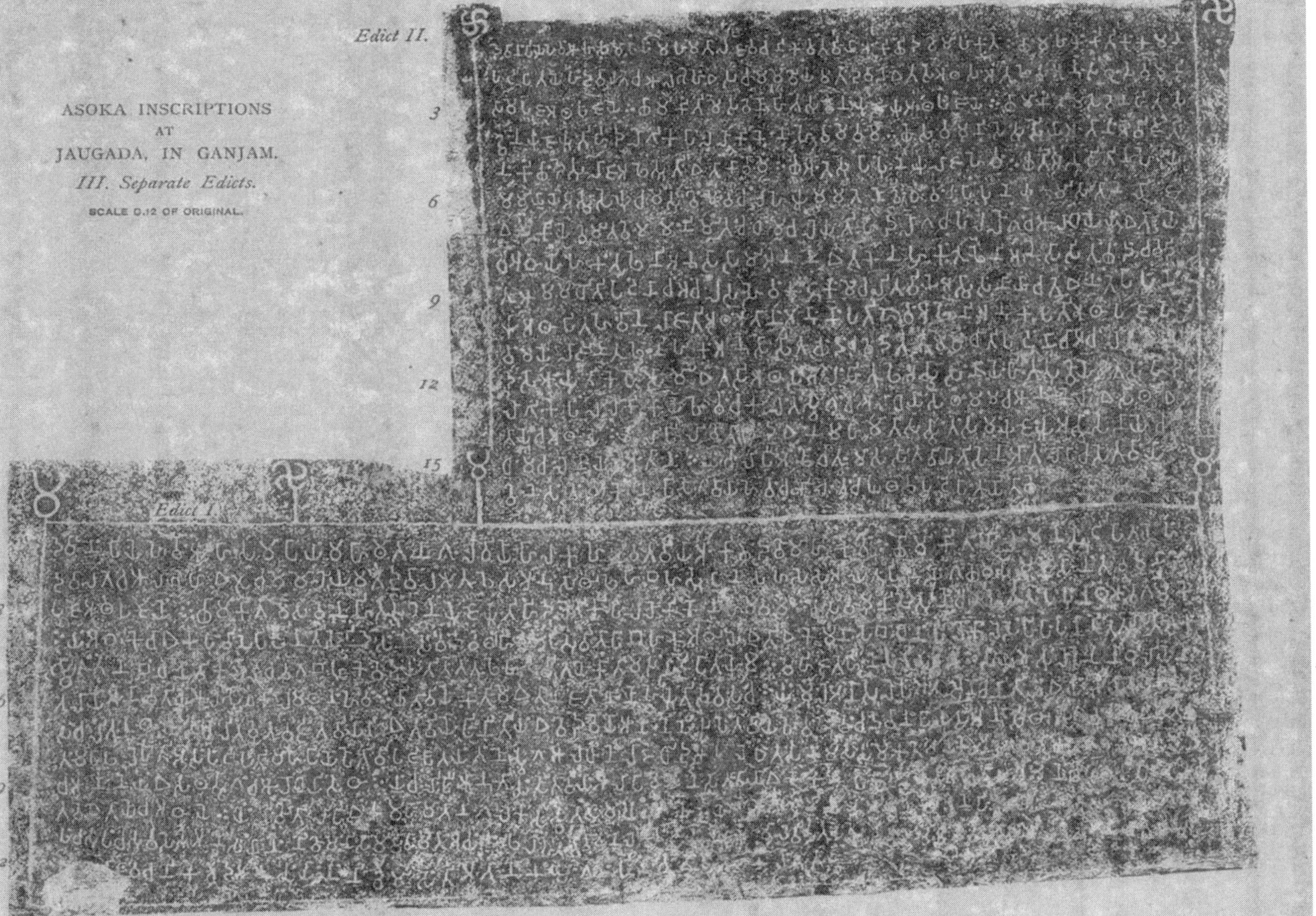

Edict I.

J. Burgess, fecit